After Maastricht

After Maastricht

A guide to European monetary union

JOHN GRAHL

Lawrence and Wishart Limited
LONDON

Lawrence and Wishart Limited
99a Wallis Road
London E9 5LN

First published 1997
Copyright © John Grahl 1997

British Library Cataloguing in Publication data.
A catalogue record for this book is available from the British Library.

ISBN 0 85315 822 3

Copy-edited, designed and typeset by
The Running Head Limited, Cambridge and London.
Printed and bound in Great Britain by
Redwood Books, Trowbridge.

Contents

Preface

The aims of this book are both expository and critical. It tries, firstly, to present students of European integration with the minimum information required to understand the current project of economic and monetary union (EMU) in Europe, whether this information concerns the historical background to the project, its political economy or the economic theories which are used to interpret it.

The other objective is to put the normal understanding of monetary union to the test of critical examination. It is argued that monetary theory in general and international monetary economics in particular are fragile and uncertain bodies of doctrine which are far from giving us a solid and reliable basis for monetary policies. Further, the history of monetary cooperation within the European Union is marked by many serious policy errors, the latest and most dramatic being the unnecessary and damaging recession of 1991–92 for which millions of European citizens paid a very heavy price. Finally, it is suggested that the plans for monetary union embodied in the Treaty of Maastricht are seriously flawed: they involve both the risk of more contractionary pressures on employment and production and the failure to grasp the opportunities which monetary union could open up of desirable reform within Europe and on a global scale.

In spite of these criticisms, the conclusion of the book is that monetary union should be pursued while attempts are made to correct the weaknesses of the existing design for a single currency and a European Central Bank. The view is taken that failure would be very damaging to European integration as such and to the hopes that integration holds out for a more stable, equitable and efficient economy. It is suggested, in particular, that Britain has little to gain and a great deal to lose from attempts to hold out against the drive to monetary integration by our partners in the Union.

The plan of the book is as follows. The first three chapters survey the relevant monetary economics. Chapter 1 deals with monetary theory and monetary policy in general; Chapter 2 with the economics of balances of payments and exchange rates; and Chapter 3 with international monetary systems. In all three discussions it is emphasised how limited and unsure our knowledge of monetary processes remains.

The next three chapters deal with the history of European monetary cooperation in the period since the Second World War. Chapter 4 takes the story up to 1979: it stresses the close interconnection between internal European monetary developments and changes in the global monetary system centred on the United States. Chapter 5 deals with the European Monetary System; in general this structure is judged to have been a failure, in spite of its contribution to price and exchange rate stability; this is because it did not encourage faster adaptation of productive systems or a more rapid growth of employment. Chapter 6 deals with the crisis of the EMS in 1992 and 1993: although many policy errors contributed to this débâcle, primary responsibility is attributed to German monetary policy which pursued narrowly national objectives in reckless disregard of general European interests.

The remaining chapters examine various aspects of the project for full monetary unification in the EU. Chapter 7 discusses the compromise between economic and political objectives on which the project rests; it is argued that this compromise makes the whole project of European construction dangerously dependent on a narrow and dogmatic programme for monetary disinflation. Chapter 8 criticises the fashionable doctrine of the independent central bank, committed to disinflation, which is embodied in the Treaty of Maastricht; it is argued, against this doctrine, that a well-functioning monetary system must necessarily balance the goal of price stability with those of financial and, more generally, output and employment stability. Chapter 9 then looks at financial integration within Western Europe in more detail; it is suggested that this process will involve serious risks of economic dislocation unless it is much more closely and carefully regulated than at present. Chapter 10 deals with the interaction of monetary and budgetary policy in the EU; it argues that the balance between these two main aspects of macroeconomic policy is already too restrictive and is likely to remain so unless there is a complete change of direction in the approach to EMU. Chapter 11 is devoted to the ways in which monetary integration within Europe may interact with trends in the world monetary and financial systems; although important possibilities for a positive contribution to global reform are detected, it is suggested that these possibilities are at present blocked by a dogmatic focus on internal price stability as the sole objective of EU monetary policy.

Chapter 12 concludes. In spite of the highly critical view of EMU adopted throughout the book, the position is taken that monetary integration is valuable and should be pursued because individual nation states today have less and less scope for autonomous economic policies and because the failure of EMU will deal a heavy, perhaps mortal, blow to the whole project of European integration which offers the most realistic prospect of reasserting social control over internationalised economic forces. In the case of Britain in particular, the argument is developed that no plausible strategy exists for employment growth or economic reform on a national basis. It should be stressed, finally, that this conclusion – EMU as the lesser of the evils that confront European populations – is tentative. The European Union may not in fact have a future as anything more than a set of market arrangements which, while they no doubt raise incomes for some social strata, also tend to undermine any forceful initiatives for a more equitable organisation of economic life; if this should prove to be the case then the Treaty of Maastricht will have destroyed the hopes which, for two generations, have inspired the movement for European unity.

Acknowledgements

This book is based on a series of lectures I delivered at the Free University of Berlin in 1994, when I held a visiting Jean Monnet post. I am extremely grateful to Professor Horst Tomann of the Free University for inviting me to Berlin and providing me with an ideal environment in which to study and discuss issues of European integration. I also benefited greatly from participating in the seminar on European monetary issues held at the Free University by Professor Claus Thomasberger and Dr Rainer Naser. Two of my colleagues at Queen Mary and Westfield College, University of London, Dr Iannis Mourmouras and Dr Raul Hopkins, were good enough to comment on parts of the book, as did also my friend Dr Crisafis Iordanoglou. Ms Eilis Rafferty and Mr Bob Burns of the Queen Mary and Westfield library gave me enormous help with the vast bibliography on monetary integration, while Ms Estelle Conway of the QMW Economics secretarial staff helped me with word processing. The concluding chapter draws heavily on joint work with Professor Sam Aaronovitch of South Bank University. The faults of the work, however, are my sole responsibility.

1

Monetary theory and monetary policy

Open questions

The aim of this chapter is to give a straightforward account of some important aspects of monetary theory and to characterise briefly the workings of monetary policy. The discussion concerns only the use of money within a closed economy; international questions are dealt with in the two following chapters. The argument emphasises two propositions. Firstly, although there have been important advances in monetary theory, many of the most important questions remain open. In particular, we do not have a clear and a widely accepted account of the degree and manner in which a money-using economy differs from the non-monetary economies which are examined in many standard models of the exchange process. Such models *abstract* from money: for example they might treat a wage-bargain as essentially an exchange of labour services for consumer goods. There are purposes for which it is legitimate to make this abstraction, but it is not legitimate when we are considering questions of macroeconomic stability where monetary forces are seen by most commentators to be of great importance.

The second proposition concerns monetary policy. Although there were strong historical and political forces behind the switch from generally accommodating to more restrictive monetary policies (from 'Keynesianism' to 'monetarism') which has taken place over the last twenty years, the scientific basis for this switch was very weak. Nor have the achievements of monetarist strategies matched up to the claims which were made for them.

Monetary theory

We can begin by referring to the *functions* of money. It is generally agreed that there are three principal functions. Money acts as:

1. a unit of account;

2. a means of exchange;

3. a store of value.

A fourth function, money as a standard for deferred payments, or means of settlement, is sometimes added but this function is often seen as deriving from a combination of the second and third functions.

In most mainstream accounts the second and third functions (medium of exchange and store of value) are seen as central, since both in principle and sometimes in practice, the first function can be separated from the next two: that is, economic agents might use one currency in actual exchange, although they calculate in terms of another.

The medium of exchange and store of value functions, on the other hand, cannot be completely separated in either theory or practice: money produces a gap between sale and purchase – economic agents sell one good or service for money and subsequently use it to buy different goods and services. It follows that money must retain its value (preserve its purchasing power) at least between the two exchanges. However, the relative importance of these two functions is one of the basic issues at stake between the broad tendencies usually described as Keynesian and monetarist. For the latter, money is a 'temporary abode of purchasing power' (M. Friedman) but is basically held for exchange, or transactions, purposes. For Keynesians, money is the liquid asset *par excellence*; the fact that it can be readily and reliably exchanged for most assets and commodities makes it safe to hold money when economic life is marked by major changes.

Money and theory

It is one thing to agree about the functions of money. This agreement does not mean that there is an agreed account of how a monetary economy works as a system. The best-known and most technically elaborate accounts of a competitive exchange economy abstract from money, and from the conditions which make it useful: such are the models of general equilibrium in the tradition of Walras, perfected by Debreu (1959) and Arrow and Hahn (1971). In these models transactions are costless and frictionless. In such a context there is no need for money – or one might equally say that all commodities act as money, since they are all recognised by, and acceptable to, every agent in the system.

For more than thirty years contemporary economic theory has been wrestling with the problem of introducing money, as an essential element, into the general theory of exchange. A key question in this enterprise is: to what extent must our understanding of the exchange economy be modified to take into account the existence and the functions of money? It is probably fair to say that we are still very far from a definitive answer to this question. On the one hand some writers suggest that the necessary modifications

2

might be relatively minor: according to Ostroy and Starr (1990) this would be the case if there were significant transactions costs in a non-monetary economy which could be reduced virtually to zero by the introduction of money so that, once money was in place, the pattern of production and exchange would be determined by real factors such as technologies, resource constraints and consumer tastes. On the other hand, if transactions costs are important to begin with then it seems implausible to suggest that they can be eliminated so easily, although money obviously reduces them.

Formal economic analysis of monetary systems faces difficult problems because several radical changes have to be made to Walrasian models in order to address the problem of money:

- *time* – since money links *successive* acts of exchange we have to envisage economic life as a sequence of events;

- *uncertainty* – a specific means of exchange would not be necessary unless at least some economic agents lacked information about the timing and nature of the exchanges in which they would be involved or the prices at which exchange would take place; hence:

- *decentralisation* – exchange in a monetary economy takes place between pairs of economic agents and not, or at least not completely, through some centralised institution such as a clearing house or organised market. (In a centralised market, for example the stock exchange, dealers can transact with each other making limited use of money – money is used as a unit of account and for the settlement of debts, but the centralised organisation of the market makes it possible for them to swap shares against other shares in their day-to-day dealings.)

These are formidable requirements. Formal economic models today are very complex but they still depend on quite drastic simplifying assumptions. It is certainly possible to cope with some aspects of these three theoretical dimensions, but it is perhaps impossible to get determinate results from a formal model which tries to include them all in a comprehensive way – one simply gets the result that more or less anything can happen.

It is at least widely agreed that the use of money is linked to the existence of *transaction costs*. One list of these costs, cited by Coase (1988), is as follows:

- *search and information costs* – these are incurred in exploring the range of possible exchanges, finding out who is offering or demanding goods and services, of what quality and on what terms;

- *bargaining and decision costs* – after market search is completed there are still costs involved in deciding on a particular transaction and agreeing it with the chosen counterpart;

• *policing and enforcement costs* – credit transactions, transactions for future delivery of some good or service, those involving a guarantee of future performance and so on are not completed at the moment of agreement between the parties; it is necessary to see that contracts are honoured.

(Although *information* is here used to categorise only one set of costs – those incurred before a transaction takes place – in a wider sense all these costs have an informational aspect.)

In general it is easy to see how the use of money would reduce all of these transactions costs: for example, search costs are reduced by the fact that one has only to find a buyer for the good or service offered who need no longer be also a seller of the goods which one wants to buy (this removes the need for a 'double coincidence of wants' which characterises a barter economy); again, the existence of a unit of account facilitates calculation and negotiations. However, what is not yet clearly established is how the use of money affects the overall working of an exchange economy.

The money–real dichotomy and Patinkin

The starting point for much postwar monetary theory was a situation described as the money–real dichotomy, which marked the state of economic thinking in the early 1950s. The theoretical dichotomy was as follows. On the basis of real factors (technologies, endowments – that is, the initial distribution of resources among agents – and consumer preferences or utility functions) one could explain, in an abstract way, the real outcomes of the economic process – that is, what goods and services would be produced and allocated – together with the *relative* prices of resources, goods and services. These *relative* prices (the prices of goods in terms of each other) were thus seen as real, or non-monetary, phenomena – they could be explained without invoking monetary forces. This meant that only one key economic variable was undetermined – the nominal price level: it was already known, for example, what wages or rents would be in terms of the goods they could purchase; all that remained was to specify at what money prices this relative price structure would be realised. This gap was filled by invoking some version of the quantity theory of money, using the relation:

$$MV = PT$$

where M is the money stock, V the velocity of circulation, T the volume of transactions and P the average money price at which transactions take place. According to quantity theory there would be, in equilibrium, proportionality between M, the supply of money and the general level of prices, P.

This theoretical position was not illogical; the same simple structure is often, quite justifiably, used today to abstract from money and think about the interaction of real economic forces. However, the situation was surely unsatisfactory from the point of view of *monetary theory* and macroeconomics. Monetary forces did not affect any aspect of economic life except the general price level; nor was there any explanation of how much of their wealth economic agents would choose to hold in monetary form.

An important theoretical intervention was made by Patinkin (1956, second edition 1965). He established a connection between money and the real economy by introducing *real balances* (money holdings measured in terms of purchasing power) into the preferences of economic agents who thus had a determinate propensity to acquire and hold money. This procedure begs some questions – money is surely not wanted for itself but rather for the various functions it performs – but it made theoretically possible a richer set of interactions between monetary and other forces. Thus, in the price-setting process (itself drastically simplified) leading to equilibrium, excess supply of or demand for money would interact with those for other goods and services; equilibrium would determine not only relative but also money prices together with the money holdings of each agent. The change from the previous, dichotomised, models was, however, minimal; the basic characteristics of Walrasian models remained. For this reason Patinkin's work attracted much criticism. It remained, however, the starting point for a lot of the subsequent theoretical work.

The Clower critique

A critique of Patinkin was developed notably by Clower (1967) and Leijonhufvud (1967). (Hahn 1965 raised similar objections). In the price-setting process each agent made offers to buy and sell conditional on a given set of prices; these demands and supplies were subject to a budget constraint so that the value of total potential sales equalled that of potential purchases. The process consisted of raising the price of goods in excess demand and lowering the price of goods in excess supply until all markets cleared. In this *tatonnement* process money was treated by Patinkin just like any other commodity. Clower argued that this failed to capture the specificity of a monetary economy. How could excess demand for some good drive up its price if there were also an excess demand for money? The budget constraint (total sales equal to total purchases, closely related to Walras' Law, that excess demand and excess supply sum to zero across the economy as a whole) misspecifies the constraints on agents in a monetary economy. Clower (1965) gives the concrete example of unemployed workers: they want to sell more labour services (excess supply of labour) and purchase more goods (excess demand for consumer goods). In the Patinkin model the corresponding price adjustment would involve not only a fall in wages but, most important, a rise in the price of consumer goods, inducing enterprises to increase output. Clower argued that the excess demand for consumer goods on the part of unemployed workers was purely *notional* – they lacked the money to make it 'effective' demand in the Keynesian sense. To reflect more accurately the constraints on agents in a money economy they have to be respecified to account for the actual role of money in exchange – the fact, as Clower put it, that 'money buys goods and goods buy money but goods do not buy goods'. This, of course, amounts to saying that monetary exchange supersedes barter and that it is therefore illegitimate to treat monetary price formation as a barter process.

Clower and Leijonhufvud were thus led to insist on a distinction between *notional* and *effective* excess demands, the latter being backed by an offer of money. An additional, *monetary*, constraint thus has to be introduced and rationalised in the account of economic equilibration.

Many developments since the intervention of Clower can be looked on as ways of trying to overcome these difficulties. A key question is: how and to what extent must standard, Walrasian, views of the exchange economy be modified in order to give a convincing account of monetary relations? Some of the more influential modelling approaches are looked at in the next paragraphs.

Non-Walrasian equilibria

This approach, developed in particular by French economists (for example, Benassy 1986), explores the consequence of trade on non-clearing markets, where prices do not adjust *prior* to exchange in ways which bring about market-clearing equilibrium. This captures a key element of the Clower critique: if at *actual* prices an agent is unable to sell, then that agent's purchases will also be constrained. Results of this line of enquiry are interesting but still incomplete. The fixity of prices is assumed rather than explained; and the role of money in the system is still very limited in these models since the new, respecified equilibria are often invariant to uniform changes in nominal prices, just as is the case in a Walrasian economy. These limitations are linked to the fact that markets are still treated as in many ways centralised –

thus in each market there may be excess supply or demand and, correspondingly, sellers or buyers may be rationed. The possibility of there being at the same time both unsatisfied buyers and sellers – which is surely possible in decentralised exchange – was excluded.

New Keynesian theories

New Keynesian writers, concerned to give more adequate microeconomic foundations to Keynesian macroeconomics, take us some way towards an explanation of the non-market-clearing prices assumed by the previous group (see the collection in Mankiw and Romer 1991). To do this they invoke imperfect competition, drawing on the classical contributions of Chamberlin (1933). Chamberlin's imperfect competition, where each producer has some local market power because customers are not fully mobile from one supplier to another, seems to correspond to one key aspect of decentralisation in economic life. On this basis, new Keynesian economists offer an explanation of rigidities in *relative* prices. This can become an explanation of rigid *money* prices if there are even small costs ('menu' costs) in making frequent adjustments to the latter. This work, however, does not directly address the functioning of economic systems as these are tackled by economists whose starting point is the Walrasian model. Rather, the new Keynesians develop partial microeconomic models which can throw light on macroeconomic stability.

'Cash-in-advance' models

Robert Lucas, in some extremely complex models, has developed another line of the Clower critique: the notion that goods exchange for money, not other goods (Lucas and Stokey 1987). The assumption is made that goods can be divided into two groups, one of which can only be purchased with money, the other not being subject to this constraint. One result is that, under certain conditions, agents will substitute the second type of good for the first. Since the second group includes 'leisure', we have confirmation that monetary disturbances can provoke unemployment. This work, however, excludes barter exchange by assumption rather than by showing why agents should reject barter in favour of monetary exchange.

Overlapping generations models

One of the weaknesses identified in Patinkin's approach was the presence of money in agents' utility functions. That is, the desire to hold money balances was treated as a *primary* datum, although logically one holds money for instrumental purposes, because it facilitates exchange. Thus the demand for money is a derived demand; money is a way of achieving 'real' objectives.

Within the context of 'overlapping generations' (a stylised representation of equilibria over time) it was shown how a demand for money as a store of value could be derived without the question-begging assumption of money in the utility function. Money would be held as a way of transferring wealth from one time period to another, even though it is intrinsically worthless. However, it proved difficult to obtain the same result when money ceased to be a *unique* store of value, that is, when there was a range of capital assets in the economy (Brock 1990).

Transactions technologies

This approach, taken by Ostroy and Starr (1990) for example, represents one of the most ambitious research programmes. The central idea is to start with a general equilibrium system, but give it two technologies: alongside the traditional production technology there would also exist a transactions technology specifying the costs of exchange. This is, in principle, a very comprehensive modelling strategy which should permit a full account of monetary functions. In reality, however, the very complexity of these models gives rise to formidable analytical difficulties in the interaction between the two technologies.

The origins of money

Some of the most interesting recent work has attempted to give a formal account of the conditions under which a monetary economy would emerge (for example, Kiyotaki and Wright 1989). Economic agents are led to denominate a monetary object and abandon simple barter, given the costs of barter exchange. Because of the complexity of the problem the search has been for the simplest possible specification of these conditions. (One needs, for instance, at least three commodities, otherwise commodities would necessarily play a symmetrical role in exchange; one needs at least three agents, otherwise the separation of purchase and sale is meaningless, as is the search for a counterpart in the exchange process.) Potentially, this work could be relevant to the international economy because, in the absence of a powerful world authority, international monetary relations emerge from the behaviour of agents themselves in, for example, the choice of a particular asset as world money. The work also illuminates the significance of money substitutes (a particularly interesting example is the now classical paper by Brunner and Meltzer 1971 on this theme). It should be stressed, however, that the formal models used are extremely stylised, and make use of many very artificial devices.

Theories of finance

To close this extremely brief and simplified look at very complex monetary models, theories of finance can be mentioned. Arising out of the contemporary transformation of financial systems, this work is expanding in volume. Some of its key themes are obviously relevant to monetary questions, since they include the negotiability of assets, the search for counterparts in exchange and so on. The limitation is that the approach is focused on microeconomics, that is, on particular markets and assets rather than economy-wide characteristics of a monetary economy.

Although much has been learned about the monetary economy through all of these modelling exercises, many of the most important issues remain open. It is possible that they cannot in fact be resolved by the use of formal mathematical models, however elaborate. It is widely agreed that a complex of factors involving uncertainty and transactions costs need to be introduced into models of the exchange economy if the operation of money is to be understood. And it is recognised, further, that these factors will modify standard results on the equilibrium of exchange economies and their efficiency. The *extent* of these modifications, and hence their policy implications, continue to be a matter of dispute. This can be seen in the very different interpretations of transactions costs within the neoclassical and Keynesian traditions.

The interpretation of transactions costs

The recognition of the importance of transactions costs in general leaves open their precise specification, and thus the key tension between Keynesian and neoliberal views remains. From the latter point of view the central questions are monitoring of contracts and the control of opportunistic behaviour (compare the work of Williamson 1985). Money obviates the need for detailed investigations of buyers by sellers and prevents economic agents from violating their budget constraints. Such a view tends to minimise the impact of money on the exchange economy: to the extent that money is an effective institution it will reduce transactions costs sufficiently to make the theorems of neoclassical economics, which abstract from such costs, approximately valid. At the same time, since all transactions give rise to such difficulties we could expect a reasonably stable relation between the demand for money in real terms and the volume of transactions. Such a view continues to be defended by, in particular, Allan Meltzer (Brunner and Meltzer 1990). However, a different focus is also possible, which would tend rather to validate Keynesian insights into monetary mechanisms.

Liquidity

It certainly seems possible to emphasise the role of uncertainty and of transactions costs as these bear on the investment decision in a changing general
context; the same applies to aggregate effects. There were considerable difficulties in formalising the Keynesian notion of liquidity preference, but Hicks
(1974) seems to have given the core of the solution. We can specify the
problem facing an investor, not in a basic two-period scheme, but using three
periods. The simplest scheme is:

Two-period scheme

Period	1	2
	Choice of portfolio	Outcome

Here any choice of investment is as liquid as any other. Hicks proposes
instead:

Three-period scheme

Period	1	2	3
	Initial choice of portfolio	More information on probable pay-offs becomes available	Outcome

Here a liquid portfolio is one which can be more easily adapted in period 2.
An illiquid position is, to a greater extent, 'locked into' irreversible investments.[1]

Money and money substitutes

Corresponding to the same line of reasoning, the range of assets which agents
consider, in a self-fulfilling way, to be liquid also depends on the extent and
nature of the uncertainties they face. With high levels of confidence a wide
spectrum of assets are considered liquid, and credit will be advanced on
them. This range can narrow if some of these assets are generally perceived as
risky.

It follows from the same point of view that liquidity preference will
depend upon the degree of balance or imbalance in the economy as a whole.
If monetary flows (flows of receipts and expenditures) are regular and predictable, this itself makes them replaceable by credit. In an equilibrated
economy most commodities and assets partake of the nature of money in the

sense that they can be easily exchanged for other things. If, however, there are exceptional and unanticipated imbalances, surplus units will be reluctant to extend credit to deficit units who will therefore be constrained to cover their position with narrower forms of money. They will be constrained to reduce expenditures or sell assets. Thus if the degree of equilibration varies for cyclical reasons, then liquidity preference will also vary over the cycle. In sum, Keynesian theorists tend to view the differences between a non-monetary and a monetary exchange economy as quite radical: the behaviour of individual agents with respect to money gives rise to new systemic properties affecting both the stability and the efficiency of the economy as a whole.

Theory and policy

The key debates preceding the decisive turn of monetary policy towards disinflation were not greatly influenced by the gradual theoretical developments described above. The theoretical discussion of *policy* began from the prevailing *neoclassical synthesis*, although synthesis may be too strong a word for the coexistence of Keynesian macroeconomic policies with an understanding of microeconomics still characterised by the real–money dichotomy. This raises questions about the microfoundations of Keynesian macro theory. Although some Keynesians adopted the empiricist position that such foundations were unnecessary (Peston 1959), it proved to be a key intellectual weakness in the postwar Keynesian order, to some extent remedied, after the policy switch, by the analytical work of the new Keynesians.

Nevertheless, we can suggest that different positions on monetary policy can be loosely related to the tension we have identified on the notion of transactions costs. For the monetarists, these are largely a question of discipline and monitoring; because they are of essentially *microeconomic* significance and well resolved by a stable monetary unit, it then becomes appropriate to neglect them. (There are close affinities between the monetarist school and the new institutionalism.) For Keynesians, on the other hand, system-wide uncertainties are central. Although money makes it possible for individual economic agents to adapt to uncertainties, particularly in processes involving long periods of time, it by no means moves us to the efficient, self-stabilising exchange economy of the neoclassical tradition. An active macroeconomic policy remains necessary to avoid financial instability and to accommodate changes in wealth holders' preference for liquid assets.

11

Other approaches

The most ambitious interpretation of formal model building in monetary economics is that an 'artificial economy' (in the words of Lucas 1977) should be constructed by mathematical means, permitting a full examination of all the functions of money and of the working of different monetary systems. This is almost certainly a chimera. The distribution of exchange over space and time, the nature of uncertainty, the flows of information among decentralised agents – these issues are so complex as to render any comprehensive mathematical representation impossible. Already the more complex models are increasingly *opaque*: the models themselves are increasingly difficult to understand; they tell us less and less about behaviour – frequently all they show is that virtually anything might happen; determinate results can only be obtained by imposing a lot of very specific, and, usually, counterfactual assumptions.

This is not to deny that formal models – often relatively simple ones – can illuminate aspects of monetary processes. But the research programme which begins with Patinkin and aims to introduce money into the Walrasian system turns out to be degenerate in that the system dissolves when the attempt is made to move it closer to reality.[2] General competitive equilibrium, under all the artificial conditions which Arrow and Debreu showed to be necessary, may be indispensable as an intellectual reference point; but its relevance to actual monetary economies is essentially negative – we learn, through the work of Clower for example, that an actual monetary economy must be different from this in several essential respects. However, the Walrasian model cannot be usefully rebuilt to embrace all these factors since determinate results in such an abstract system cannot be obtained without exactly such an array of counterfactual simplifying assumptions. If, on the other hand, the applicability of the model is taken for granted then the notion of general competitive equilibrium is *hypostatised*, assumed, without evidence, to correspond to some reality, in a way which can only be explored in ideological terms.

In this context, it is of interest to consider other approaches. Three examples will be taken. They have in common, firstly, that they place less faith in formal models. General theoretical relations are explored, but to put these into some relation to reality what is required is specific information of a historical and institutional kind. Secondly, each approach tends to reject the problematic of an integration of monetary and real exchange as this is understood in the mainstream literature. All three offer significant insights, although it is not clear whether their own research agenda have a future.

Neo-Austrian theory tends to reverse the standard line of reasoning *from* rational economic agents *to* the use of money. Rather, a well-functioning monetary system, like other institutions, is seen as constituting the rational agents who cannot be considered as existing separately from and prior to this institutional framework. There are clear connections to the heavy stress on monetary institutions found in the writings of the Ordoliberals in postwar Germany. Neo-Austrians place great emphasis on disequilibrium processes but, in spite of this, the macroeconomic aspects of their doctrine are not well developed; and the cycle theory of Schumpeter, which often serves them as a macroeconomic framework, cannot be regarded as offering an adequate account of monetary disturbances. (For a similar view, which includes some macroeconomic theory, see the writings of Arndt, for instance, 1994.)

Post-Keynesian theory has developed the notion of a monetary production economy, where 'real' exchange is an abstraction from calculation in monetary terms. Price formation in this view is intrinsically monetary, and real exchange ratios, relative prices, only have a secondary and derivative influence on economic behaviour. The view of prices that results – usually some version of a cost plus mark-up theory – has empirical validity. A second important aspect of post-Keynesianism is its insistence on the 'endogeneity' of money in modern economies – money enters the economic system through the credit operations of commercial banks, private agents, whose behaviour can only be indirectly influenced by the authorities. This influence is usually seen as working through short-term rates of interest rather than in terms of monetary quantities – a point on which post-Keynesians can claim to have had the better of their monetarist opponents.

Neo-Marxist writers have attempted to address the relative neglect of monetary questions in the Marxist tradition. The basic standpoint is that the economic institutions of modern society are alienated from true social purposes to become aims in themselves – thus the accumulation of capital, of wealth in monetary form, dominates and distorts the satisfaction of needs. The work of the French *régulation* theorists, Lipietz (1985) and Aglietta (see Aglietta and Orléan 1982), has been particularly suggestive: for these writers, contemporary monetary disturbances arise from the dislocation of the growth model ('accumulation regime') which guided the development of Western economies in the postwar decades. The restoration of monetary stability would be conditional on transition to a new stability in long-run economic development as a whole. An extreme, but interesting example of such work can be found in the writings of Cartelier (for example Benetti and Cartelier 1980) who tries to theorise an economy in which money is the only generally valued and desired object of exchange activity.[3]

One characteristic that these heretical schools of thought have in common is to place exceptional emphasis on money as a *unit of account*, as the necessary basis of economic calculation. Their common merit is to situate monetary process in *historical* context, within a set of institutions and practices which cannot be derived axiomatically but, rather, have to be considered as the outcome of a specific and in some ways contingent process of development.

Monetary policy

Monetary policy attempts to influence the issue of money – the amount which is put into circulation and the conditions under which this occurs. In modern industrial economies this influence is indirect, since most money is not issued by governments or publicly controlled central banks but by private companies – that is, commercial banks and other financial companies – and most money takes the form of deposits with these banks. Correspondingly, most transactions are paid for by transfers from one such account to another.

This private, commercial bank money is largely created by these banks themselves, as they lend. An individual or a non-financial company borrowing from a bank makes over to the bank a claim on that individual's or company's resources. This is usually a non-liquid claim, in that it would be difficult to sell because of risk and the difficulty of ascertaining the probability of default. The claim becomes the commercial bank's asset; in return the borrower is given a claim over the bank – the bank's liability, a deposit. This can be easily used for transactions because most agents in the economy will accept a claim on the commercial banking system as payment for any goods or services they are selling. If the payee is content to hold such a deposit – rather than changing it to notes and coin or cancelling it against a previous debt to the banks – then the original act of lending has increased the quantity of money.

If banks as a whole increase their lending, the quantity of money held by the public will then tend to rise. There are limits to this process: if depositors prefer to hold other assets, or if debtors switch their borrowing away from the banks, then the quantity of money would decrease again. For example, a company might sell shares in order to pay off its bank overdraft; the individuals or other agents who bought the shares would transfer claims on the banks from their accounts to that of the company concerned, which would cancel them against its overdraft. As this took place money would be annihilated – the process is known as *disintermediation*, because the banks are no longer acting as intermediaries between the creditors (the new shareholders) and the

14

debtor (the company in this case) concerned. In spite of the possibility of dis-intermediation, it is by no means automatic, so that commercial banks in general are able to expand or contract the quantity of bank deposits held by the public, as they increase or reduce their lending.

How can this process be influenced by governments? This is basically possible because, although most money is privately issued, there are important forms of money which are issued by the state – by Treasuries and central banks. This central bank money, sometimes called *high-powered* money, takes two main forms: the notes and coin held by the public are often central bank money; more importantly the commercial banks themselves hold deposits, or similar claims, on the central bank. Central bank money is even more acceptable than commercial bank money, in that there are some transactions where commercial bank money may not be accepted. This is the case for payments to the state, where the state may ultimately require settlement in central bank money: one might pay one's taxes with a cheque on a commercial bank, but it is then open to the authorities not simply to hold a deposit with the commercial banking system, but to require settlement in high-powered money, so that the commercial bank would have to hand over cash or run down its own deposit with the central bank.

Similarly, high-powered money will always be accepted in payments among banks themselves, whereas there will be limits to the extent that one private bank will hold deposits with another. (There are also, in general, rules limiting such deposits.)

We can say then that, although most money is issued privately, it is issued *under the constraint of convertibility* into central bank or high-powered money. Commercial banks must be ready to pay their depositors with state money if they are required to do so; corresponding to this dominance of state money, it is state money also which constitutes the basic unit of account.

The constraint of convertibility permits the central bank to affect the overall issue of money, even though the money it itself issues may be a very small fraction of the total. The availability of central bank money determines how easy it will be for commercial banks to meet this constraint, and thus is a factor in their own issue of money.

The basic tools of monetary policy are thus the terms on which central bank money is issued – that is, the conditions under which the central bank itself borrows and lends. Very roughly we can distinguish two such policy instruments: open market operations, through which the central bank borrows and lends on credit markets; and discount policy, which concerns the terms on which the central bank lends directly to the commercial banking system. The first of these is a more impersonal, market-oriented instrument; the second has a slightly more interventionist character. In addition, central banks or other monetary authorities regulate commercial banks – they lay down operating rules which have to be followed and supervise banks to ensure that rules are actually observed.

In general, it is believed that the rate of interest at which the central bank lends will have a very important effect on the rates at which commercial banks lend, and hence the money creation process. Monetarists have sometimes argued that a similar close relation held in quantitative terms; that the amount of high powered money that was issued would control the quantity of money issued by commercial banks. This kind of proposition is much more debatable.

The demotion of monetary policy

It is fair to say that in the decades following the Second World War the key instrument used to control monetary flows in industrialised economies was not monetary policy as such – that is, it did not directly concern the terms on which money was issued – but, rather, fiscal policy – public sector spending and taxation. It was generally thought, under the strong influence of experience during the Great Depression of the 1930s, that fiscal measures provided a more direct and reliable control over aggregate demand – expenditures on goods and services of all kinds. Taxes, by lowering incomes, would reduce expenditure flows, while public spending, by increasing company revenues or household incomes, would increase them. Behind this approach to policy lay several beliefs about the way the economy worked. It was believed that the quantity of money as such (however money was defined) had little influence over total spending because the velocity of circulation, the number of transactions covered by a given amount of money, was highly variable and because it was usually easy to make transactions with various forms of credit rather than money itself. Interest rates were not seen as having a big impact on either consumer spending or investment expenditures. Many of these beliefs were inherited from the 1930s when monetary policy as such had seemed ineffective in fighting recession, while state spending seemed a more promising response and had indeed proved to be so when war expenditures rapidly restored full employment in the 1940s. In retrospect, however, these empirical regularities did not prove as reliable as was thought.

Meanwhile, monetary policy as such underwent a certain demotion. It became a secondary, supportive tool of policy used firstly to keep the banking and credit systems as stable as possible, secondly to maintain interest rates at a low level – with the aim of encouraging growth and investment. The control of inflationary pressures was a concern of policy but it was felt that fiscal policy, the main instrument used to manage total spending in the economy, was the most potent weapon against inflation.

Two key tensions can be identified in the postwar Keynesian structure. At the theoretical level, there was a split between microeconomics and macroeconomics. The behaviour of individual households, enterprises and markets continued to be understood in terms of the neoclassical economics developed in the late nineteenth century. The premises of this theory – market equilibrium and full information – were, however, radically inconsistent with the main results of Keynesian macro theory, which was based essentially on a pragmatic specification of aggregate empirical regularities rather than on a clear theory of individual behaviour. This was the problem of the *micro-foundations* of Keynesian theory, which only began to be addressed as Keynesian policies themselves came under increasing attack.

The second tension arose from increasing problems of economic policy and performance. By the late 1960s these were legion: growth rates were declining; productivity increases were becoming harder to obtain; the international economy was more unstable as the leadership exercised by the US became less effective. However, macroeconomic discussion increasingly focused on rising rates of inflation: it was asserted by critics of the Keynesian approach that the active use of fiscal policy to sustain output, together with a passive, accommodating, monetary policy, was the source of increasing inflation.

The orthodox Keynesian position thus faced increasing difficulties in the spheres both of theory and of policy. Nevertheless, it can be argued that it rested on a valid insight – that market economies are not self-stabilising and that therefore only an active macroeconomic policy can create the necessary conditions for the efficient functioning of individual markets and enterprises. Experience since the abandonment of Keynesian policies after 1980 has done nothing to undermine this view, although the task of stabilisation certainly seems much more complex and difficult than in the past.

Monetarism

In spite of the cloudy nature of theory, a sharp and so far decisive turn in the conduct of monetary policy was taken in most Western economies around the end of the 1970s. Monetary policy, which had tended broadly to accommodate inflationary pressures in the name of financial stability, was dramatically tightened. The indicators of monetary policy also changed – from interest rates to various monetary and credit aggregates. Simultaneously there was a reduction in the use of fiscal policy for the achievement of high rates of activity (with the important exception of the Reagan period in the United States).

In technical terms this switch took place gradually: through the 1970s monetary authorities payed increasing attention to monetary aggregates (one of the first to do so being the German Bundesbank). More substantially, however, the change centred on the readiness to accept high real rates of interest. The Thatcher experiment in Britain can be seen as the first clear example. Of quite global significance was a similar change in the US – the 'Volcker shock'. Appointed to the chair of the Federal Reserve Board (the US central bank) in the summer of 1979, at the end of the same year Paul Volcker launched a determined effort to control the growth of the money stock in the US. A direct consequence of this was that interest rates were allowed to go to very high levels. It also turned out that interest rates became particularly volatile.

The Volcker shock was a decisive event in the 1980s, and many of the events and upheavals of that decade can be seen as a working out of its consequences. Two important consequences can be used as illustration: the precipitation of a persistent crisis of indebtedness in the developing countries; and economic pressure on state expenditures and budget deficits in the Western European countries. If there were certainly strong political and historical pressures making for a move to more restrictive macropolicies in Europe, it is also true that external pressures, from the US, helped to make a continuation of previous policy unsustainable.

The switch in policies which took place has to be seen in a much wider context than that of monetary policy alone. Monetarism was an integral part of a far-reaching neoliberal project which aimed to expand the scope of market processes and limit state intervention over wide areas of social and economic life. The technical views of monetarists may not be the most important consideration in this wider context: it may be the case that, contrary to appearances, the essence of their position concerned, not money, but the labour market; it amounted to a readiness, or even a desire, for much higher levels of unemployment as the basis of a renewed discipline over working people. This is not the place for a general discussion of the neoliberal project. It may be conceded that a movement successful in influencing policy worldwide over more than a decade, and in making thoroughgoing reforms of economic institutions, was in some ways a necessary response to the problems of the era. At any rate there had emerged quite fundamental obstacles to the pattern of state intervention which had developed in Western democracies from the

Second World War. Nevertheless, this writer continues to view neoliberalism as essentially a form of social reaction, whose (to be hoped, temporary) political triumph does not make it valid as an agenda for economic reconstruction. The results of a decade and a half of neoliberal reform are hardly encouraging: violent instabilities; development blocked by debt crises in many of the poorest countries; in the industrialised world whole populations demoralised by unemployment, inequality and insecurity.

The following remarks are confined to the narrower, purely monetary aspects of the policy shift. It has already been pointed out that monetarists did not all neglect fundamental questions about the role of money and its conditions of existence. In particular Karl Brunner and Alan Meltzer (1971), both of monetarist persuasion, produced one of most developed accounts of the role of money in exchange. However, monetarists in general tended to *minimise* the differences between a monetary economy and the, purely real, exchange economies analysed in the neoclassical tradition. The transactions costs which are emphasised are largely microeconomic – a question of ensuring that individual agents do not violate their budget constraints – rather than complex, system-wide phenomena; and it was believed that a well-functioning monetary system greatly reduced these costs. Thus it was logical for monetarists to argue that money was essentially neutral – except, in the short run, the employment of factors of production and the relative prices at which goods and services are exchanged depends on real economic forces – that is, on technologies, preferences, and endowments of productive resources. At the same time, however, it was argued that errors in monetary policy could have profoundly adverse cyclical effects and, indeed, the severity of the Great Depression in the 1930s was traced to such errors. Correspondingly, it was argued that monetary forces provided the exclusive explanation of the general price level and inflation. This argument was expressed in terms of the *quantity theory of money* – the theory that aggregate expenditures in money terms were closely determined by the amount of money in circulation. In accordance with the underlying view taken of transactions costs it was believed that the velocity of circulation of money, which could be seen as the ratio of the transactions undertaken in a given period to the transactions balances which were held to finance them, tended to be stable (a stable function of money incomes and a small number of other variables).

Further premises were needed to complete the monetarist position and to establish the monetarist policy agenda. It was argued that, monetary disturbances apart, free-market economies were intrinsically stable so that there was no great scope for discretionary macroeconomic policy to increase growth rates or levels of employment. Finally, the supply of money was seen as being subject to control by the authorities, so that restrictive monetary policies offered an unproblematic method of stopping inflation; the costs of such a policy, in lost output and employment, would be small and transient.

Behind this, more or less coherent, theoretical structure a more diffuse but influential set of social beliefs can be detected which did much to legitimise the monetarist policy agenda. The crisis of the Keynesian epoch was traced to excessive state intervention and to the growing power of organised labour in what was interpreted as a situation of 'overfull' employment. Thus a rise in unemployment was not just seen as a temporary cost of disinflation; it was welcomed by some groups as a means of restoring discipline in the labour market and in employment relations. Similarly, a non-accommodating monetary policy was seen as the occasion for a thoroughgoing attack on what was perceived as excessive public spending and state intervention. In broad social terms, then, monetarism was a strategy for the general reassertion of the market economy and its disciplines.

This ideological and political context helps to explain the persistence of monetarist strategies in spite of what must be regarded as extremely negative practical results. Experience has not dealt kindly with the tenets of monetarist doctrine. A host of difficulties has complicated and obstructed attempts to define, measure and control the quantity of money in circulation; the market economy has proved much less stable than was anticipated, and in fact the monetarists' perception of its intrinsic stability can best be seen as a misinterpretation of the Keynesian epoch when active policies guaranteed an otherwise unobtainable degree of stability. The costs of monetary restriction have proved anything but transient; rather, the turn to such policies was associated with a permanent rise in unemployment levels. Although inflation has been brought down, it has by no means been eliminated and continues to threaten Western economies.

However, the dominant response to these failures has not been to abandon, but rather to reformulate, monetarist strategies. For example, the notion of an independent central bank has been elaborated to respond to problems of monetary control without giving up the objective of achieving a thorough disinflation by monetary means. Correspondingly, there is an attempt to rescue the core of monetarist theory: many of the more detailed empirical assertions are no longer heard, but the notion is still prevalent that, in the medium term, money is neutral and the real economy is determined only by real economic forces. As will be seen this reconstructed monetarism has had an enormous influence on the recent strategies of the European Union.

20

Further reading

The account given here of mainstream theories draws on the comprehensive survey in Friedman and Hahn (1990) but much of this is very technical; for a more accessible discussion see Stevenson, Muscatelli and Gregory (1988). For a neo-Austrian view of money see Horwitz (1992); post-Keynesianism is surveyed in Arestis (1996); for a neo-Marxist view, Lipietz (1985). A fascinating study of monetary policy, drawing on British experience, is Dow and Saville (1990).

Notes

1. Makowski (1989) has shown how, using this approach, we can consider separately decisions by investors (whose response to uncertainty is delay) and by savers (who do not lower their required yields in response to declining demand for credit because they know that future information will release investment and push up interest rates). Thus a decline in investment which is perceived as temporary may not reduce long-run rates of interest. If the information/uncertainty concerns the whole working of the economy – involving the direction of economic advance in some Schumpeterian sense – then an increased preference for liquidity will have macroeconomic consequences. Note that since the supply of liquid assets takes place, predominantly, through the extension of credit by commercial banks, their supply is likely to be constrained by the same uncertainties that increase liquidity preference. In this sense, liquidity preference cannot be identified with the demand for money as understood in monetarist theory: it concerns not the supply of real output but the disposition of portfolios.
2. For the concept of a research programme see Lakatos (1970).
3. One way of expressing the limitations of much monetary theory is to refer to the problem of *price formation*. To show that money has real effects involves, in most views of the matter, demonstrating that *nominal* prices, that is, prices in money terms, have a certain inertia so that varying flows of money expenditures can impact on the *quantities* of goods and services which are sold. Now the mainstream tradition in economics does not possess an agreed theory explaining this phenomenon and has difficulty dealing with it because its central doctrines give a non-monetary account of *relative* prices which conflicts with it: if, for example, we explain real wages (that is, wages measured in purchasing power) by non-monetary factors, then money wages must simply vary

with the price of the goods they buy and cannot display the required stickiness. (For a list of the many, very different, theories of nominal price rigidity which are entertained today see Blinder 1994.) Post-Keynesian and neo-Marxist approaches both reject this problematic of relative prices as fundamental and attempt to construct theories in which nominal prices are the basic phenomenon and relative prices become secondary.

2

Exchange rates and the balance of payments

Imprecise theories

The monetary systems of different countries interact through the balance of payments (the net flow of transactions between countries both for trade and investment) and the exchange rate (the terms on which one monetary unit can be exchanged for another). This chapter gives a simple account of the standard theories which deal with these interactions. Today, international trade and investment flows are so large that, at least for small countries, the most important aspect of monetary policy is its impact on external economic relations. Over the last three decades, investment flows – including massive, short-term, speculative movements – between countries have become so large that their effects on exchange rates dominate those of trade, at least in the short run. These effects are not well understood and even the most elaborate economic models find it difficult to predict how changes in monetary policy will affect exchange rates. Even though the general direction of exchange rate pressures is known, their scale and timing are impossible to predict.

Demand and competitiveness

In the 1950s the standard approach was focused on the current account of the balance of payments (that is, essentially on trade in goods and services) because private international investment was low and subject to tight controls. The balance of payments was seen then as determined by the level of demand at home and abroad (higher home demand, for example, would pull in imports and move the current account towards deficit) and by competitiveness (which is reflected to a great extent in the relative price of traded goods and services). Exchange rates were fixed over long periods of time but were adjusted to correct for fundamental disequilibria, understood as substantial changes in competitiveness. In general the impact of disequilibria on stocks of money and assets was regarded as small enough to be neglected. Monetary policy within individual countries was shielded from external pressures by exchange controls on foreign investment. These stopped wealth holders from exploiting differences in the rate of interest among countries.

Mundell-Fleming

The Mundell–Fleming model, developed in the early 1960s, attempted to integrate external relations, both trade and financial flows, into the analysis of monetary policy. It recognised that private international capital flows were of increasing importance. In spite of its limitations, Mundell–Fleming models remain the standard method of analysing medium-term changes in the balance of payments and/or the exchange rate.

The starting point was the IS–LM model of monetary policy in a closed economy. In this model the IS function shows how much expenditure economic agents will want to undertake at different rates of interest; the LM function shows how much expenditure the banking system will be ready to *finance* at different rates of interest. The two functions together therefore determine the level of expenditure (and, hence, on Keynesian lines, the overall level of economic activity) together with the level of interest rates. The government's budgetary and monetary policies are seen as changing the IS and LM curves respectively: tighter fiscal policy, tending to reduce spending, will lower both expenditure and the rate of interest; tighter monetary policy, reducing the availability of finance, will lower expenditures while raising interest rates.

How are these processes affected by external trade and investment flows? The Mundell-Fleming model offers a medium-term analysis of this question, making the key assumption that monetary authorities cannot *sterilise* the effects of payments disequilibria. Sterilisation is an operation to isolate domestic monetary conditions from the effects of intervention on foreign exchange markets. If the government or central bank has fixed the exchange rate, or is even just trying to influence it, it will have to buy or sell its own currency against foreign exchange when there is a payments disequilibrium at the target rate. This involves the issue of 'high-powered', state money and thus affects internal financial conditions. For example, in an economy with an export surplus the commercial banks will accumulate foreign exchange. They can sell this for domestic currency at the central bank and thus acquire reserves which enable them to expand their lending. To sterilise this inflow the central bank can increase its own borrowing and avoid a general relaxation in credit conditions.

Over the medium term such sterilisation may be difficult, basically because it prevents correction of the initial disequilibrium. In the same example, a non-sterilised inflow into the successful exporting country will encourage spending at home; this will tend to increase imports and move the country back towards balance. Sterilisation blocks this automatic adjustment process, thus the initial surplus will persist. The Mundell-Fleming model assumes that sterilisation does not take place, so that domestic credit conditions will alter to eliminate external imbalances. (In practice, however, the limits on sterilisation are not clear cut. They are also asymmetric – a deficit country which is losing foreign exchange reserves will tend to reach the limits of sterilisation before a surplus country, which is accumulating reserves.)

On the basis of no sterilisation we can derive the following contrast, according to whether a government is trying to fix or manage the exchange rate or allowing it to float (find its own level on forex markets).[1] Under fixed rates, a country with an inflow on balance of payments must be relaxing its monetary policy as it purchases foreign exchange; under floating rates it allows an appreciation of the exchange rate which will choke off the excess demand for domestic currency by discouraging sales of exports or assets to other countries. Similarly with outflows: they lead either to tighter monetary policy (fixed rates) or depreciation (floating rates). The standard results are then as follows:

Capital internationally immobile – starting from a balance of payments equilibrium a country relaxes either fiscal or monetary policy. In a closed economy there would be a rise in expenditure and output but now the rise in home demand leads to an outflow (in this case on current, trading, account only). This is met under fixed rates by a tightening of monetary policy which eventually returns domestic expenditures to their original level. Under floating rates there is a depreciation which corrects the outflow by stimulating exports and discouraging imports. Thus only if a lower exchange is accepted can macro policy be used to increase the level of internal activity; otherwise there is a balance of payments constraint on the growth of domestic income.

Capital internationally mobile – in this case it is necessary to distinguish between fiscal and monetary policy. A fiscal expansion tends to raise domestic interest rates. Thus it has opposite effects on current and capital accounts: the first deteriorates as higher domestic spending increases net imports, but the second tends to improve as investment funds are attracted from abroad. Under the standard (but not always plausible) assumptions that international capital is in elastic supply and that there is no perception of increased risk as the country becomes more indebted, the investment inflow will be able to balance the continuing deficit on current account with only very small changes in interest rates. Under fixed rates, non-sterilised intervention will alter credit conditions to secure this balance, reducing capital inflows if they are more than needed to compensate for the current account deficit.

Under freely floating exchange rates, by contrast, there is no such induced change in credit conditions, because there is no exchange market intervention. The equilibrating variable becomes the exchange rate. While there is upward pressure on interest rates, capital inflows, exceeding the deterioration on current account, drive the exchange rate higher. Net export demand falls – until total demand in the home economy is brought back to its original level.

Monetary expansion on the other hand increases domestic spending while tending to reduce interest rates. There is thus a tendency towards deficit on both current and capital account. With fixed rates and non-sterilised intervention the outflow is eliminated by an induced tightening of monetary conditions which negates the original stimulus. Under floating rates, however, the exchange rate depreciates to generate a current account surplus and this is matched by a sustainable outflow of investment funds.

In this way we arrive at the well-known assignment rule of Mundell-Fleming (M-F). Under fixed rates only fiscal policy can influence the domestic level of activity; with variable rates, only monetary policy can be so used.

Direct application of this kind of analysis has to pay attention to the assumptions. In the case of capital mobility it is assumed that the financial assets of different countries are very good substitutes for each other; at the same time, however, their different moneys are not at all substitutable – expenditure in each country requires the use of domestic money so that there can be a stable relation between internal activity and the demand for domestic monetary assets. These conditions come closest to being met in large, strong economies, and it is these economies which provide the clearest examples of the most surprising M-F result – the tendency of a fiscal expansion to harden the exchange rate. A separate theory has to be developed for small open economies, subject to much tighter constraints on their international borrowing. Despite its abstract nature the M-F model does help to explain the increased potency of monetary policy in the contemporary world of floating exchange rates and mobile capital.

Monetarist views

The M-F model was originally constructed on the standard Keynesian assumptions that prices were relatively fixed while changes in demand had an important effect on the level of real output. Early monetarist discussions of monetary policy and the foreign exchanges retained the equilibrating mechanisms of the M-F model while altering its supply-side structure. Output is now determined by real forces at a level corresponding to the 'natural rate of unemployment'. Monetary policy affects goods and asset prices. Under fixed exchange rates there follows a monetary theory of the balance of payments, which is seen as bringing the supply of money into equilibrium with the (stable) demand for it, at home and abroad. A relaxation of monetary policy provokes an outflow, which will simply continue if sterilisation is used to avoid changing this policy; without sterilisation the outflow will force policy back to its original stance. Under floating rates, with exchange intervention assumed to be absent, countries can choose their own monetary policies at the cost of accepting the corresponding exchange rate movements. Equilibrium exchange rates were seen as being determined by purchasing power parity (PPP) – a unit of domestic currency will exchange for foreign currency with the same purchasing power.

When the degree of abstraction of this model is neglected it can lead to serious errors. For example, real economic growth, because it is seen as supply-determined, is supposed to strengthen the exchange rate or the balance of payments. In practice only extremely competitive economies display this behaviour except in the very long run. There are also empirical difficulties with PPP, as with most 'neutrality' propositions of the same type. The idea of convergence to PPP remains important for medium- and longer-term analysis of exchange rates but it hardly fits actual developments at all. Even when we make a distinction between tradable and untradable goods (the 'law of one price' can only logically be held to apply to the former at an international level), price indices do not give a very good representation of a country's competitiveness; and most manufactured goods are sold in imperfect markets where prices are not rapidly equated. We can accept that there is a medium- to longer-term competitiveness constraint on the exchange rate (or balance of payments, if rates are fixed) both in theory and practice, but reliable indicators of competitiveness are difficult to construct. For this reason, the current account itself, de-emphasised by economists of this school who treat it as a purely monetary phenomenon, may remain an important signal of competitiveness and not just of monetary conditions.

The central weakness of the monetarist approach is its claim that floating exchange rates could restore national autonomy in monetary policy. This is logically true if, by floating rates, one denotes a 'clean' float with no official intervention on forex markets. However, the claim is devoid of practical significance unless the demand for national money is a stable function of domestic variables such as nominal GDP. If private agents regard domestic and foreign monetary assets as close substitutes then the ability to fix the domestic money supply does not give the authorities a powerful policy instrument.

The principal contribution of this type of theory was probably that it emphasised portfolio aspects of the foreign exchanges, at a time when increased international capital flows were indeed making this more important. Thus for monetarists, it was a secondary matter whether the outflow provoked by monetary expansion took the form of imports or investment abroad. This goes too far, but it is true that investment flows, rather than trade flows, became decisive for short-run exchange rate movements and dynamic theories of the foreign exchange are essentially a branch of financial economics.

Exchange rate dynamics

The models so far considered focus on medium-term equilibria and tell us little about adjustment. In the short run, however, the speeds of adjustment of different variables are very different – exchange rates (or capital flows, if rates are fixed) vary from minute to minute, while the output, trade and price variables linked in the specification of macroeconomic equilibria only change slowly. The approach developed from the late 1970s has been to treat the exchange rate as a price on a financial market; in the standard view exchange rates adjust instantaneously, via the rational expectations of market agents, to all news bearing on long-term equilibrium. On this basis, Dornbusch (1976) showed that exchange rates might overshoot in the course of adjustment. For example, consider a country, Britain say, which lowers interest rates; the expansionary monetary policy implies a lower exchange rate in the medium term. But international wealth holders arbitrage continuously among different currencies. They will only hold assets which bear a lower rate of interest (say, a deposit in a British bank, or British Treasury Bills) if the currency concerned is expected to appreciate, thus giving a profit on the exchange rate movement which compensates for the loss of interest. It follows that sterling cannot slowly fall to its new equilibrium; it must drop immediately, overshooting the new equilibrium by enough to produce this subsequent expected rise. The Dornbusch model was thus regarded as helping to explain volatility in forex markets. (A different model, using a similar methodology, was the portfolio balance theory: whereas Dornbusch assumed that goods prices could only adjust slowly towards a medium-term equilibrium, this held that imports and exports might be slow to adjust the current account to a new equilibrium position – in both cases exchange rates change instantaneously and may overshoot.)

Now it is surely correct to look at exchange rates as determined on speculative financial markets. The overwhelming share of forex transactions today are financial in nature, having little or nothing to do either with trade or with long-run fixed investments. But the rational expectations/efficient markets view of financial prices does not fit the facts particularly well. (For the general difficulties with this view of competitive financial markets see Chapter 9.) In the specific case of foreign exchange, Dornbusch models do not explain the actual degree of volatility. This can be seen by considering the relation between spot and forward exchange rates.

Interest rate parities

If the spot exchange rate is S_t (units of home currency per unit of foreign currency), the home interest rate is r and the foreign interest rate is r_f, then a money market investment of one unit of home currency will yield $(1 + r)$ units after one time period.

If the same amount is placed in the foreign currency it will yield $(1 + r_f)/S_t$ units of foreign exchange. If a well-organised forward exchange market exists then a wealth holder can eliminate risk (*cover* the position) by contracting *now* to sell the proceeds at a fixed forward rate F_t. This means that the foreign placement yields, without exchange rate risk, $(F_t/S_t)(1 + r_f)$ units of home currency. Arbitrage between the two markets should equalise these pay-offs, so that

(1) $$(1 + r) = (1 + r_f)(F_t/S_t)$$

This is the covered interest rate parity condition.

As an illustration, Britain is the home country with interest rate (r) 5 per cent per annum; Germany the foreign one with interest rate (r_f) 10 per cent per annum. The spot exchange rate (S_t) is 0.4 pounds per D-mark. A British wealth holder can thus obtain £1.05 after a year for each pound placed in the domestic financial system. Or he can obtain 2.5 D-marks at the spot exchange rate, which will become 2.75 DM after a year if placed on German credit markets. The British wealth holder can contract now to sell these proceeds for sterling, at the rate F_t, obtaining 2.75 F_t in pounds. Since arbitrage between the two positions is both quick and easy, these yields must be the same. Thus, from (1)

$$F_t = \{(1 + r)/(1 + r_f)\}S_t \text{ or here}$$

$$F_t = \{(1.05)/(1.10)\} \times 0.40 = 0.382 \text{ £/DM}$$

The forward rate for the D-mark must be at a *discount* to sterling (that is, it is cheaper to buy D-marks forward than spot). This is a general rule: the currency which has the lower interest rate is at a forward premium. This discount/premium exactly matches the interest rate differential. Note that the arbitrage needed to maintain this relationship is instantaneous – the spot purchase and forward sale of D-marks, in the example, can be executed at the same time.

Empirical investigations confirm that relationship (1) holds almost invariably when an organised forward market exists for the exchange of two currencies. It would be surprising if this were not the case – one would wonder why wealth holders were satisfied with a lower return when, without risk, they could obtain a better one in another currency.

Uncovered parity

If wealth holders are risk-neutral (that is, they care only about the average yield from their assets, not by how much it might vary around that average) or, less implausibly, if financial markets permit diversification which eliminates most risk, then the same relationship should hold between exchange rates and interest rates, even when it is *uncovered*, that is, where the foreign exchange proceeds of a placement are not sold in advance. We would then have

$$(2) \qquad (1 + r) = (1 + r_f)\{E[S_{t+1}]/S_t\}$$

where $E[S_{t+1}]$ is the expected exchange rate at the end of one period. Once again, it can be suggested that arbitrage should impose this relationship – if it does not hold then one can expect to make money, on average, by switching between the two currencies. It is important, however, that this is an expected gain, subject to risk, not the instantaneous locking-in of a gain as in the 'covered' case.

Relations (1) and (2) imply that today's forward rate, F_t, should equal the expect future spot rate $E[S_{t+1}]$. If expectations are *rational* in the sense used in economic theory (expectations make optimal use of currently available information and correspond to optimal forecasts), this implies that the forward rate is an unbiased predictor of the future spot rate. Were this not so, then the following opportunity for gain exists: one contracts to sell foreign exchange forward if the expected depreciation of the currency concerned exceeds its discount on the forward contract; one closes the position, by buying foreign exchange on the spot market when the forward contract is due. Provided this new spot rate S_{t+1} actually is lower than the forward rate – that is, the depreciation does exceed the forward discount – a profit is made. (The same reasoning applies if a currency's expected appreciation exceeds its forward premium; in this case one would contract to buy the currency forward.)

In the same example as before, if one did not actually expect the mark to fall to £0.382, but rather expected to hold its current value £0.40 or even to appreciate, then one might buy D-marks forward, i.e. contract to buy them for sterling in a year's time say, at £0.382. If one's expectations were fulfilled and the spot rate stayed at £0.4, one could close the contract by selling the D-marks against sterling at that price, thus obtaining a profit of 0.018 pounds for each D-mark. A speculator whose base currency was D-marks could achieve an equivalent result by selling sterling forward and buying it spot to close the position.

Empirical investigation has not, in general, supported the hypothesis that F_t is an optional predictor of S_{t+1}. In particular, the current spot rate, S_t, seems to predict S_{t+1} as well as F_t, or even better.

In the light of these problems one can either reject the theoretical paradigm (fully rational economic agents, equilibrated asset markets) or appeal to *risk premia*. For example, investors on both sides might be deterred from the operation described above if they regarded the D-mark/sterling exchange rate as so volatile as to involve unacceptable risks. (In this case, risk is likely to mean different things for agents with D-mark liabilities on the one hand, or sterling liabilities on the other.) The introduction of such risk premia makes the theory compatible with the evidence but considerably reduces its empirical content, since the premia cannot be observed directly and vary a great deal over time. In practice they can only be inferred *ex post facto* by the degree to which forward exchange rates over- or underpredict future spot rates. In fact, no account of exchange rate dynamics has performed better in prediction than a simple random walk (Meese and Rogoff 1983, cited by Williamson 1993):

$$S_{t+1} = S_t + u_t$$

where u_t is a random shock. (Similar difficulties arise in the analysis of other financial data involving arbitrage over time: stock market prices are not good predictors of future dividends: nor do long-run interest rates give good predictions of future movements in short-run rates – these problems are raised again in Chapter 9.)

The consequence of these problems is that there are difficulties with standard models of exchange rate dynamics (those of Dornbusch, and more complex recent developments such as the attempt to explain the movements of exchange rates within officially declared fluctuation bands).[2] All these standard models rely on a version of long-run, 'rational', forward-looking, calculation of future variables which is not supported empirically by any relevant evidence. The 'overshooting' of equilibrium positions which is possible within these models is an order of magnitude smaller than the actual turbulence which is often experienced on foreign exchange markets and other organised asset markets.

Theories of disequilibrium

Even within the paradigmatic theory of rational expectations and market clearing, there are some models which try to explain trading at prices which are divorced from the 'fundamental' forces which are assumed to correspond to a full-information equilibrium.

One example is the notion of a 'rational bubble'. In a probabilistic context, where there is a small probability of a large price fall, and a large probability of a continuing profit to be made on an asset, it may be advantageous for speculators to hold it although they are aware it is overpriced in 'fundamental' terms. An analogous type of reasoning has been applied to currencies – the so-called 'peso problem' with reference to the Mexican currency – where devaluations are in the long run inevitable but are still very unlikely in any given period. In practice these models are difficult to verify: we cannot specify 'fundamental' factors with precision and the same speculative movements may be based on erroneous expectations rather than this kind of 'bubble'.

Similar difficulties arise with sunspot models. Here operators misinterpret the nature of the fundamental determinants of an asset's value, but their erroneous theory becomes self-fulfilling.

The absence of a convincing theory

The era of volatile exchange rates, which began with the abandonment of fixed dollar parities in 1972–73, offers many examples of exchange rate movements which defy explanation by economic theory (for the general empirical failure of exchange rate models see Meese 1990). The most important case is probably the behaviour of the US dollar following the change in American monetary policy in 1979 (the 'Volcker shock'). Over the years 1980–85 a cumulative dollar appreciation occurred which was so large as to be difficult to relate to any 'fundamental' factors (such as changes in competitiveness, in international trade patterns or in rates of return in different countries). By 1985 the overvaluation was, on any sensible view of these fundamentals, quite unsustainable. In the light of such phenomena some writers, notably De

Grauwe (see De Grauwe and van Santen 1991), have been led to abandon the efficient markets paradigm. One way of doing this is to introduce notions of bounded rationality which place some events or factors beyond the awareness of agents; another procedure is to recognise that, contrary to the paradigm, market agents are not unanimous and do not all make the same type of calculation. One interesting innovation of this kind is the idea of 'stop-loss' trading where a subgroup of agents liquidate any positions which are showing more than a certain loss, even though they expect long-run movements which would produce a profit (Krugman and Miller 1992). Such behaviour can increase the volatility of markets. Similarly, it can be recognised that there are information asymmetries even in well-organised asset markets which make it tempting for some agents to *imitate* the behaviour of others whom they regard (perhaps mistakenly) as being better informed. There are possibilities of cumulative disturbance in such cases (Orléan 1986).

These more complex accounts may give us more convincing explanations of exchange rate movements. They seem, however, to exclude any precise prediction because there is no longer any clear relation between market prices and 'fundamentals', because the dynamics of market may be so complex ('chaotic') as to make prediction impossible even in principle, and because behaviour is continually modified by learning processes, there being no stable regime which everyone comes to understand.

Further reading

Jones and Kenen (1985) is a full survey of international monetary theory at an advanced level. Williamson (1993) gives a conspectus of exchange rate theories in the course of a discussion of the ability of governments to influence exchange rates. Argy (1994) is a thorough text on international macroeconomics. On exchange rates, including the wide gap between theory and observation in this field, see Krugman (1989) and Frankel (1993).

Notes

1. In fact, the distinction essential to the model is between a completely fixed exchange rate and one that is variable: the variation might be brought about by changing a fixed (but adjustable) parity rather than by floating the currency. This point is important in practice but not for the exposition in the text.
2. For these theories see Krugman and Miller (1992a). Although extremely elegant in form there are many difficulties with them – in particular they require market agents to be able to identify a single-valued,

'fundamental' factor determining exchange rate movements. One aspect of the problems facing both economic agents in foreign exchange markets and economic analysts is that it is almost impossible to specify such a fundamental factor in a definite way. The obvious candidate for the role, purchasing power parity, only exercises an imprecise influence over long periods of time.

3

International monetary regimes

International money

Within all countries today the form of money is determined by the state. Although in advanced countries it is actually commercial banks (private organisations) which supply most money, they do so under the constraint of maintaining convertibility with state-issued (fiat) money.

In an international context, however, there is no authority which can impose a monetary unit; thus the designation of an international money requires the consent of the agents (private and public) who make use of it. At an early stage of development of the world economy the agents concerned were primarily merchants, but with the development of modern nation states, national governments came to have a large interest in the international moneys that were used and the terms on which their national money could be exchanged for others. Thus, in an international context, we can consider each of the functions of money as being doubled according to whether the agents involved are private or public (national governments). Krugman (1992, p167) gives the list in Table 3.1. (It should be noted that private international exchange media are different at retail and wholesale levels. Although companies and individuals can change any currency against any other, most large-scale switches today are still via dollars.)

Table 3.1 Functions of international money

	Private	Public
Medium of exchange	Vehicle	Intervention
Unit of account	Invoice	Peg
Store of value	Banking	Reserves

Interactions and externalities

As soon as monetary relations within countries become a concern of public policy, international monetary relations do also, because of the interaction of national policies. Thus policy choices in one country have spillover effects on

others: there are thus externalities (positive and negative) and, at least potentially, coordination problems.

The basic analysis of these difficulties can be illustrated by the case of two
countries, each aiming for a strong balance of payments with the other and
prepared to use high domestic interest rates (or any other unpleasant policy
instrument) to achieve this. If there is no collusion between governments the
process that results can resemble the classical game theoretical account of a
prisoner's dilemma: the outcome will be high interest rates in both countries,
although the same balance of payments figures could have been achieved with
lower rates. A similar structure can result if the target of policy is the
exchange rate rather than the balance of payments. The analysis can be
extended, with technical difficulties, from two to more countries. Both inflationary and deflationary games can be examined in these terms: the former
could involve a sequence of competitive devaluations; the latter a scramble to
build up gold or foreign currency reserves via high interest rates.

Note that if the preferences of the countries concerned become sharper –
they attach more importance to balance of payments targets, for example –
then the policy conflicts we have discussed can become a straightforward
inconsistency: it becomes impossible for all countries to achieve their targets.
This is often referred to as the $(n-1)$ problem: among n countries there are
only $(n-1)$ degrees of freedom for exchange rates (or balances of payments).

Regimes

An international monetary regime can be regarded as an attempt to resolve
problems of policy interaction in an institutionalised way through a system of
rules. The rules designate international money, the terms on which it is
issued and the conditions under which it is converted into national moneys.

The objectives of such a system are often specified as the three goals:
adjustment, liquidity, confidence. The first two of these form a pair and
specify how the system aims to insert national economies into the overall
structure. There is necessarily a balance between liquidity and adjustment –
that is, between the extent to which deficit countries are refinanced and the
extent to which they are constrained to adjust their positions. For national
governments this results in a specific external constraint. Because extremes
are unworkable these two objectives must be balanced – adjustments without
any refinance would return us to a barter economy because each import item
would have to be immediately covered by corresponding exports, while over-
generous refinance would lead to widening disequilibria.

The third objective, confidence, seems to result from the fact that there is no overall world government which imposes monetary arrangements. These therefore have to inspire confidence in the agents who make use of them, although of course different agents can reject the rules of the regime to different degrees. The breakdown of a regime is likely to be associated with crisis, or at least turbulence and instability. The appropriate analogy within national economies is probably financial disturbance, which follows a loss of confidence in private debts.

Finally, one can repeat the point made in Chapter 2 about mainstream analysis, which sees institutional arrangements as a way of reconciling or coordinating the decisions of rational agents. But there is some value in the opposite approach of the neo-Austrians for whom institutions construct rationality – in this case the external rules of the game help to organise and rationalise the behaviour of national authorities. Similarly, post-Keynesian views suggest that basic expectations of the future cannot be formed individually and then reconciled in a process of market exchange. Orderly exchange will only be possible if there are widely shared conventions about the stability and continuity of the arrangements which provide a framework for the system.

The main interest of this book is in the regimes introduced on a regional basis within Western Europe, but in the present context we will examine the two best-defined global monetary regimes: – the international gold standard and Bretton Woods. The focus will be on two interconnected issues:

- to what extent do these regimes depend on asymmetric power relations – the issue of dominance;

- to what extent does the functioning of monetary arrangements reflect the changes in real economic development – the issue of neutrality or of money–real interactions.

The international gold standard

Cohen (1978) characterises international monetary systems along the following dimensions:

- centralisation–decentralisation

- discretion–automaticity

- asymmetry–symmetry.

In principle the international gold standard can be seen as lying at the extreme point of all these contrasts: it was a decentralised system without supranational institutions; it made adjustment of imbalances to a large extent automatic and it implied at least in principle the same forms of constraint on all participating countries. For these reasons it appeals to some free-market conservatives. Adjustment took the form of specie flow – a loss of gold by deficit countries which subjected them to deflationary pressure. The use of the standard policy instrument, the short-run rate of interest or discount rate, could delay immediate loss of gold by attracting short-run capital inflows, but only by exercising deflationary pressures on domestic expenditures and thus promoting adjustment. While it was in operation all participating currencies had essentially fixed exchange rates as they were all convertible into the same unit of account (gold) on fixed terms.

One can note first the restricted range of the system both in time and place. Only Britain (after it went back on gold following the Napoleonic Wars) was on a pure gold standard throughout the nineteenth century; other countries used silver, bimetallic standards or inconvertible currency. The collective choice of gold as a common standard, towards the end of the century, resulted from a conflict which pitted debtors and some of the primary producing countries against creditors and the stronger industrial interests. Silver, which tended to depreciate for technical reasons, was the easy money choice, gold a hard currency strategy. These choices by different countries were, however, interdependent as the demonetisation of silver in one country tended to reduce its price further and depreciate the currencies of countries remaining with a silver standard.

The pure gold standard was also spatially restricted. The only countries on the standard throughout the period of its international predominance were those which had achieved a relatively advanced and continuing process of industrialisation. Thus the gold standard is closely associated with the 'second industrial revolution' and with the countries, such as Germany and the United States, which were in its forefront.

The danger menacing the liquidity of a pure gold standard is that an increase in the supply of money will require either gold production or price deflation – the first being slow and the second difficult. In fact the liquidity of the period was largely autonomous of immediate moves in the gold stock. Two main forces were at work: within the advanced countries financial innovation, in the form of the rapid growth of commercial banking, was reducing the share of the public's monetary holdings which took the form of gold. In Britain these developments gradually bypassed the attempt made by Bullionists to control the quantity of paper money, notably through the Bank Act of 1844, which proved unworkable in times of crisis.

In the international context transactions were covered by a system of credit based on London. Thus confidence rested to a large extent on the strength of London-based mercantile and financial interests and on the ability of London, in an emergency, to settle its debts in gold. Technically this could sometimes be difficult since the Bank of England in fact operated with a rather small gold reserve. At times of pressure, when withdrawals from the London financial system exceeded deposits, London would reverse the flow of gold by increasing the short-run interest rate ('Bank rate'). As the dominant player in the game London enjoyed key advantages:

- the still remaining industrial pre-eminence of Britain, which meant that it could settle its debts, in the medium term, with industrial exports which were in strong demand;

- Britain's position as a net creditor, able to sell assets to meet liabilities;

- the political and military control exercised over the empire, particularly India: these countries were essentially forced onto a 'gold-exchange' standard where they swapped their gold stocks with London in exchange for sterling-denominated reserves (de Cecco 1984).

Adjustments in principle worked by imposing automatic contractionary pressure on economies with a net outflow, and corresponding and symmetrical expansionary pressure in surplus countries. Although there were devices used to mitigate automatic contractionary pressure (manipulations, within limits, of the gold price or the terms on which gold was coined, temporary suspensions in weaker countries) it is true that participating countries did not attempt to operate fully independent monetary policies. (Tariffs were also used to stabilise payments.)

A fully discretionary policy was operated essentially by London, which manipulated Bank rate; it is sometimes argued that British policy was functional for the system as a whole since when the British economy slowed down it imported less goods but directed larger flows of capital abroad. Capital flows were curtailed when the British economy tended to overheat. Thus Britain's partners could always obtain sterling, either by exporting to, or by borrowing from, Britain. However, this functionality perhaps was more obvious for the core, industrialising countries, than for those of the periphery (Lewis 1978). In the core, the cycle tended to be synchronised so that the movements of British short-rates were not necessarily inappropriate for other countries.

However, it has been argued by Panic (1992) that the classical (or neo-classical) specie flow adjustment mechanisms were essentially irrelevant among the group of rapidly industrialising countries which succeeded in operating a gold standard continuously between the 1870s and the First World War. The reason was that major inflows of long-term capital, on a scale never matched since, suspended the deflationary pressure which would otherwise have fallen on deficit countries. Flows came from France and above all Britain, which was closely integrated in financial terms with the most important recipient – the United States. According to Panic, flows on this scale obviated any important resort to the specie-flow mechanism to correct temporary imbalances. The success of the industrialisation process then made it possible to service the debts incurred.[1] Countries where industrialisation was blocked, or interrupted, were on the other hand unable to maintain the discipline of the gold standard. Population movements were a complementary adjustment process to the capital flows – taking social pressure off the countries of emigration such as Scandinavia and Britain, and essential to the industrialisation process in North America.

Thus it could be argued that the classical gold standard was a managed rather than a fully automatic system; that it rested on British hegemony; and that it functioned successfully because it was compatible, financially, with the needs of a particular phase of development.

A final point of interest concerns the breakdown of the international payments system in 1914. It was clear that a major European war would fundamentally disrupt international transactions – what is significant is that, initially, this brought excess liquidity to London as demand for other currencies collapsed. This was the case even though Britain was a combatant and imperilled by the conflict. One could say that an international increase in liquidity preference made it easier to issue British liabilities, even though Britain was at the heart of the system which went into crisis. A similar paradox seems to have marked the weakening of US economic leadership in the 1970s and 1980s: the same factors which weakened the US, because they led to system-wide uncertainty, could well increase the demand for US dollars as the established store of value in the world economy.

Although the interwar period saw some attempt to reconstruct a well-functioning multilateral monetary system, this proved abortive. The British restoration of convertibility in 1925 made inadequate provision for the loss of British competitiveness by attempting to restore the old sterling-dollar parity. A less ambitious restoration of gold convertibility in France proved more durable. Attempts were made to economise the need for gold by making more use of gold-convertible currencies as reserve assets, but no stable pattern of central bank behaviour emerged. National governments did not fully dismantle the control mechanisms adopted during the war and tended to pursue much more autonomy in domestic monetary policy. Finally capital flows proved to be fundamentally destabilising at the time of the Depression of 1929 since US capital outflows were cut off at the same time as the US market contracted – thus debtor countries could secure their positions neither in goods nor in internationally acceptable money.

The disorder which followed the 1930s involved competitive devaluations, floating, suspensions of convertibility in a manner which hindered international trade and investment and hence economic recovery. (A certain minimum coherence was eventually introduced by the Tripartite Agreement of 1936 between Britain, France and the US.)

Bretton Woods

The postwar period saw a further attempt to stabilise and organise international monetary relations. Once again there was a certain amount of conflict in the design of the system, on this occasion between Britain and the United States. Britain, now an international debtor, argued for a less restrictive and more symmetrical set of arrangements than in fact emerged. The original design can be seen as a gold-exchange standard,[2] but in an institutionalised setting and where the rules of adjustment were clearer and both confidence and liquidity were more stable. Apart from a declining proportion of reserves held in sterling, this was essentially a gold-dollar system.

In contrast to the gold standard, it was initially characterised by considerable autonomy of national monetary policy rather than by very extensive capital flows. (It is generally considered that with fixed exchange rates either monetary autonomy or free flows of capital are possible but not both.) The rules of adjustment were reasonably clear – a deficit could be met temporarily out of reserves or credits, then by policy adjustment (tighter monetary or fiscal policy); a fundamental disequilibrium – involving essentially an incompatibility between internal and external balance at the given exchange rate – could justify a change of parity.

The free convertibility for trade purposes which was written into the system was delayed until the second half of the 1950s, after an abortive attempt at sterling convertibility in 1947, in the belief that European currencies were so weak *vis-à-vis* the dollar that convertibility would lead to uncontrollable outflows from European countries. This delay itself, however, reflected US confidence in its own long-term strategy and had some constitutional basis in the 'scarce currency' clause of the International Monetary Fund (IMF) agreement. This does mean, however, that the period during which the system was in full operation was rather less than two decades. In the period of its operation there was an immense growth of trade, particularly trade centred on the Western European countries.

Two interrelated forces can be identified which tended to undermine the arrangements established at Bretton Woods. The first is the position of the US as the centre of the system; the second concerns the increasing constraints on national policy.

US leadership

The rules of the system made gold the ultimate form of world money, while most international money functions were in practice fulfilled by the dollar. From one point of view, repeatedly argued by Robert Triffin (1961), this situation was itself unstable. Increases in world liquidity, necessitated by the growth of trade, were accommodated by a growth of dollar assets – that is, of claims on the US banking system. But this very growth called into question the convertibility of dollars into gold. Liquidity and confidence were therefore necessarily counterposed in this system. And in fact the gold-dollar relation came under pressure quite early – during the 1960s the convertibility of dollars into gold was limited more and more; ultimately a parallel free market in gold was established alongside a controlled market to which only national central banks had any access. On the other hand, the premium on this free market was initially quite small.

Although Rueff (1967), whose diagnosis resembled that of Triffin, argued for a return to a more classical gold standard (a view which had some influence in France), Triffin himself argued for a supranational reserve asset, not related to gold, which would be issued by an international authority. Although the IMF did eventually introduce SDRs as a new reserve asset,[3] they have never had more than a supplementary role alongside various national currencies and dollars.

Triffin's position can be seen as a rejection of hegemony in international monetary relations. Kindleberger (1987) adopted a more optimistic view of such asymmetries. He argued that concern with the US balance of payments was exaggerated. What was often seen as an alarming deficit was in fact a current surplus, more than matched by an outflow of long-term investment. In Kindleberger's view, this was a standard banking operation – the US was borrowing short and lending long, and in this way supplying liquidity to the world economy. (The French, in particular, found more polemical terms to describe this asymmetric position of the US.) Kindleberger also took a more positive view of US hegemony in international affairs. He suggested that the hegemon played the role of lender of last resort to the world economy – a function normally performed within national economies by the central bank, which prevents a loss of confidence in one asset or one debtor from spreading to the system as a whole. Kindleberger suggested, in an influential study of the 1930s, that one problem had been exactly the absence of such a hegemon: Britain was no longer able to fulfil this stabilising role and the US was not ready to assume it. However, even from this point of view, the US did in practice fail to perform its leadership functions in the course of 1971 – rather than tighten US policy, President Nixon imposed controls on outward investment and an import surcharge, both moves incompatible with the lender of last resort role.

What both Triffin's and Kindleberger's views leave open to question is the relation between hegemonic stability and the real economic performance of the US. Clearly the very success of the international economy weakened the relative position of the US. (At the end of the Second World War it had had the quasi-totality of both the world's monetary gold and its industrial production.) But there also developed a distinct malaise within the US economy, of which the most discussed phenomenon was a productivity slowdown in its manufacturing industries, the sign (according to many) of quite basic problems within the American socio-economic model. (For a discussion of these real economic problems see Marglin and Schor 1990.)

The response of the US economy to these difficulties was, in the first instance, inflationary. This can be seen simply as a customary policy response – by the government and the monetary authority. However, it could also be suggested that the established price-setting and wage-setting practices always had an inflationary potential which emerged openly once productivity growth slowed down.

Clearly the Bretton Woods structures tended to generalise these inflationary effects, since other currencies were pegged to the dollar and thus prices tended to rise in other countries as a result. On the other hand, delays in the response of import prices dampened them to some extent.

A crisis of rigidities?

The Bretton Woods system is generally summed up as involving fixed exchange rates against the dollar. So far we have looked at the notion that it was the denominator of the system – the US dollar – that was the basic cause of its instability. It was increasingly argued, however, that the key problem was the first term of the definition – the fixed rates – rather than the unit in terms of which the fixed rates were expressed.

In fact it is not clear that fundamental balance of payments disequilibria grew in scale while the fixed rate system lasted. There were certainly differential rates of inflation, but although these were a source of difficulties in the 1960s, they were not much larger than in the 1950s. Bretton Woods generated inflationary pressures in the US, but it also had real disciplinary effects on inflation trends in other countries. It is also true that some of the pressure that developed in exchange markets reflected fundamental loss of confidence in the dollar as much as any disequilibrium on the current account – both forces were driving up the D-mark.

Nevertheless, the pressure of incipient balance of payments constraints on national economic policy was tending to grow. This was firstly just because of the increased volumes of trade relative to output – disequilibria could no longer be controlled by relatively minor switches of output from domestic markets to net exports. Secondly, international capital had become increasingly mobile – a tendency which restricts autonomous national monetary policies under fixed exchange rates by making possible large outflows from countries with low interest rates to countries with higher ones: thus countries suffering an outflow would have to reverse their policies or accept a devaluation. At the same time, any currency perceived as overvalued could become the target of massive, and essentially risk-free, speculation (the famous *one-way bet* offered by a fixed parity system).

Such capital mobility developed gradually – when the Bretton Woods system was inaugurated there were comprehensive controls both on capital inflows and, especially, outflows in most countries. During the 1950s the main international flows of capital were official, in the form of intergovernmental lending unlikely to destabilise exchange rates. Liberalisation concerned especially inflows of direct investment and portfolio investment, particularly from the US. Countries with strong balance of payments positions, such as Germany, also found it convenient to liberalise outflows, rather than accumulate reserves. This could be seen as a way of tightening monetary policy a little.

But international capital mobility was also a function of the growth of trade and direct investment themselves. Trade credit obviously had to be permitted and 'leads and lags' in payments for trade could generate substantial movements in creditor and debtor positions. In addition, trade revenues and profits on direct investment often escaped capital controls and became internationally mobile funds. The rapid development of Eurodollar, and then other Euro-currency credit markets, during the 1960s facilitated these trends by making it much easier to borrow and lend funds outside national banking and credit systems. The funds exchanged on such markets are usually exempt from capital controls by virtue of their origin.

Thus, as opposed to the classical gold standard, which rested on capital mobility and was tendentially weakened by the growth of national monetary policy, Bretton Woods existed in symbiosis with active, usually expansionist, national policies and was tendentially weakened by capital mobility.

The balance between the two aspects of the Bretton Woods crisis is a difficult and important issue. If one accepts the position that the problem was fixed rates, then the key problem becomes a question of difficulties in adjustment, which are much mitigated by exchange rate flexibility. Problems of liquidity and confidence are secondary in this perspective, indeed it is often argued that the international capital markets themselves supply the necessary liquidity.

From the other point of view, the central difficulty was not adjustment of disequilibria as such, but the difficulty of reconciling confidence and liquidity. Here the emphasis tends to be on the strength and efficiency of underlying monetary institutions – including those which issue internationally acceptable forms of money. Thus it is a lack of organisation and control at the global level which is the key problem, and not the lack of flexibility for individual countries. The necessary solutions are then a matter of politics, not markets. Although this second point of view is less fashionable than the first, it corresponds better to the experience of international monetary relations since the demise of Bretton Woods, which have displayed continuing disorder.

There is a link of association between the two problems of confidence in the dollar and balance of payments adjustment in that the transformation and gradual liberalisation of international finance, like the productivity slowdown, was an expression of economic tensions within the US. In many ways the emergence of a global financial system was the outcome of twin processes of deregulation and internationalisation in a US banking system originally under close public control but tending increasingly to escape from it. Thus it might be suggested that a stronger and better-controlled economic performance by the US could have avoided not only a crisis of confidence in the dollar, but also excessive pressure on the fixed parities, by exercising control over the international financial system.

Another way of looking at this contrast of views is suggested by Paul De Grauwe (1989). He argues that until the failure of Bretton Woods, national and international monetary systems had developed in analogous ways: from the disorganised issue of different moneys on a competitive basis; to agreement on a common standard (gold); to the promotion of one money issuer to central prominence – the role of the central bank as it evolved within private banking, the role of the US within Bretton Woods; and finally to the gradual supersession of gold by state-issued money. At this point there is a divergence between the two paths of development: whereas national systems develop through explicit political control and the substitution of fiat money for gold, the international system moves to a plurality of monetary units, scrutinised and perhaps controlled by a sophisticated set of financial markets. It is difficult to justify such different lines of development. If they are inconsistent, which is the correct path? Should political control over monetary processes within nation states be attenuated, or do we require strong international political institutions to stabilise and direct the global monetary and financial system?

In the period since the break-up of Bretton Woods the first view has predominated, but precisely as a result of that dominance and its effects on policy, it is the second view which is coming to seem more persuasive.

It should be emphasised that the Bretton Woods era, in spite of the emerging crisis, was one of exceptionally fast and stable growth – especially in Western Europe. The much less structured and less organised arrangements which have prevailed since have been far less conducive to sustained development.

Further reading

McKinnon (1993) is a short historical overview of international monetary systems; De Grauwe (1989) gives a complete account of international monetary developments. On the gold standard see de Cecco (1984) and the collection edited by Eichengreen (1985). Panic (1992) relates the problems of the gold standard to those of contemporary Europe. On the break-up of Bretton Woods and its aftermath see Black (1985). On general questions of international monetary systems see Cohen (1978) or, for more recent views, Steinherr and Weiserbs (1991).

Notes

1. Note that, although there were few barriers to capital movement among leading countries, many of them made use of tariffs during the early phase of industrialisation. This tended to ensure that international borrowing was used to acquire productive equipment rather than consumer goods.
2. A gold-exchange system is one in which gold is the ultimate denominator but where a large part of international reserves are held in the form of

other currencies, thus economising on the amount of gold needed to support a given level of international exchange. This kind of system was tried, unsuccessfully, after the First World War.

3. The SDR (special drawing right) is a form of international reserve created and issued by the IMF. Its value is determined by a fixed basket of national currencies. In principle, SDRs could evolve into the main form of international money but in practice only small quantities have been issued. The ECU plays a somewhat analogous role within the European Union.

4

Monetary integration in Europe

Internal and external history

Since the Second World War, European monetary integration has had a very chequered history, marked at some times by progress, at others by regression or stagnation. It will be argued that this history can only be understood in the context of external monetary conditions – that is, essentially, the context set by developments in the US. Considerable progress was made when US conditions were favourable and US policy actively encouraged European cooperation. As US leadership became less effective, difficulties arose for the Europeans, who were able to limit, but not to avoid, damaging consequences from the growing disorder in international finance and payments. Internal conflicts, especially differences among France, Germany and Britain, have so far prevented the European Union making a significant contribution to the reconstruction of the international order.

Schematically, the history of European monetary integration can be divided into four phases, corresponding very roughly to decades; in each case the global/US circumstances differed. In the 1950s, the European Payments Union (EPU) restored internal convertibility even though the massive predominance of the US and the problem of dollar shortage led to restrictions on the external convertibility of European currencies. In the 1960s, with convertibility restored, European monetary integration essentially reflected global integration through the workings of the gold–dollar system; in consequence, the growing problems of this global system started to provoke tensions within Europe. In the 1970s, in a climate characterised by recurrent dollar depreciation, European efforts to secure a measure of internal stability, through the exchange rate system known as the 'snake', were largely unsuccessful. In the 1980s, which opened with a dramatic reversal of US policy, the European Monetary System (EMS) represented a more ambitious, but ultimately unsuccessful, attempt to promote internal integration. This chapter will discuss the first three phases, leaving the EMS itself to the next chapter.

The European Payments Union

In the early postwar years international transactions and payments were subject to multiple restrictions and controls. In consequence international payments within Europe were largely balanced on a bilateral basis. The resulting situation was analogous to barter, in that exports to one country could not be used easily to balance imports from another. By the late 1940s this difficulty was inhibiting the initially dynamic trade among Western European countries. The obvious solution – to make payments in dollars (or gold) – was obstructed by the inconvertibility of European currencies into the dollar.

The prevailing view on convertibility was that the weaknesses of European economies and the strength of the US were so extreme that free convertibility into dollars would lead to instability – either to massive devaluations or to the need for severely contractionary policies. The failure of an early attempt by Britain to restore dollar convertibility in 1947 was seen as corroboration of this view, since Britain's economy was at the time much stronger than those of continental Europe.

A recent reassessment of the period by Eichengreen (1993) sees social and political constraints on convertibility as more important than narrowly economic ones. He suggests that, especially after a general devaluation against the dollar in 1949, convertibility was feasible, but that it would have tended to undermine the growth-oriented compromise between capital and organised labour which was reached in the postwar period. This view is perhaps not so different from the conventional one: devaluation to permit convertibility would have raised profits at the expense of real wages, while monetary stringency would have reduced employment and growth rates. In other words internal economic balance would have been impaired by free convertibility; the balance of political forces, however, was such as to rule out a sacrifice of internal objectives to external ones.

The solution found was to make European currencies convertible into each other, while external convertibility was delayed. The agreement to do so took the institutional form of the European Payments Union of 1950. It was sponsored by the US agency associated with the Marshall Plan – the Economic Cooperation Administration. This was characteristic of US strategy at the time, which saw European integration as complementary to the long-run US objective of a liberal world order.

It is significant that the EPU did not merely establish internal convertibility and multilateralism. It also provided extra liquidity for European trade by organising international credit. Each participating country was assigned a quota, divided into five sections. Deficit countries were allowed to make payments up to 20 per cent of quota by credit from the EPU; of the next 20 per cent they could cover 80 per cent by borrowing from the EPU but had to clear the remainder in gold (or, equivalently, dollars); the third 20 per cent of quota had to be covered 40 per cent by gold, 60 per cent by borrowing and so on. Similarly, surplus countries accepted payment up to 20 per cent of quota in claims on the EPU – these claims, of course, being convertible into all member currencies, but not gold. For the next 20 per cent they received payment partly in gold (or dollars), partly in claims on the EPU and so on.[1] There was a certain asymmetry in the treatment of surplus and deficit countries: for the initial slices of quota, the former received more externally convertible money (dollars or gold) than the latter were required to pay. This discrepancy was covered by an initial loan to the EPU from the US. Thus the scheme both introduced multilateral clearing (in fact administered by the Bank for International Settlements, which is based in Geneva) and extended credit to permit trade expansion. In this second respect it proved more far-reaching than subsequent experiments, which have not attempted to influence the liquidity of international payments.[2]

Robert Triffin (1966), one of the main architects of the system, claimed for it the following achievements:

- elimination of bilateral trading arrangements;

- encouragement of intra-European trade;

- mobilisation of existing bilateral claims.

It is noteworthy that the introduction of the EPU proved particularly valuable to West Germany. A strong economic expansion had begun in Germany following the currency reform of 1948. This had led to a trade deficit; the credit arrangements of the EPU (together with a discretionary credit beyond those corresponding to the rules) helped to finance this and to permit the cancellation of debit and credit items with other countries (Gros and Thygesen 1992, p7).

The EPU can be regarded therefore as a successful European initiative, which modified, on a regional basis, the workings of the global payments system inaugurated at Bretton Woods, and which promoted integration via intra-European trade. The system, however, failed to develop, largely because of hostility towards it by Britain. Within a few years, most countries were at the limits of their quotas, either in a deficit or a credit direction, and thus payments had to be made in dollars – so that the EPU ceased to provide additional liquidity. It could only have done so by developing rules to govern the adjustment and finance of continuing disequilibria (beyond those already inscribed in the general rules of the IMF). This never happened. Meanwhile, large-scale outflows from the US tended to eliminate the sharp shortage of dollars, so that restrictions on convertibility into dollars for trade purposes were gradually eased and finally abolished at the end of 1958.

With dollar convertibility the original *raison d'être* of the EPU disappeared. At this point the British insisted on dissolving it, rather than redefining its role and continuing it as a channel for the coordination of monetary and exchange rate policy. This was certainly a blow against European integration, since Western Europe at this point lost its most developed monetary institutions (see Triffin 1966, Chapter 11).

Dissolution may also have been based on a miscalculation of Britain's own interests. The British government was impatient for convertibility and did not like the discipline of the EPU, since the requirement to make a certain percentage of payments in hard currencies restricted its official financing.[3] Britain may also have regarded its own position as exceptional because of the survival, within the Commonwealth, of the old sterling-exchange system whereby a large number of countries held reserves in sterling. This seemed to provide liquidity for Britain, although the system eroded rapidly in the next decade, effectively ending the role of sterling as a reserve asset. Throughout the 1960s British economic policy was recurrently constrained by balance of payments difficulties, which culminated in the devaluation of 1967, so that the bid for full independence may have been an error.

The EPU represents the high point of US leadership in European monetary organisation. The US acted from a position of strength and, by taking a long-run, strategic view, was able to accommodate European interests while promoting two of its key objectives: an eventual liberalisation of payments and the development of intra-European cooperation.

Europe on the dollar standard

The provisions for monetary cooperation which were written into the Treaty of Rome (1957) were sketchy and did not set out a clear project for integration in the monetary sphere. Only convertibility for current transactions was required and this was limited by a safeguard clause for countries with balance of payments problems; similarly, other countries might be authorised to take temporary protective measures against a country which 'distorted' competition through a big devaluation; beyond this, member states were enjoined to treat macroeconomic policy as a matter of 'common concern' but Community action was dependent on unanimity and thus remained an intergovernmental issue. Thus for the first twelve years of its working the

European Economic Community (EEC) concentrated on real aspects of integration and took little action on monetary issues. One could say that during this period European monetary integration merely reflected the global arrangements determined, above all, by the US and given institutional structure through the IMF. Thus Western European currencies were fixed in terms of each other by virtue of all being pegged to the dollar. (As a result the margins of fluctuation between two European currencies were twice those allowed – plus or minus 0.75 per cent – against the dollar).

As the Bretton Woods system came under increasing pressure, European countries experienced negative effects, but the views they took of the developing crisis tended to differ. In Germany the system came to be perceived as a source of imported inflation – as private capital became more and more mobile it was increasingly difficult for Germany to sterilise inflows and maintain a relatively conservative monetary position; in fact (as is suggested by the Mundell-Fleming theory) monetary weapons were self-defeating – if German interest rates rose there were enormous purchases of D-marks and German banks were thus put in a position to make large increases in their lending.[4] France also had objections to the working of the system but these were much more directly political. The De Gaulle presidency saw the role of the dollar as an instrument of economic domination by the US – for instance it was suggested that the big investments of US multinationals in Europe were in fact financed by the Europeans themselves through their readiness to hold reserves in the form of dollars.

Nevertheless, for most of the 1960s monetary and exchange rate developments were relatively stable, compared to what followed. For example when the EEC adopted a unit of account for the denomination of its official receipts and expenditures, it seemed natural to equate this unit to the US dollar, and this was done by assigning the unit a notional value in gold equal to that of the dollar.

European monetary arrangements in the 1960s were thus still determined by a global framework in which the dollar was predominant and the US exercised leadership. In contrast to the previous decade, however, the ability of the US to preserve stability was increasingly open to question.

The Werner Report

As the Bretton Woods structure began to crack, serious monetary tensions appeared also *within* Western Europe. One of the first expressions of the developing crisis of the dollar was repeated and increasingly frequent speculative movements into D-marks. These in fact compelled several D-mark revaluations (against the wishes of both Federal government and the Bundesbank), as well as episodes when the D-mark was allowed to float. Even more than the attack on the pound in 1967, these events signalled the emerging power of the international money and credit markets. Unprecedented sums – billions of dollars in a single hour – flowed across D-mark foreign exchange markets in periods of tension.

Nevertheless, emerging plans for monetary integration in Europe, agreed in principle by the Council of Ministers at The Hague in 1969 and embodied in the Werner Plan of 1970, were predicated on the continuation of the relatively stable external environment which had characterised most of the 1960s. It seemed a relatively small step to unify currencies which were already closely linked to each other by the Bretton Woods system. Unlike the Delors Report twenty years later, the Werner Report did not argue for a sudden centralisation of competence for monetary policy at the end of a transitional period. Rather, the assumption was that speculative, short-run, capital flows from one member state currency to another would gradually be liberalised while national policies were subject to increasing degrees of central coordination so that autonomy in monetary policy could be transferred slowly between levels. (The Report is reproduced in Steinherr 1994.) It was expected, however, that real economic convergence, among what were then only six members with five currencies (since Belgium and Luxembourg have a monetary union), would obviate the need for sharply differentiated policies.

The key issue in the debate on projected monetary union was between the 'monetarist' and 'economist' positions and was reflected in contrasting memoranda by Raymond Barre and Karl-Otto Pöhl. The terms 'monetarist' and 'economist' were used in a specific sense to refer to opposing positions on the integration process. The 'monetarist' view, held by France, was that monetary union could be the path to more complete economic integration in general and thus to a convergence of economic performance and economic policy in the member states. A single money would make many integration processes much easier than they had been before its introduction. The 'economist' view was the reverse and expressed (especially German) reservations about the project. To this school of thought, rapid monetary integration, without preconditions, was a leap in the dark and could promote serious instabilities if the ground was not well prepared. Rather, convergence of real economic conditions and of economic policies should be achieved gradually – monetary union would then come as the culmination of the integration project, not as its starting point. The position of the two countries altered little between the Werner Report and the Delors Report some twenty years later. France still laid emphasis on the voluntaristic construction of European monetary institutions; Germany continued to insist on a lengthy preliminary process of stabilisation, to avoid inflationary pressures or financial disruption within the integrated monetary zone which would finally emerge.

D-mark appreciation

A compromise on the timing of monetary integration was in fact agreed by the Council of Ministers in 1970, which set a target date for full monetary union within ten years. This ambitious objective, however, soon became a dead letter as the Bretton Woods system finally collapsed: in the summer of 1971 the US formally repudiated the convertibility of the dollar into gold; by March 1973 a final attempt at fixed parities had broken down and most major industrial countries floated their currencies against the dollar. A period of ten years began which was marked by the recurrent weakness and depreciation of the dollar. The consequence of this proved to be repeated distortion of exchange rates *within* Europe, because movements out of the dollar tended to be towards, not Western European currencies in general, but D-marks (and to some extent Swiss francs) in particular. Thus these currencies appreciated most both against the dollar and other European currencies. This change in internal exchange rates created difficulties because it did not reflect any change in the trading relations among European countries or in the relative competitiveness of their economies. Deflationary pressure resulted in Germany, while other countries saw an unwanted reduction in their D-mark exchange rates, which tended to push up costs. The internal exchange rate shifts also disrupted the workings of the Common Agricultural Policy by turning what were intended to be equal farm prices into unequal ones.

Why did dollar weakness have this differential effect on European currencies? The question seems important in both theoretical and policy terms. One answer is to say that D-mark appreciation resulted from various contingent factors: Germany's balance of trade surplus and its record of stable prices lowered the risks of holding D-marks; the fact that it did not operate foreign exchange controls (while most of its European partners did) guaranteed that foreign depositors would be able to withdraw funds from German banks and credit markets when they so desired. From this point of view, purchase of German financial assets was a risk-reducing diversification of portfolios. If there were suitable reforms in other countries – lower inflation, open capital markets – funds would flow into lira, French francs and Irish pounds just as easily.

However, there is a contrasting explanation, which stresses the monetary origins of these disturbances: they originated in a loss of confidence in the established form of international money, and reflected a search for a more reliable *monetary* asset. From this point of view, the focus of speculation on one or two particular currencies was to be expected, because what economic agents were seeking was a widely acceptable medium for international trade and investment. The search for such an alternative *monetary* asset tends to concentration rather than diversification of speculative purchases because the very fact that other agents are buying D-marks confirms the general acceptability, the international liquidity, of D-mark assets. Movements into alternative monetary assets thus seem to be inherently cumulative. This second point of view is related also to the discussion of the forces behind the break-up of Bretton Woods; it is consonant with the position that the essential problem concerned the dollar as an international form of money, rather than the rigidities of fixed exchange rates as such.[4]

The snake

As opposed to the Werner Plan, which proved to be merely a theoretical proposal,[5] practical efforts at European monetary cooperation during the 1970s took the form of the 'snake' – an attempt to stabilise intra-European exchange rates. The mechanism was set up in the wake of the Smithsonian agreement. This was an ill-fated attempt to return to fixed parities against the dollar even after the link with gold had disappeared – in effect to put global payments onto a straightforward dollar standard. In the hope of limiting speculative pressure on the new fixed rates, wider permitted bands of fluctuation were introduced of plus or minus 2.25 per cent. Since these were bands of fluctuation against the dollar, the implied fluctuations between two European currencies were twice as large. The snake began as a modest attempt to narrow these internal fluctuations. The currencies of participating countries, while remaining within the wider dollar bands, would be held to narrower fluctuations among themselves. This procedure was known as the 'snake in the tunnel' from the way it was pictured on a graph – the tunnel was the space between maximum and minimum dollar rates; the snake was traced out by the joint movements of European currencies within this band.

The Smithsonian agreement soon broke down. Continuing balance of payments disequilibria and recurrent speculative attacks forced frequent parity changes, and major industrial countries resorted to floating their currencies against the dollar. (Britain, typically, was one of the first to do so.) However, the attempt to maintain stability within Europe was continued so that the snake survived even although the tunnel had vanished.

Thus throughout the 1970s European countries attempted to stabilise internal rates. The result was in general a failure because of the strong pressures towards D-mark appreciation. As suggested above, these pressures did not stem directly from developments in international trade, but from recurrent loss of confidence in the dollar. Wealth holders (individuals, enterprises and banks), even though they might have no interests in Germany or trade with it, nevertheless purchased D-mark assets as an international store of value and investment medium. Since the same effect did not apply to Germany's partners in the snake, they were frequently faced with an unpleasant choice between accepting a very large loss of competitiveness in dollar markets outside Europe, or of abandoning their fixed parities with the D-mark. Thus all of Germany's partners (except Belgium and the Netherlands) at one time or another departed from the snake – in the case of France, there were several attempts to fix exchange rates, each of which failed (for details see Britton and Mayes 1992).

The same developments also placed considerable pressure on the German economy. During the 1950s and 1960s, the D-mark had been *undervalued*, promoting German exports as the locomotive of an enormous industrial expansion and generating continuous current account surpluses. Increases in German wage rates together with rapid D-mark appreciation now reversed these cost relationships. A period of industrial restructuring began which reinforced mechanisation and automation, increased German specialisation in higher-quality exports, particularly of capital equipment, and moved many labour-intensive processes to other countries with lower wage costs. Although this restructuring process successfully reshaped German competitiveness it tended also to increase unemployment, and macroeconomic control of the process was imperilled by sudden sharp appreciations of the D-mark. Since the snake in general failed to stabilise internal European exchange rates, these appreciations put unpredictable pressure on German export markets inside as well as outside the EEC.

In general, events in this period indicated that the problems with Bretton Woods had been more far-reaching than the mere rigidities introduced by fixed exchange rates, since the lack of a stable form of world money continued to perturb international economic relations even after fixed rates had disappeared.

Further reading

A concise account of the history of European monetary integration can be found in Gros and Thygesen (1992). A more detailed account is in van

Ypersele and Koeune (1984). For the EPU see Eichengreen (1993, 1995) and the longer study by Kaplan and Schleiminger (1989).

Notes

1. When a country had exceeded its quota – either in deficit or surplus – it made or received subsequent payments in dollars or gold.
2. These credits may have been necessary for the scheme as a whole, otherwise member countries might have been tempted to restrict imports or artificially promote exports within Western Europe in the hope of using the resulting surplus to acquire US goods. Such a scramble for internal surpluses could have discouraged the growth of trade.
3. Britain had made a previous attempt to exit from the EPU as early as 1953, but this proved premature. It should be added that Germany also came to take a negative attitude to the EPU because it rapidly became a large creditor in Europe, particularly of France, and the EPU tended to expand this lending more than it thought desirable (Giersch, Paqué and Schmieding 1992, p113). Polster and Voy (1995) argue that German policy was almost always impatient with European institutions in the field of monetary relations.
4. This pattern of exchange rate fluctuation persists to this day: a rise in the dollar weakens the D-mark *vis-à-vis* the French franc, while a fall hardens it.
5. Gros and Thygesen (1992, Chapter 1) point out that institutional developments in monetary integration at this time also proved disappointing. A European Monetary Cooperation Fund was established (usually denoted by its French acronym FECOM), consisting of the heads of member state central banks; however, it was never an effective channel of cooperation or policy coordination because the central bankers were not prepared to accept the intended guidance from the Council of Finance Ministers, ECOFIN. FECOM met as a relatively unimportant additional item at the regular meetings of world central bankers under the auspices of the Bank for International Settlements.

5

The EMS

From the snake to the EMS

By the late 1970s it was clear that the snake had failed to produce monetary stability in the European Community – largely because of the upward pressures on the D-mark. These essentially led to it becoming a simple D-mark zone, within which few other countries could achieve satisfactory foreign exchange rates. On a proposal from Commission President Roy Jenkins, the search began for a stronger institutional framework, which would promote a better balance of member state interests and which could respond more flexibly to external pressure.

The main architects of the new system were French President Giscard D'Estaing and German Chancellor Schmidt. It is important to note that the far-reaching coordination of policies envisaged by these leaders went beyond monetary policy. They also worked for a general macroeconomic expansion within Western Europe, with Germany, as a major creditor country with a very strong balance of payments, playing the leading role.

The European Monetary System which emerged was agreed by the European Council in Bremen in 1978 and came into effect early in 1979. Britain was a signatory to the agreement, but chose not to participate in its main element, the Exchange Rate Mechanism (ERM).[1]

The Exchange Rate Mechanism

In practice the ERM was the most important aspect of the EMS. It was an agreement for the joint determination, and collective defence, of a set of fixed exchange rates among participating countries. The commitment to maintain agreed exchange rates, alterable only by agreement, and to defend them collectively made the EMS a more centralised system than Bretton Woods had been in practice.

The proposed exchange rate mechanism involved two sets of constraints on exchange rate fluctuations, known as the parity grid and the divergence indicator. The parity grid was simply a consistent set of cross-exchange rates among the currencies. Each currency would be allowed to fluctuate 2.25 per cent up or down against any of the others. An exception was made for the

Italian lira, which had fluctuation bands of plus or minus 6 per cent. This exception reflected the high and variable rate of inflation in Italy, which made its exchange rate harder to stabilise.

When the limit of fluctuation between any two member currencies was reached, there was an obligation on both central banks concerned to intervene in the forex markets to maintain the parity. Thus the central bank of the weaker currency country was required to purchase its own currency; that of the stronger currency country would buy the other currency with its own. This double obligation was new – it had not existed either under Bretton Woods or the snake. Certainly strong central banks had frequently come to the assistance of weaker ones, but such assistance had typically been discretionary, not obligatory.

To permit central banks to defend their currencies effectively, a very short-term financing facility was agreed, which would provide unlimited (in principle) credit to permit forex intervention. These credits were organised through FECOM, the committee of central bank presidents, which supervised the technical functioning of the system. The credit was made unlimited to avoid setting an obvious target for speculators, who might otherwise be tempted to attack when a credit ceiling was close to being reached. These arrangements can also be looked on as a concession by Germany, since they imposed an obligation on strong currency countries to lend to weaker ones.[2] The repayment of credit could, if necessary, be extended, but such extension was not automatic.

The second constraint on the system as designed was the divergence indicator. This measured the movement of one currency not against another individually, but against all the others taken together. The limits here were set at 75 per cent of the limit on the parity grid: thus a country's currency reached its divergence threshold if it moved 75 per cent towards the parity limit against a basket of the other currencies weighted according to their importance. No measures had to be taken automatically to correct divergence, but there was a presumption that policy changes were required in the divergent country – that is, it should raise interest rates relative to the rest or take other measures to strengthen its balance of payments if its currency was weak, and it should relax policy if its currency was diverging upwards.

The discipline implied by the divergence indicator was, in formal terms, symmetric. It would apply not only to appreciating currencies, but also to depreciating currencies, which would thus be required to consider anti-inflationary measures, such as more restrictive monetary policy. However, in practice it represented another concession by Germany as it was essentially designed to prevent the values of other currencies being pulled up against the dollar by the strength of the D-mark. Thus the divergence indicator had a certain general resemblance to the 'scarce currency clause' written into the Bretton Woods agreement, which permitted other countries to defend themselves against a strong dollar. Had it proved an effective instrument it would have solved the $(n-1)$ problem by a kind of majority vote of the ERM economies: the central tendency of their policies would have determined overall monetary conditions – for instance the general level of interest rates or the average exchange rate of the EC currencies in general *vis-à-vis* the US dollar.

However, the divergence indicator never seems to have had a significant influence on events. This was because the polarity between Germany and the rest which it assumed did not occur: partly this was because, unexpectedly, the first period of the ERM coincided with a phase of dollar strength and D-mark weakness. Thus the effective constraint was always the first one – the parity grid.

The role of the ECU

During the 1970s a form of international money, the ECU (European Currency Unit) developed in the EC. As was pointed out in Chapter 4, the Community had initially used a unit of account, made equivalent to the Bretton Woods dollar by giving it, notionally, the same gold value. With the break-up of Bretton Woods, the link between the dollar and gold was broken. Neither on its own was convenient for accounting purposes in the EC as the dollar tended to depreciate against European currencies while the price of gold, once a free market was established, rose rapidly and fluctuated wildly. In consequence a new accounting unit, the EUA (European Unit of Account) was introduced in 1974. This was a 'basket', defined by the value of specified sums of member state currencies. With the introduction of the EMS, there was an attempt to extend the uses of this unit as a transactions medium, rather than a pure accounting device. It was renamed the ECU in 1979. By 1981 some commercial banks had introduced ECU accounts and payments – largely used for transactions with the EC itself – and some international borrowers began to issue ECU-denominated debt, which offered lenders a way of spreading risks over EC currencies (van Ypersele and Koeune 1984; Britton and Mayes 1992).

Within the EMS, the ECU was given a different significance in the various functions of the system:

• For the parity grid the ECU, was in principle, the denominator. Thus cross-rates were derived from the parity of the two currencies concerned against the ECU. In practice this made no difference – the rates against the D-mark would have worked in the same way. And to make actual calculations, dollar rates were often used: thus the dollar value of the ECU was calculated from the dollar rates of individual currencies.

• For the divergence indicator similarly, measurements were in principle in ECUs. Since the ECU itself included each of the currencies, divergence ranges had to be smaller for important currencies such as the franc and the D-mark which constituted a large part of the ECU's value. Otherwise these currencies would have fluctuated more against the others, pulling up the ECU when they appreciated.

• Some steps were taken towards making the ECU a reserve asset. Participating countries deposited 20 per cent of their foreign exchange reserves with FECOM against ECU credits. However there were two limits on this role. Firstly, the ECU-foreign currency swap was temporary – three-month deposits being repeatedly rolled over rather than constituting a permanent reserve fund. Secondly, there were (and are) no spot markets on which ECUs can be used for foreign exchange intervention: they have first to be dismantled into their component currencies in order to intervene on forex markets.

• Starting from its use by the EC, the ECU developed a certain role as a private investment medium: private agents began to raise loans in ECUs on international capital markets (although it can be noted that the use of ECU accounts was for some years prevented in Germany by banking laws). These were long-term loans for the most part, and there was no possibility of official intervention, open-market operations, on this market, because (as will be seen) there was no strong European monetary institution with influence over financial markets. Thus the private and public uses of the ECU were cut off from each other – an important limitation on its monetary role (Aglietta 1986).

• ECUs were used as a payments vehicle – a means of exchange – essentially only by the Community itself. To enable this, European commercial banks did develop their payments systems, so that accounts could be denominated and cheques cleared in ECUs. For nearly all payments except those to the official bodies of the EC, however, this involved packaging ECUs from national currencies and then unpacking them before they could be used for transactions.

To summarise, the ECU developed a limited role as a unit of account and as a store of value. But it remained very underdeveloped as a medium of exchange. The definition of a monetary policy through the ECU – influencing ECU/dollar exchange rates or ECU interest rates – was never really attempted.

A complicating factor was that the ECU included non-participating currencies such as the pound sterling and the drachma – thus it was complicated to use it as a denominator for the participating ERM currencies. Also, the basket has been periodically altered, to prevent the German mark from making up an ever-increasing fraction of its value as the D-mark is repeatedly revalued.

Thus the ambition to organise the EMS around a Community reserve asset remained unfulfilled.

The institutional phase

The Bremen agreement went beyond the mere establishment of the ERM to include the setting-up of a common monetary institution – this was to be the 'institutional phase' of the system. In fact this phase was never reached, although it should in principle have followed within two years of the start of the ERM. The functions of the European Monetary Fund were never well defined but its function essentially would have been to centralise a large part of the dollar and gold reserves of the EC countries and, on that basis, to operate a common external monetary policy by laying down a foreign exchange rate strategy *vis-à-vis* the dollar. The institutional phase was aborted largely because of German reluctance to centralise monetary power without a much more far-reaching political agreement among the member states. In fact, as we shall see, the political conditions for such a development were inauspicious during the early 1980s. (For details of the institutional phase see van Ypersele and Koeune 1984.)

The result, however, was both an economic and a political failure – the $(n-1)$ problem for the EMS was never resolved. That is, in order to achieve the internal exchange rate stability among the original seven currencies (D-mark, franc, Belgian/Luxembourg franc, kroner, lira, punt, guilder), only six policy instruments were required. The remaining degree of freedom could have been used to lay down an overall policy for the system – either a monetary aggregate, a nominal interest rate or an external exchange rate, or some trade-off of these three – but such a collective position was never defined. The method of achieving this could either have been asymmetric – with, for example, Germany laying down the overall objective – or more symmetric – for example an average interest rate could have been specified for the system, with individual countries using the differentials between their own rates and this average to control their exchange rates.

This absence of a common position may have been an advantage in the original, very loose, system since it allowed considerable divergence in member state positions. In the subsequent period, however, it became a weakness and eventually led to the disruption of the whole system.

Phase I – the island of stability

It is generally recognised that the ERM began as a very limited structure, imposing a minimum of constraints on member states, and that it gradually evolved towards a much more ambitious attempt at monetary integration. Schematically, we can distinguish a phase I and phase II system, differing in several dimensions (Table 5.1).

In the first phase, then, what was attempted was essentially short-run exchange rate stability and thus the reduction of volatility. If a conflict developed between the existing exchange rate parities and the policy stance of a member state, it would be the parity that was sacrificed. For example, France

Table 5.1 Stylised view of changes in the EMS

	Phase I: island of stability	*Phase II: competitive disinflation*
Constraints on national policy	limited	severe
Realignments	frequent	infrequent
External conditions	strong dollar	weak dollar
Capital controls	intensively used by weaker countries	dismantled
Rules	original	amended (Basle-Nyborg)
Order	bipolar	unipolar
Predominance of	domestic policy	system-wide constraints
Overall objective	short-run stabilisation	medium-term disinflation

devalued the franc three times between 1981 and 1983 in order to accommodate the expansionary objectives of the early Mitterrand years.

One reason that the system endured in spite of this lack of coordination was that the D-mark was relatively weak during the first phase. The enormous speculation in the dollar between 1980 and 1985 tended even to an undervaluation of the D-mark (Table 5.2). Thus countries with less competitive economies and higher inflation rates experienced less difficulty than might have been anticipated in pegging their currencies to the D-mark.

Table 5.2 Dollar/D-mark exchange rate

1970	1972	1974	1976	1978	1980	1982	1984	1986	1988
3.66	3.19	2.59	2.52	2.01	1.82	2.43	2.85	2.17	1.76

Source: OECD

The relative success of the system also depended on continuing capital controls in several member states. Belgium, for example, continued to operate dual dollar exchange rates, with investment dollars more expensive than trade dollars. Both France and Italy continued to operate controls on foreign exchange – in the French case these were even facilitated by the virtually complete nationalisation of the banking sector at the start of 1982. Thus there remained significant differentials between franc interest rates within France and those on the Euro-currency markets. At times external interest rates were pushed very high (on occasion franc rates on short-term loans went above 1,000 per cent) in order to discourage sales of the franc without this having an automatic effect on borrowers within France.

During this period asymmetries in the system were limited. Several studies (for instance Weber 1991) indicate that the ERM cannot be simply characterised as a D-mark zone; whether policy is examined in terms of monetary aggregates, interest rates or sterilisation of inflows, it is incorrect to see a pattern of German dominance to which other countries simply adapted. Rather, following Weber, it may be more appropriate to characterise the system as bipolar. One group of countries – Belgium, Denmark and the Netherlands – did attempt to align their policies closely with those of Germany. The others, Italy and Ireland, tended to follow the lead of Paris. Germany was not closely constrained by the system in these years but it did not dominate policy formation in the system as a whole.

The success of the system lay essentially in reducing short-term volatility and preventing the overshooting of exchange rates. This seems to have occurred by influencing expectations rather than reintroducing volatility elsewhere – thus short-term fluctuations in interest rates did not increase to offset foreign exchange pressures; rather these pressures were themselves reduced, at least over short time periods. Speculation against the parities was limited: on the one hand by controls; on the other by the frequent, small, realignments which did not offer large profits to speculation. In practice the commitment required by the system was not very large: it amounted to saying that devaluations and revaluations would be small, rather than saying that parities would be defended come what may.

Franco–German divergence

Nevertheless, the achievements of the system in this period appear to be modest, given the scale of the difficulties that emerged for member state economies. Their coordination was limited to short-term forex stabilisation, and did not affect macroeconomic policy more generally. In fact we can even talk of a decline in general policy coordination. The main factor here was a wide divergence between French and German policies, each of which became more focused on more narrowly internal questions.

The agreements of Schmidt and Giscard had, as has been already noted, gone well beyond monetary stabilisation and involved an attempt – to be led by Germany – to expand the European economy as a whole. Both these personalities were soon removed from the scene. The German expansion was a factor in the removal of Schmidt who came into conflict with the Bundesbank over his budgetary programme. Macroeconomic problems in Germany were exacerbated by the Volcker shock of 1980 and the oil price rises of 1980. Together these produced a large current account deficit in Germany which, whether justifiably or not, intensified the Bundesbank's preoccupation with retrenchment. Interest rates were increased sharply and the central bank opposed Schmidt's borrowing programme (in a bizarre attempt to circumvent Bundesbank restrictions on German finance, Schmidt even attempted to raise money from the Saudis, but this proved abortive). The conflict was a key factor in the switch of allegiance of Schmidt's coalition partner, the FDP, to the right-wing CDU/CSU. A conservative government thus came to office committed to both tighter monetary control and fiscal retrenchment (Herr 1991).

In France meanwhile, policy moved in exactly the opposite direction. The presidential and then legislative elections of 1981 inaugurated a

Keynes/Marx experiment within a strictly national framework. A major fiscal expansion, with accommodating monetary policy, was combined with an ambitious programme of public ownership designed to transform the whole economic and social system. Both aspects of French strategy focused on the domestic economy. It was intended to override external macroeconomic constraints through the use of controls, while reducing French dependence on foreign investment and technology. The failure of this strategy was probably inevitable as the industrial policy was misconceived – it was not possible to reduce the specialisation of French leading industries without impairing efficiency. However, external shocks intensified the difficulties – worldwide recession and rising international interest rates led to substantial balance of payments pressures. In the discussions preceding the reversal of policy in 1983, the ERM was a key issue. The left-wing minority which wanted to continue the experiment pressed for France to leave the mechanism; the dominant forces within the majority, however, were not prepared to risk a rupture with the EC. Rather, the French socialists abandoned the goal of 'growth within one country' and began to reformulate their more ambitious objectives in terms of long-term, European, developments rather than as immediate policies for France itself (Muet and Fontenau 1990).

This extreme divergence of policy during the early 1980s, with the two key members of the Community going their separate ways, indicates that a close coordination of macroeconomic policies was perhaps infeasible. It was only the failure of 'growth in one country' that began to focus attention again on the possibilities of common action. Nevertheless, a very high price was paid by Europe for its lack of a common stance. In the wake of the Volcker shock the European economies entered the deepest postwar recession up to that time. Unemployment climbed to very high levels, from which no full recovery has yet occurred. Subjected to extreme financial pressures, governments turned towards retrenchment – again in an uncoordinated way which provoked negative spillovers on each other.

Europe and Volcker

In late 1979, under the chairmanship of Paul Volcker, the US Federal Reserve turned to a policy of monetary restriction, influenced by (if not absolutely in accordance with) the doctrines of Milton Friedman and the Chicago School. The first results were much higher and more variable interest rates and a sharp, but short, recession. However, with the inauguration of Ronald Reagan as US president in 1981 very large tax cuts were introduced, under the influence of the 'voodoo' version of supply-side economics. The administration took the absurd position that these would be self-financing because they would bring about an economic miracle. At unchanged interest rates such a fiscal expansion would have led to a big increase in money and credit. The central bank under Volcker raised interest rates again, for a longer period; in fact there was now open conflict between the fiscal and monetary authorities in the US. Although monetary policies were modified and gradually relaxed from the late summer of 1982, generally tight credit conditions persisted in the US for several years. On an international scale the results were high interest rates and an immense rise in the value of the dollar. (Krugman 1994, Chapter 8, argues that the policy shift was an emergency reaction to double-digit inflation rather than indicative of any profound change in doctrine.)

It may seem common sense to say that a dramatic tightening of monetary policy in the US would cause problems in Western Europe. However, there is a theoretical difficulty in analysing this effect which was pointed out by Fitoussi and Phelps (1988) in their account of the European recession. According to the most widely used model (that of Mundell and Fleming, see Chapter 2), a rise in external interest rates should in fact have had an expansionary effect on Western Europe. The Mundell-Fleming model indicates that, with floating exchange rates, the medium-term consequences of such a shock would be a depreciation of European currencies together with an expansion of European exports to the US. European interest rates would increase but only, if we assume unchanged monetary policy in European countries, as a consequence of the substantial rise in output and employment induced by export-led growth. To this result, the kind of dynamics developed by Dornbusch (1976) would add the possibility of a temporary overshoot – that is, the initial gap between high US interest rates and low European rates would require a slow appreciation of European currencies – and there would be a larger immediate fall of European currencies to make this possible.

In reality, however, there is no doubt that the US move had deflationary consequences for Europe, and even the subsequent US tax cuts under President Reagan's audacious 'supply-side' measures did not compensate the Europeans for these effects. There are several plausible explanations for what happened:

- *The 'dirty' float.* Although European currencies were floating against the dollar, this by no means implied that European governments were indifferent to the dollar exchange rate. In fact they attempted to limit the depreciation of their currencies by tightening monetary policy. In this case the appropriate version of the Mundell-Fleming model might be the fixed exchange rate version, which would indicate that European interest rates would rise by direct monetary contraction rather than by an increase in exports and production in general.

- *The speculative rise of the dollar.* There is little doubt that, even allowing for a Dornbusch-type overshoot, the dollar was pushed to unsustainable levels. This certainly stimulated European exports, but it did so with a considerable lag. Meanwhile it intensified the concern of European governments to limit depreciation and government spending.

- *Fiscal policy in Europe.* The new regime of high real interest rates, arising from lower inflation and higher nominal rates, provoked an attempt to stabilise government budgets. During the 1970s, Keynesian deficit spending had been easy to finance because low interest rates meant that inflation was wiping out the real value of public debt. This relation was now reversed: interest payments and public debt became the fastest-growing component of public expenditure, and other forms of expenditure were squeezed (Table 5.3). (This effect is even detectable in Britain, where a major fiscal squeeze limited public borrowing at the cost of a more intense recession than elsewhere.)

- Interactions between financial systems. The simplified form of the Mundell-Fleming model assumes that, even when capital is highly mobile, distinct national monetary policies are possible. However, there is no clear dividing line between monetary and other assets, so that it is doubtful whether this distinction between money and other liquid forms of capital is valid. National authorities might in principle be able to control narrow forms of money (currency and deposits of the central bank), but if the

Table 5.3 Financial pressure on European governments (percentage share of interest payments in total public expenditure)

	1979	1980	1981	1982	1983	1984	1985
Germany	2.3	2.7	3.3	4.1	4.8	4.9	4.9
France	1.7	1.7	2.5	2.4	3.3	3.7	4.0
Italy	10.6	11.2	12.0	13.9	14.4	15.2	14.5
UK	2.8	3.1	3.3	3.2	3.1	3.3	3.4

Source: OECD

public regards other domestic assets as close substitutes for foreign assets, a rise in external interest rates might alter the relation between narrow money and broader measures of liquidity. In particular, the rates of interest on medium-term and long-term borrowing might be driven higher by foreign pressures even if very short rates are kept relatively low.

- *Supply-side effects.* Standard models confine the effect of interest rates on output to demand-side influences (influences on expenditure). However, as Fitoussi and Phelps (1988) were among the first to point out, high real interest rates may also destroy productive possibilities. In particular, enterprises have to pay more attention to cashflow and less to long-term profitability. Thus they raise their mark-ups – the margins between their costs and their prices. If wages and other resource costs do not immediately fall, there will be a decline in production even at constant levels of demand.[3]

- *The second oil shock.* Because oil is priced in dollars, the rise of the dollar multiplied the effect on Europe of the second major rise in oil prices in 1979–80. This in itself lowered demand in Europe while increasing inflationary pressures. It also provided governments with another motive to tighten policy.

It is probably fair to summarise Volcker as having caused a global *liquidity shock*, a widespread attempt to turn other assets into money or near-money in the face of increased uncertainty. Standard analysis would suggest that such a shock, if not resolutely combatted by monetary expansion, would raise interest rates, discourage investment and lower employment in the short to medium term at least. The key problem for Europe was that the form of money in question was the US dollar, which they themselves did not issue, while US policy was based precisely on restriction rather than accommodation.

Thus the switch in US policy had a major contractionary effect on Europe. The lack of coordination among European countries then proved very costly. As each tightened policy, pressure increased on all the others, through higher interest rates and declining export demand. It is not difficult to see that a coordinated response might have limited the damage. Had the European countries agreed on an interest rate policy, they could at least have avoided adding internal, European pressures to the external shock. The very existence of such a policy would have increased the confidence of governments that, even if the dollar appreciated, they would not find other European currencies appreciating also. Perhaps lower European interest rates would, for a while, have encouraged an even faster rise in the dollar. But it is most unlikely that the boom of the dollar would have been worse overall – in practice it went on rising to quite absurd levels, for five years. In fact a well-defined and confident response by the Europeans might have made both market operators and the US government reconsider their positions. The Europeans would have been declaring that US policy was too tight and that the dollar was becoming misaligned; they would have contested the increasingly dysfunctional role of the dollar in the international monetary system. What actually took place – a disorganised response aimed at limiting foreign exchange pressures on individual countries – may have added to the market's belief in the primacy of the dollar.[4]

Thus the judgement on the first phase of EMS that is suggested here is much more severe than that usually presented. It is true that cooperation within the ERM reduced volatility. But the cooperation did not go very deep. Beneath it there remained a wide divergence of fundamental strategy – especially between France and Germany – which led to what was perhaps the greatest coordination failure of the postwar period. The price of this failure was a recession whose after-effects continue to impair the performance of the European economies.

Phase II – competitive disinflation

By the mid-1980s the whole climate of Western European policy had changed decisively. Attempts to fight unemployment with traditional Keynesian weapons had fallen into desuetude. Rather, macroeconomic instruments were increasingly directed towards disinflation and the stabilisation of public finances. Real economic targets, growth and employment, were now pursued with supply-side reforms of a neoliberal kind: deregulation; privatisation; labour market flexibility; tax cuts, particularly for business and qualified workers. Corresponding to this shift in approach at national level, the significance and objectives of the EMS also began to change.

There are, of course, a number of historical factors behind this shift. The fundamental factor was perhaps the breakdown of the Keynes-Ford model of economic growth, which had performed so well in the phase of European industrialisation from 1945 to 1970 but which was now no longer capable of generating rapid increases in output and productivity.[5] Recent macroeconomic events helped to turn the search for reform in a neoliberal direction. The French Marx-Keynes experiment had clearly failed; while early, although in the event largely illusory, success for the monetarist exercises of Britain and the US won prestige for this approach.

This misreading of the British and US policy was to some extent the consequence of developments in the foreign exchange markets. In both countries an early result of monetarism was a rise in the exchange rate. This appreciation was not a question of foreign trade (although North Sea oil was a factor in the British case); it resulted from high interest rates and from the confidence international wealth holders placed in right-wing governments. An overvalued exchange rate can do great damage to export industry and to a country's competitiveness, but it also produces short-run benefits which can mask these effects for a while. A high exchange rate raises incomes and at the same time slows down inflation (in both cases because import prices are reduced). In consequence, the monetarist experiments were able to point to impressive early successes, although these were in fact mortgaged on a future loss of competitiveness.

A further general factor in the European turn towards monetary restriction was the Volcker shock itself and the much higher interest rates it led to. Although the very high interest rates of the early 1980s were subsequently reduced, they remained at historically high levels. Since monetary restriction had succeeded in reducing inflation, real interest rates remained at exceptional levels. In these circumstances, standard Keynesian remedies for unemployment – which involved public sector deficits – were very difficult to finance.

In the context of this switch in policy orientation, the objectives of the EMS came to be redefined. As all participating countries now declared inflation to be public enemy number one, they were much more concerned to avoid exchange rate depreciations. At the same time a firm link to the D-mark was seen as reinforcing a currency's anti-inflationary credentials.

The most important example of this policy switch was that of France. The new, restrictive, French strategy became known as competitive disinflation. This explicitly subordinated the objective of full employment to that of price stability. The idea was to reduce the rate of inflation by restrictive measures. If this was done at fixed exchange rates and more successfully than in other countries, then France would gain a competitive advantage from its lower prices and net exports would increase. It was hoped that this would reverse the tendency to higher unemployment which the strategy certainly implied.

Of course, a quicker and more reliable way of stimulating net exports would have simply been for France to devalue, but this was rejected because of its tendency to produce both direct inflation and a climate of inflationary expectations based on the view that more devaluations would follow. Although this was certainly a reasonable conclusion from previous French experience, the disadvantages of the devaluationary alternative were, perhaps, overestimated, in the same way that the costs of disinflation in terms of unemployment were underestimated (for a critical analysis of the strategy see Fitoussi *et al.* 1993, Blanchard and Muet 1993).

A second difficulty with the strategy lay in its potential implications for the Community as a whole. If several other countries imitated France and attempted to improve their net exports by restrictive policies, then a contractionary game could result, forcing down everybody's inflation but at substantial costs in terms of employment and with the hoped-for gains in exports proving illusory for the players as a group. In fact such a contractionary spiral did not appear because there was a general improvement in growth rates in Europe in the late 1980s; however, it remained a risk and may have been an aggravating factor in the disruption of the EMS in the early 1990s.

With the new preoccupation with exchange rate stability, realignments became less frequent and practically ceased after 1987.[6] Thus it was not internal policy which was adapted to external constraints, but rather the other way round. Two factors increased the potential difficulties of maintaining fixed exchange rates in this second phase. Firstly, the US dollar began to depreciate and, as the usual consequence, the D-mark began once again to increase its role as an international money. To begin with, this was probably a welcome development: the dollar had been seriously misaligned and this had inflated import costs for European countries. Gradually, however, dollar weakness started to threaten the same kind of tensions within Europe as had been experienced in the 1970s. Secondly, European governments began to dismantle their foreign exchange controls. Partly this was in accordance with the now prevalent free-market theories – Britain had done the same immediately after the election of a Conservative government in 1979. The process was accelerated by the '1992' market completion programme of the European Community. This required the free movement of funds within the EC, but since there was never any question of the countries (such as Germany or Britain) which no longer operated controls reintroducing them, the only way to allow free internal capital flows was through a complete liberalisation which would abolish restrictions on both internal and external movements. This liberalisation was agreed by the Council of Ministers in 1988. All foreign exchange controls were to be lifted by 1 July 1990 (with an extension until July 1992 for weaker economies such as Spain).[7]

The liberalisation of capital flows meant that to defend a weak currency it was necessary to change domestic policies – that is, most usually, to raise domestic interest rates. Previously it had been possible to raise interest rates for non-residents, while, at least for a short period, domestic debtors were shielded. This was no longer possible.

Basle-Nyborg

In this new climate of more determined disinflation, the central banks which operated the exchange rate system agreed, in 1987, on a change of rules. The agreement was aimed at strengthening the ERM, which was increasingly seen as a success, and at tightening the discipline which the mechanism imposed on participating currencies. This was in general consonant with the readiness of countries to accept more constraints on their domestic policy, in the name of disinflation.

There were two main elements to what became known as the Basle-Nyborg agreement. Firstly, the short-run defence of the parities against market pressures was strengthened: on the one hand by making provision for longer-run credit to central banks under pressure; on the other hand, by agreeing to make more use of intra-marginal intervention. The meaning of the latter is as follows. The original EMS rules required central banks of two countries to intervene on the foreign exchange markets when the exchange rate between their currencies reached the limit of its permitted band of fluctuation; the weaker bank would buy its own currency while the stronger bank sold its own money against the other. However, intervention only at the margins of fluctuation is dangerous because it comes late and inevitably has a suggestion of emergency action, which can have the perverse effect of further undermining confidence. For this reason central banks often prefer to avoid the limits of the system being explicitly tested, by intervening well before they are reached. The agreement now was to make more use of such intervention (although the supporting central bank was not put under a direct obligation to do so) and to provide credits for such operations.

These measures strengthened the collective defences of the system. They can be seen, in principle, as concessions by Germany because Germany was most likely to be the lender in extending credit to other central banks and most likely, also, to be intervening in foreign exchange markets to support other currencies. (In practice, however, Germany does not seem to have intervened much within the margins of fluctuation – that is, it tended to wait until it was obliged, by the formal rules, to support another currency.)

The second element of Basle-Nyborg, however, can be seen as a concession to Germany. It stated that central banks would not rely on foreign exchange market intervention alone to preserve the parities of the ERM, but that they would make more use of interest rates. What this suggested is that countries whose currency was under pressure would raise interest rates, thus reducing spending and economic activity in their own countries in order to improve the trade balance and persuade international wealth holders to hold their currency. This commitment represented the new willingness of European countries to subordinate internal to external economic objectives, in the name of price stability. It meant in practice that they would align their monetary policies with that of Germany.

The issue of German dominance

It was suggested above that the way the ERM began, and the failure of its 'institutional phase', left the $(n - 1)$ question in suspense. In other words, it was left unclear how overall monetary policy would be set within the system. The divergence indicator pointed to the determination of policy by general, but uncoordinated, decisions – whatever monetary stance was adopted by most members would become the rule. However, the divergence procedure was never effective in practice and after Basle-Nyborg it was, in effect, abandoned.

The question of overall policy was not too pressing in the early years of the EMS because the system was so loose – essentially member states could pursue independent policies and use realignments to adjust the exchange rate accordingly. However, after the new orientation of the system, with realignments avoided and internal policy geared to stabilising exchange rates, the question of overall direction came up again. In principle, this could have been resolved by an EMS agreement on monetary policy (that is, on the general movement of interest rates, or on external exchange rates against the dollar or on the growth of some measure of the money supply, or – more practically – on some trade-off among these three targets). However, no such agreement was ever reached, even informally, and it is most doubtful whether the political basis for it existed.

The argument here is that the $(n - 1)$ problem was resolved through the classic method of hegemony, and that Germany now had the ability to set the parameters of the system as a whole. However, this judgement needs to be elaborated because most detailed studies have pointed to the opposite conclusion: that Germany did not dominate policy formation in the ERM and that it is therefore wrong to characterise this as a D-mark zone.

The statistical studies of the question (Fratianni and von Hagen 1990, Weber 1991) investigate three issues. The first is whether German leadership determined the supply of money within the system. Since there are so many difficulties with relationships concerning money supply, this issue is perhaps not particularly significant. The second, probably much more important question, concerns interest rates. Was the overall level of interest rates within the system determined unilaterally by the Bundesbank? The weight of empirical investigation suggests not. Thirdly, the issue of sterilisation has been explored: the focus here is on the interaction of external and internal aspects of monetary policy – that is, exchange rate parities and the internal supply of credit. Sterilisation denotes an attempt to separate internal and external aspects. A central bank whose currency is under pressure will be buying in its own money on the foreign exchange markets; this tends automatically to reduce the supply of central bank money and thus to restrict credit and increase interest rates. If these domestic consequences are unwelcome the forex operations are sterilised by putting additional credit back into the domestic economy, so that domestic borrowing and lending is insulated from the external pressure. Similarly, a central bank with a strong currency might seek to avoid pressure to expand the domestic economy arising from the foreign exchange market. Although it would be selling its own currency against foreign exchange, it would try to take corresponding amounts out of internal circulation by borrowing from the public or restricting loans to commercial banks. The basic allegation, then, was that while other EMS countries did not, Germany did sterilise foreign exchange inflows so that, unlike the others, it tried to set monetary policy independently of the exchange rate parities, rather than adapting its policy to the constraints of the system. However, once again the weight of evidence seems to be against this hypothesis. Extensive sterilisation was practised by all participating countries, not just Germany.

However, the present argument does not conflict with this evidence because of the issue of timing. It is not asserted that the ERM was, from the start, a D-mark zone, only that it tended to become so towards the end of the 1980s. The account of Weber (1991) seems convincing: while the ERM began as a bipolar system, with countries loosely aligning their policies either on France or on Germany, from 1987 onwards it *tended* to become unipolar – with all members focusing on their D-mark parities. Even the second phase did not begin with any forceful assertion of German dominance: German interest rates were relatively low, and since other countries were trying to fight inflation, they did not experience German policy as too much of a constraint – their internal and external targets tended, roughly, to coincide.

However, when German policy tightened (before, but especially after unification), all this changed. The ability of Germany to set the general direction of monetary policy was dramatically asserted and the other countries had to struggle, in the end unsuccessfully, to adapt. In fact, in the absence of a collective agreement on European policy, this hegemonic pattern was always likely to emerge. Other countries even made a virtue of necessity, claiming that a stable link to the D-mark helped to stabilise their own price levels and build confidence in the disinflationary process. (This should, in principle, have made it easier to reduce inflation because workers and employers who were ready to moderate their wage demands and their prices would be confident that others would do the same. In practice, however, there is little evidence for such a D-mark confidence spillover; it proved harder than policy-makers anticipated to 'borrow' the reputation of the Bundesbank; see Egebo and Englander 1992.)

Thus German dominance, always a possibility, only became a fact from 1989 onwards and led to a process of monetary restriction. (Gardiner and Perraudin 1993 give a more detailed chronology but see German leadership as established from 1987 with a brief interruption in 1990.) After three years of deepening recession, the system was totally disrupted, amounting, in practice, to a monetary disintegration of Western Europe; this constitutes the theme of the next chapter.

Further reading

Gros and Thygesen (1992) sum up knowledge on the eve of the crises of 1992–93. For a select bibliography of a vast literature on the EMS see De Grauwe and Papademos (1990); for a survey of literature see Bank of England (1991). The history of the EMS is laid out in Collignon (1994) part I.

Notes

1. This decision was taken by a Labour government, concerned that the ERM would make devaluation difficult. It was, ironically, adhered to by the incoming Thatcher administration in 1979; for them, a fixed exchange rate would have obstructed the planned monetary squeeze by preventing sterling appreciation.
2. Note, however, that the Bundesbank secured assurances from the Federal government that it would not be compelled to put domestic price stability at risk by intervention obligations under the EMS. If such a situation threatened, the government would take pressure off the Bundesbank either by securing a revaluation of the D-mark or, if need be, suspending the Bundesbank's obligation to intervene. It is relevant to what subsequently happened that the first recourse – to a realign-

ment – was not in the power of the government to deliver, unless other countries agreed. Hence, the only way out would be to cut off support for a weak currency. It is not clear that this undertaking was compatible with the Bremen agreement (Emminger 1986, cited by Eichengreen and Wyplosz 1993).

3. US fiscal policy under Reagan, which was recklessly expansionary – although it was met by higher interest rates – gave some relief to US enterprises by allowing them to write off many interest rate costs against tax. Such fiscal cushioning of enterprises against the credit squeeze was not nearly as common in Europe (Fitoussi and Phelps 1988, p67).

4. It should be noted that the dramatic tightening of US policy at the end of 1979 was not a purely US decision; European interests were represented at least once. A high level American delegation met with German Chancellor Schmidt and Bundesbank president Emminger in Hamburg in September 1979. The American side, led by Volcker, were concerned about dollar depreciation and proposed joint intervention to hold the dollar in a target range. The Germans said that they would under no circumstances accept an overshoot of their money supply targets as a result of increased intervention. It is worth quoting the interchange between Emminger and Volcker. The latter asked, 'Is it your opinion that American interest rates are not high enough?' Emminger replied that many US commercial bankers had told him that they were not worried by high rates provided they could refinance themselves at the Federal Reserve. He declared that US inflation was essentially a matter of the money supply. 'Exactly', agreed Volcker, to Emminger's surprise, 'the really decisive factor is the money supply.' It is to be doubted, in view of subsequent events, whether general European interests were adequately represented at this encounter by the Bundesbank model for the coming European Central Bank (Emminger 1986, pp390–8).

5. For a discussion of the emerging economic problems of industrialised economies in these terms see the work of the *régulation* school, for example Boyer (1990) and Lipietz (1987). This writer has tried to argue, from this point of view, that the growth of monetary disturbances in the West is inseparable from failures of its productive system (Grahl 1988).

6. There was a small alteration of Italy's central rate at the same time as Italy moved from wider to narrower bands, but this did not amount to a devaluation.

7. For details of this decision see Chapter 9.

6

The crisis of the EMS

Débâcle

At the beginning of the 1990s the EMS enjoyed unprecedented prestige. Increasingly it was seen as central to the macroeconomic strategy of EC member states; new countries – Spain, Britain, then Portugal, joined the exchange rate mechanism while Nordic countries still outside the Community became 'unofficial' members by pegging their own currencies to the D-mark. On the basis of the EMS, the project of monetary unification in the Community was revived and became the centrepiece of the Maastricht Treaty negotiated through 1991. Less than two years later the system was in complete disarray. Repeated foreign exchange rate crises had driven Britain and Italy out of the mechanism, compelled Sweden and Finland to float their currencies, forced several devaluations and the reintroduction of capital controls elsewhere, and finally led to the widening of fluctuation bands from plus or minus 2.25 per cent to the huge range of plus or minus 15 per cent, which was widely regarded as a virtual abandonment of the attempt to control exchange rates. At the same time the tentative recovery in employment and output growth which had occurred in the late 1980s gave way to a damaging, Europe-wide recession which brought unprecedented levels of unemployment.

This chapter examines the reasons for this débâcle. There were policy errors in several countries which weakened the system, but it will be argued that the key problem was the failure to define a constructive, growth-oriented, monetary policy for Western Europe as a whole. Since, by the early 1990s, the EMS had become a hegemonic system, led by Germany, this means that German monetary policy bears a heavy responsibility for what happened.

Theories of foreign exchange crises

During the 1980s a theory of foreign exchange crises first advanced by Krugman (1979) was gradually extended and elaborated (for a survey see Blackburn and Sola 1993). The focus of Krugman's model is on the *timing* of such crises – the fact that they do not, as the notion of efficient markets might lead one to expect, break out as soon as underlying monetary policy is perceived to be incompatible with a fixed exchange rate. This delay is possible because of the foreign exchange reserves which a country possesses and which it can use to defend a fixed exchange rate, even though its domestic policy may be so inflationary as to be incompatible with the maintenance of that rate in the medium term. Krugman envisages sterilised forex intervention which fails to reduce the growth of the money supply so that the underlying equilibrium exchange rate, determined by competitiveness, is gradually falling. Only when there is a clear gap between this potential equilibrium rate and the fixed rate which is being defended by intervention, so that speculators have the prospect of a clear profit, will remaining reserves be immediately exhausted in a speculative attack and a depreciation result.

Although this is a suggestive model, there are many difficulties in relating it to empirical foreign exchange disturbances. In particular, governments – at least in industrialised countries today – do not have a fixed endowment of foreign exchange reserves, controlled by international agencies such as the IMF. They are able, in fact, to borrow reserves on the Euro-currency markets. In these circumstances the limit to the defence of a fixed parity is more difficult to specify. On the one hand there may be limits to the government's readiness to undertake intervention and thus build up a debtor position; on the other hand the international credit markets themselves may impose a limit if the solvency of the government is called into question, by requiring very high interest rates on further credits. A second complicating factor is that markets will examine not only current policies but the path of future policy: in particular, if it is seen that the political costs of a restrictive monetary stance are rising, because of unemployment, then a relaxation may be seen as more likely. Self-fulfilling speculative attacks are also possible in certain versions of these models: policy may be sustainable provided the exchange rate does not fall under suspicion, but not otherwise.

There is a further difficulty in applying the model to the specific case of the ERM. The ERM was an agreement only on *internal* exchange rates – thus its defence required only currencies issued by the participating countries themselves. In principle, then, market speculation could never break EMS parities if all member central banks were fully committed to maintain them. (Intervention in practice would often require dollars, but this does not seem to involve a severe difficulty – to defend a weak currency one would buy it for dollars while a strong currency was sold to obtain them.) However, the fact that external currencies were not needed certainly does not mean that the ERM could be made invulnerable to market attack. Consider first the case of sterilised intervention, so that each country attempts to insulate domestic monetary conditions from the working of the foreign exchange markets. A country whose currency was under consistent pressure would exhaust its own reserves and become increasingly indebted to its partners, while strong currency countries would attract consistent capital inflows and accumulate unlimited claims on the weaker one in their own reserves. Eventually either the solvency of the weak country would be called into question, or the strong country would not be prepared to extend unconditional credit.

Unsterilised intervention would be a different matter, since it would tend to force the monetary policies of the different countries into compatibility with the given exchange parities. Interest rates would be driven up in the weak country and down in the strong one until the differential was sufficient to relieve the pressure on the first – by improving its trade balance and attracting capital inflows. But the actual pattern of this intervention seems to be indeterminate and its consequences doubtful, since the EMS has no norm or reference interest rate relative to which such adjustments should be made. Although an interest rate reduction in the strong country might be the way to remove tensions in the exchange rate mechanism, it was much more likely that interest rates would rise in the weaker one. In fact, there was no way to require a strong currency country – in practice, Germany – to undertake such a relaxation. (For a study which applies several such models to the EMS crisis see Eichengreen and Wyplosz 1993.)

There are no clear rules about sterilisation or its absence in the EMS. But the whole functioning of the system in the second phase tended to rule out unsterilised intervention by Germany. Germany was declared to be the nominal anchor of the system and the other countries explicitly stated their readiness to follow the lead of the Bundesbank. In such circumstances the onus would fall on countries under pressure to raise their interest rates. Thus we could conclude tentatively that:

- the fundamental limit on the EMS parities was the readiness of countries under pressure to raise interest rates and the degree to which this relaxed tensions in the system;

- but during any period of high tension the key tactical factor was the scale and strength of German support on the foreign exchange markets.

The apogee of the system

After 1987 there were no realignments within the EMS for five years – until the crisis of the lira and sterling in September 1992. The only exception was a move of the lira to the narrower band regime of plus or minus 2.25 per cent; this was associated with a small realignment of its central rate but did not require an actual depreciation. In 1989 Spain adhered to the system, adopting the wide band option for the peseta, and in 1990 it was followed by Britain which also opted for wide bands. At the same time an increasing number of non-EC countries pegged to the D-mark – disinflation via the D-mark became the common macroeconomic strategy of all Western European countries. The emerging perspective was of a relatively rapid and unproblematic transition to monetary union without major adjustment of prevailing exchange rates. Increasing confidence in the stability of the system was expressed by the decision of EC member states, within the framework of the Community's market completion programme, to dismantle the remaining controls on foreign exchange transactions.

The most obvious success of the system was in the achievement of *nominal convergence*. Inflation rates had been brought down from double-digit levels at the beginning of the 1980s to low single digits (Table 6.1).

However, the assessment of the markets continued to require substantial interest rate premia on the non D-mark currencies. These rates were

Table 6.1 Consumer price inflation (per cent per annum)

	Germany	France	Belgium	Netherlands	UK	Italy	Denmark
1980	5.5	13.6	6.7	6.5	18.0	21.1	12.3
1981	6.3	13.4	7.1	6.7	11.9	18.7	11.7
1982	5.3	11.8	8.7	5.9	8.6	16.3	10.1
1983	3.3	9.6	7.7	2.7	4.6	15.0	6.9
1984	2.4	7.4	6.3	3.3	5.0	10.6	6.3
1985	2.2	5.8	4.9	2.3	6.1	8.6	4.7
1986	−0.1	2.7	1.3	0.1	3.4	6.1	3.6
1987	0.2	3.1	1.6	−0.7	4.1	4.6	4.0
1988	1.3	2.7	1.2	0.7	4.9	5.0	4.6
1989	2.8	3.6	3.1	1.1	7.8	6.6	4.8
1990	2.7	3.4	3.4	2.5	9.5	6.1	2.7
1991	3.5	3.2	3.2	3.9	5.9	6.5	2.4
1992	4.0	2.4	2.4	3.7	3.7	5.3	5.5

Source: OECD

consistent with confidence in the parity of the Dutch guilder but they also suggest that substantial risk premia were being exacted for most other currencies, although the relative position of the French franc seemed to be improving (Table 6.2).

In retrospect, however, it is clear that the underlying situation was particularly fragile, and that in many ways the structure of exchange rates established in 1987 was unsustainable. Two examples can be given of these fundamental problems: the cases of Italy and of Britain.

Table 6.2 Long-run interest rates

	Germany	France	Italy	UK
1987	6.2	10.2	10.6	9.6
1988	6.5	9.2	10.9	9.7
1989	7.0	9.2	12.8	10.2
1990	8.8	10.4	13.5	11.8
1991	8.5	9.5	13.1	10.1
1992	7.9	9.0	13.7	9.1
1993	6.5	7.0	11.3	7.5

Source: OECD

Italy – destabilised public finance

During the 1970s Italian policy-makers used inflation systematically to avoid a severe economic crisis. Large-scale industry, under great pressure from trade union militancy, was unable to restructure to the same extent as in other EC countries; social and political pressures led to a rapid growth of state expenditures which could not be balanced by the inefficient tax system. In spite of these difficulties, repeated exchange rate depreciation maintained the country's competitiveness and encouraged the exports of Italy's flexible and innovative small business sector.

At the end of the 1970s, as in many other Western European countries, there was a turn to stabilisation. Industrial rationalisation accelerated and the gap between primary government expenditures and tax revenues began to be closed. Over the next decade the system of rapid and complete indexation of wages which had accelerated inflation was reformed and then finally abolished.

One sign of the attempt at more rigorous policies was Italy's participation, from the beginning, in the ERM; another was a move to give the Bank of Italy more independence by releasing it from the legal obligation to purchase short-term government debt.

The first results of the stabilisation were impressive, and it seemed as if Italy had succeeded in braking a rapid inflationary process without an excessive cost in terms of lost output and employment (for an assessment of disinflation in Italy see Giavazzi and Spaventa 1989). However, two major problems remained which compromised Italy's commitment to a fixed exchange rate after 1987. Firstly, inflation, although greatly reduced, remained higher than in Italy's trading partners. Pressure on competitiveness was resisted for a time by tax reforms favouring the tradable goods sector but such stopgap measures only provided temporary relief. Secondly, accumulated government debt led to a very great interest rate burden on public finance, even though current expenditures and tax revenues had been brought into balance. In the past Italy had essentially used inflation as a source of public revenue. This was made possible by *financial repression*: a number of controls, including foreign exchange controls, had been used to make Italian wealth holders hold large quantities of government debt, even though the interest received gave insufficient compensation for inflation; very high reserve ratios were also imposed on the commercial banks, forcing them to hold more central bank money than they would have chosen to. The liberalisation of finance in general and the dismantling of foreign exchange controls in particular made such measures increasingly ineffective. Also the process of disinflation itself intensified the costs of servicing public debt as real interest rates were raised – both by high nominal rates, and by the very success that was obtained in lowering inflation. As a result, price stabilisation led to a destabilisation of public finance: total public debt rose to more than 100 per cent of Italian GDP and interest payments became an ever-growing component of public expenditure. In a chaotic political climate which hindered the drastic measures needed to resolve these problems, the exchange rate *vis-à-vis* other EMS currencies was bound to become unsustainable.[1]

The British adventure

By the mid-1980s the very restrictive monetary policies which had led to recession in Britain in 1980 and the following years had, in essence, been abandoned. Monetary control remained the official position but no clear method was found of implementing monetary policy; an attempt to tie policies to those of Germany had, ironically, to be abandoned because sterling tended always to become too strong under such a regime, since international wealth holders at this time took a very rosy view of Thatcherite Britain. In practice an uncontrolled and inflationary credit expansion developed. One factor behind this was financial deregulation, which led, in particular, to a speculative rise in housing and real estate prices. At the same time personal saving fell to very low levels as consumers obtained access to credit on less restricted terms.

The severity of the preceding recession helped to sustain the boom – in particular, the recession had produced a strong current account surplus which was then dissipated in the following years. By 1988, however, policy had clearly become unsustainable: inflationary pressures had developed and the balance of payments was deteriorating at an alarming rate. Given the government's commitment to tax reductions and its emphasis on monetary policy, the only instrument available to deal with the situation was the rate of interest. A drastic tightening took place, in which interest rates almost doubled to reach 15 per cent at the end of 1989.

This proved to be an extremely crude weapon. Real economic activity slowed very fast, leading to a very deep recession between 1990 and 1992. Unemployment rose, as did company liquidations. In the housing and construction sectors there was a severe crisis: high mortgage rates closed off housing demand; the speculative excesses of the 1980s had produced an excess supply of commercial property which pushed down rents and site values and brought activity almost to a dead stop. On the other hand, the balance of payments responded only very slowly to this treatment. In 1989 the deficit had been at the alarming level of 5.4 per cent of GDP; two years later it was still almost 2 per cent.

Within the ruling Conservative Party there had been a long debate on participation in the ERM. Like other issues connected to the European Community, the ERM seemed to focus deep conflicts in political beliefs and strategies among Conservatives. Mrs Thatcher had repeatedly delayed British participation. In October 1990 she finally agreed.

What seems clear is that the eventual timing of Britain's link to the ERM involved a considerable element of opportunism.[2] Recession was deepening and financial distress widespread. It was necessary to reduce interest rates but confidence in Britain was now fragile and there was a danger that any rapid or substantial easing of monetary policy would provoke a large depreciation of sterling. Adhesion to the ERM in October 1990 offered an escape from this dilemma – since the exchange rate was now underwritten by the system as a whole, and particularly by Germany, it became possible to reduce interest rates with more security. In fact rates were rapidly brought down until they were barely above those in Germany by the autumn of 1992.

How competitive was Britain?

Britain (apparently unilaterally, contrary to the spirit of the EMS) chose a central parity of 2.95 D-mark to the pound. It used the option of wider fluctuation bands (plus or minus 6 per cent) in recognition of the uncertainties affecting the British economy. In fact, the actual rate was initially well above this central value. The view seems to have been taken in the markets that the parity could be defended successfully at least in the short run; given this assumption, the interest rate margin above other ERM currencies tended to draw in capital. However, there was from the start considerable doubt about whether this parity was sustainable in the medium term.

The evidence was difficult to interpret. If price data was used, as in standard assessments of competitiveness, then Britain's position could seem relatively favourable: as compared with its competitors, export prices were substantially lower than they had been at the beginning of the 1980s. However, fluctuations in economic performance had been so wide that it was difficult to calculate an equilibrium position. At the start of the 1980s Britain had indeed posted substantial current account surpluses, but these were to be attributed rather to the recession than to competitiveness.

At the time Britain entered the ERM the current account was in colossal deficit – over 5 per cent of GDP in 1989, still over 4 per cent in 1990 in spite of a drastic slowdown (Table 6.3). There was a sharp division of opinion on the meaning of current account figures. Those of neoliberal persuasion tended to argue that the deficit simply corresponded to an inflow of capital; if one took an optimistic view of the working of private credit markets and assumed that they were normally both stable and efficient, then this inflow corresponded to genuine profit opportunities within Britain; it would not take place unless there was confidence that the corresponding debt would be serviced and repaid through the future development of the British economy.

It is certainly true that the development of international capital markets had made a fundamental change to the meaning of the balance of payments. Deficits no longer had to be financed largely by official credits from other governments as had still been the case in the early 1960s; finance now was essentially a market-based, private sector, process (for a discussion of the meaning of the balance of payments in this new context see Allsopp, Jenkinson and O'Shaughnessy 1990).

Nevertheless, one could still justify concern over very large deficits if a

Table 6.3 How competitive was Britain?

	Export prices relative to world prices (1987 =100)	Balance of payments current account as % of GDP	
1980	119.5	1.5	
1981	116.7	2.5	
1982	109.5	1.5	
1983	104.4	0.9	
1984	100.9	−0.2	
1985	104.1	0.5	
1986	98.8	−0.8	
1987	100.0	−2.0	
1988	106.4	−4.8	
1989	103.0	−5.4	
1990	103.6	−4.2	Britain joins ERM
1991	102.7	−1.8	
1992	105.9	−2.7	

Source: National Institute Economic Review

more sceptical view was taken of the efficiency and stability of credit markets. Private agents might make incorrect or myopic assessments of the security of international loans; then a deficit could signal problems of competitiveness not fully or correctly assessed on the markets. Externalities among credit transactions could lead to dangers of instability not immediately apprehended by individual agents. From this more critical standpoint, the deficit might signal future problems in maintaining the exchange rate at the chosen parity. In fact, the most careful studies of the problem indicated that 2.95 DM represented a substantial overvaluation of the pound, in that at this rate it would be impossible to combine internal and external equilibrium over the medium term. It is this second, more critical, assessment that was justified by events.[3] Britain, just like Italy, was operating an ERM parity that was not sustainable. The difference between the two cases lay essentially in the nature of the underlying imbalances. In Italy the key problem was public finance; in Britain, it was the private sector, which was characterised by overindebtedness.

The squeeze

From what has been said so far, it follows that the position of Britain and Italy in the ERM at the beginning of the 1990s could not be sustained. These exchange rates, at least, would have to fall. It seems likely that other countries, such as Spain, were in a similar case. Nevertheless it is also true that tensions in the system were severely aggravated by the course of European monetary policy – which was determined, because of its hegemonic position, by Germany.

The policies of the Bundesbank during this period are often related to German unification. It is certainly the case that unification posed unique problems for German policy. However, it should also be noted that interest rates had been on a rising trend in Germany from the beginning of 1988 (for a German view which de-emphasises the impact of unification, see Spahn 1995). Germany's partners were subjected in fact to over four years of continuously rising interest rates in the key country of the system (Table 6.4). The impact of this squeeze was intensified by the fact that US policy over the same period was continuously relaxed, so that European currencies tended always to harden against the US dollar.[4]

However, the enormous shock of unification certainly created quite unprecedented policy problems in Germany. In spite of some initial optimism it rapidly became clear that the new German Länder, which had previously made up the German Democratic Republic, were in an extremely weak economic position, and that huge transfers of public money from West Germany would be needed both to reconstruct their economies and to stabilise the social situation and avoid massive, dislocative, flows of population to the rest of the country. How were such transfers to be financed? Substantial tax increases were imposed on the Western population but there was also a considerable rise in public borrowing and the government deficit. This fiscal shift had a potent effect on aggregate demand (contrary to some stylised critiques of deficit spending) and led to a substantial increase in West German output and employment.

At the same time Germany's habitual balance of payments surplus disappeared as both financial resources and productive capacity were diverted from external towards internal purposes.[5]

Table 6.4 The squeeze

(a) short-term interest rates

	Germany	France	Italy	UK
1987	4.0	8.2	11.5	9.7
1988	4.2	7.9	11.3	10.3
1989	7.1	9.3	12.7	13.9
1990	8.4	10.2	12.4	14.8
1991	9.2	9.7	12.2	11.5
1992	9.5	10.5	14.0	9.6

(b) consumer price inflation

	Germany	France	Italy	UK
1987	0.8	3.3	5.3	4.4
1988	1.4	2.9	5.7	5.1
1989	3.1	3.6	6.5	5.9
1990	2.7	3.2	5.9	5.3
1991	3.9	3.2	6.8	7.2
1992	4.1	2.6	5.3	5.1

(c) 'real' short-run interest rates: a – b

	Germany	France	Italy	UK
1987	3.2	4.9	6.2	5.3
1988	2.8	5.0	5.6	5.2
1989	4.0	5.7	6.2	8.0
1990	5.7	7.0	6.5	9.5
1991	5.3	6.5	5.4	4.3
1992	5.4	7.9	8.7	4.5

Source: OECD

The Bundesbank regarded these developments as carrying a serious risk of inflation (it may also be the case that it was concerned about the weakness of the balance of payments – it has historically been an objective of German monetary policy to sustain a surplus). The fiscal deficit and the high level of demand thus became the occasion for a further tightening of policy.

This response in monetary policy is open to criticism on several grounds. There was, first, a technical problem. The Bundesbank, at least officially, related its policy to the monetary aggregate, M3, as a target. All the experience of monetarist experiments indicates how unreliable such indicators can be – especially when there is a major structural change such as that constituted by unification. At times during the period of monetary squeeze, the use of M3 may have been contradictory in that an overshoot of the money stock was used to justify high interest rates, while these high rates themselves induced capital inflows and thus further swelled money holdings.

More fundamentally, the long period of high interest rates may well have been misjudged, even if one considers it as a purely national, German, policy. The post-unification boom gave way to recession in the West; unemployment, which had been falling slowly, started to rise again. However, as a means of discipline on other economic agents, monetary policy failed in its objectives: the Federal government was not constrained to fiscal tightening; the unions continued to contest policies which they regarded as imposing too much of the burden of unification on labour; with increasing insistence the Eastern Länder demanded substantive equality with the rest of the country and rejected the triumphalist tutelage of the political class in Bonn. Eventually, monetary policy was reversed and from the summer of 1992 there was a slow, but increasingly determined, relaxation, in spite of monetary aggregates which continued to overshoot target values.[6] Many commentators saw this relaxation as a function of the impending elections; the reputedly 'independent' central bank may well have had a marked political preference for the continuation of conservative government and have wished to improve Chancellor Kohl's chances against the Social Democrats.

However, what is clear is that monetary policy, whether or not it was appropriate for Germany, clearly subordinated European to national objectives. At most, the ERM was perceived in Frankfurt as an encumbrance, an undesirable constraint on German policy. Early in the process of tightening the Bundesbank did what it could to counteract any such constraining effect. The central bank's portfolio was adjusted to hold more short-run financial assets. This was in preparation for a determined sterilisation of any monetary inflows induced by the squeeze – that is, to insulate German policy from the effects it had on Germany's ERM partners (Neumann 1994).

For those partners the squeeze was disastrous. Already these countries were committed to disinflation, which they were pursuing as forcefully as their domestic economies could stand. Now, in order to protect their ERM parities, they were compelled to tighten their own monetary policies, month after month, during a period of over four years. As German rates rose, the very progress which these countries had made in lowering inflation started to work against them, as it increased the real costs of borrowing. Since it was still necessary for their currencies to offer a risk premium over German interest rates they were caught both ways – by rising nominal interest rates and falling inflation, which together produced a credit squeeze much more intense than in Germany itself, although their productive structures and labour forces were much less able to bear such pressures.

The real but fragile recovery which EC economies had displayed in the late 1980s was brought to a halt – European unemployment, after a period of precarious stabilisation, resumed its upward trend.

In exculpation of this anti-European policy, apologists for the Bundesbank argue that ERM participants were offered an alternative. From 1990 onwards the Bundesbank offered a certain reduction in interest rates if other countries would agree to a general depreciation against the D-mark. For Germany this would essentially have meant a change in monetary instruments rather than monetary policies: a stronger D-mark would push down costs and constrain demand, so that interest rates themselves would not have had to do so much of the work of disinflation. Other countries would then not have faced such a severe squeeze (for the Bundesbank's point of view see *Central Banking* 1995).

What this position ignored was that, by 1990, a stable link to the D-mark had become the centrepiece of economic policy in all ERM countries. This was the essential 'anchor' for domestic policy and the guarantee of a consistently disinflationary stance. Depreciation would mean writing off a major investment of political capital; it would deprive ERM countries of the central element of their economic strategies while undermining confidence and credibility in whatever strategies were introduced as a substitute. These countries were bound to resist a general realignment as strongly as they could.

Meanwhile the Germans themselves did have an alternative, and one that was probably very rational from their own point of view as well as that of their partners. This was simply to accept slightly faster rates of inflation and monetary expansion for a few years than they would have desired.

The shock of unification – clearly a unique, non-repeatable, event – provided every justification for making such an exception: the damage it would have done to the Bundesbank's credibility was surely small; it would have reduced, at least temporarily, German industrial competitiveness but in this it would only have been equivalent to a revaluation of the D-mark. Both inside Germany and in Western Europe such an approach would have created space and time for a more deliberate and orderly response to the new problems of German unification and the transformation in Eastern Europe. The rejection of this alternative represented a parochial focus on domestic developments, to the neglect of problems in other countries – in fact, it was almost an expression of contempt for Germany's ERM partners.

It should be repeated that there were no German policies which could have avoided a major realignment in the ERM, involving the devaluation of, at least, the lira and sterling. The Bundesbank was not responsible for the depreciation of these currencies. It does, however, bear a heavy responsibility for the circumstances in which realignment took place, for the number of countries which were ultimately affected and for the fact that what happened was not a mere realignment but came close to a break-up of the EMS itself.

Firstly, German interest rates, in a quite simple, predictable and direct way, produced the Europe-wide recession (Table 6.5). Recession followed from the credit squeeze as night follows day. The recession itself made the adaptation and preservation of the ERM doubly difficult. It has been pointed out that the key weapon which countries could use to defend their parities was the rate of interest. Since rates now had to move substantially merely to match German policy it was much more difficult to raise them further without unacceptable effects on internal activity. At the same time the use of fiscal policy to compensate for monetary tightness was impeded by recession and the consequent pressure on public sector deficits. As the use of interest rates became more painful, it became less credible – market agents perceived the costs of a credit squeeze and drew the correct conclusion that the political pay-off to devaluation was increasing by the day.

By the beginning of the 1990s Western European countries had in fact converged on a highly integrated and interdependent monetary strategy, centred on the D-mark as the core currency. This meant that the German authorities had, in practice, been given responsibility for monetary conditions throughout the region. The disruption of the ERM is a consequence of German failure to meet that responsibility.

The role of the markets

It has already been stressed that the ERM parities which had been essentially determined in 1987 were unsustainable, as was also the parity for sterling chosen by the British government in 1990. At the same time German policy further aggravated and generalised tensions in the system. Given these

Table 6.5 The recession

Growth rate of real GDP, per cent per annum

	Germany	France	Italy	UK
1987	1.4	2.2	3.1	4.8
1988	3.7	4.3	4.1	4.3
1989	3.4	3.8	2.9	2.1
1990	5.1	2.2	2.2	0.5
1991	3.7	1.1	1.4	−2.2
1992	1.5	1.9	1.1	−0.9
1993	−0.5	1.0	0.8	1.4

Unemployment, per cent

	Germany	France	Italy	UK
1987	6.3	10.4	10.3	10.4
1988	6.3	9.9	10.8	8.5
1989	5.6	9.4	10.6	7.1
1990	4.8	9.0	9.9	7.0
1991	4.2	9.5	10.2	9.1
1992	4.5	10.1	10.2	10.8
1993	6.0	10.8	10.6	12.3

Source: OECD

judgements, there is little point in seeking for independent explanations of 'turbulence' or 'speculation' in the foreign exchange markets. The markets in most currencies had been liberalised gradually over a long period, and this process was deliberately consummated in the context of the Community's single market programme after 1985.[7] In these circumstances the price of currencies was inevitably determined by expectations of future exchange rate movements. The sanction of the markets on any obvious disequilibrium was quite unavoidable.

Rather, the key question is different: why was the markets' attack on ERM parities so long delayed? What forces suspended market pressures on the system until the autumn of 1992, when, on any unbiased estimate, the established parities were already doomed? This has come to be known as the problem of the 'excess credibility' of the system. Two types of explanation seem plausible; they do not necessarily conflict, but may indeed reinforce each other.

Firstly, one can develop an argument within the standard interpretative paradigm of rational expectations and efficient financial markets. From this standpoint the key issue is changes of regime and learning processes. It is acknowledged by the proponents of these theories themselves that correct estimates by market agents of future developments depend on a full understanding of the policy regime which is in force and that such an understanding is based on time and experience (Sheffrin 1983, p14). The ERM was a moving target in many ways – the system was continually evolving in terms of its rules, its functioning and the policy objectives which it was made to serve. Hence there is nothing paradoxical at all in a lag between the actual emergence of a major disequilibrium and the realisation by market agents of its full nature and extent. In fact, the learning process involved has been described in plausible ways. From 1987 many observers of the system tended to focus on a restricted, and hence potentially misleading, group of variables. The latter form of the ERM was interpreted, quite correctly, as an exercise in disinflation and this led to an excessive emphasis on inflation rates as an indicator of the system's success. Only later was it realised that the convergence of inflation rates did nothing to guarantee the compatibility of price *levels* needed to preserve trade equilibrium. It was also gradually realised that the capacity of governments to defend parities by altering their policies had been greatly narrowed by the German credit squeeze (Vaciago 1993).

A second, more Keynesian, interpretation of market behaviour would begin with the notion that individual agents are not capable of constructing stable, well-defined, views on the future of the institutional frameworks in which they must operate. Rather, they derive their individual expectations on such questions from conventions with their origin in social processes. If one takes this view then market expectations about the ERM seem to have been influenced by the political developments around Maastricht and monetary union. The Community managed to maintain its political momentum through the elaboration of the monetary unification project, based on an optimistic view of the future of the ERM leading to a single currency within a relatively short period. If this was in fact the future then limited disequilibria in the exchange rate system might not be of great significance – the move to a single currency would make it necessary to correct disequilbria by other means than exchange rate changes. The political resurgence of the Community from the mid-1980s and the previous success of the ERM encouraged a climate of optimism. What, ironically, took place was a reversal of the relationships between politics and economics: although, originally, the political project of monetary union was justified by the practical success of the ERM, in the end it was the other way round – the continuing stability of the ERM now depended on the belief that EMU was on the immediate political agenda.

Some support for this interpretation of events can be found in the apparent importance of political events in the developing crisis of the ERM from the summer of 1992. In June of that year the Danish electorate rejected Maastricht in a referendum. This had absolutely no implications for the current working of the ERM, but it did place a question mark on its conventionally accepted future in the transition to EMU. This event, whether or not it had any fundamental significance, certainly seems to have triggered a wave of speculation against the existing parities. Similarly, the final destruction of sterling's position was related, at least in its timing, to the impending French referendum on Maastricht and the growing fear that there would be a majority against ratification. What seems to have happened over the summer of 1992 was the dissolution of a clear conventional picture of the future of the ERM as a triumphant march towards a single currency. When that convention vanished there was no longer any rationale to sustain the ERM parities in the marketplace.[8]

The departure of the lira and sterling

Throughout the summer of 1992 a ferocious attack was mounted on sterling and the other vulnerable currencies of the mechanism. Intervention by the Bank of England was at an unprecedented level – much greater sums were committed, for example, by the Bank of England alone than had been used by the major industrial countries as a group in organised intervention against the dollar in 1985. Some 160 billion dollars' worth of D-marks were sold against sterling over a period of three months (Bank of England 1992). The fact that this did not suffice to stabilise the exchange rate demonstrated the virtually unlimited ability of the international financial system to finance foreign exchange operations.

The first cracks in the system in fact affected non-members of the ERM (thus countries without access to its collective defence mechanisms) who had pegged their currencies to the D-mark. Finland, badly affected by economic disorganisation in the former Soviet Union, was forced to float the markka on 8 September, despite having pushed interest rates to 17 per cent.

Germany offered no relief to its partners. In July 1992 it once again raised interest rates. It financed countries under pressure through the European Monetary Cooperation Fund (as it was obliged to do) but confined its own support operations to the minimum – intervening only when a weak currency was actually on its floor level. Even so it was compelled to intervene heavily in September when its holdings of foreign currencies increased by some 80 billion D-marks – almost a doubling. At the same time it pressed very hard for a comprehensive realignment of parities (at times it may have contravened the code of central bankers by being excessively public and explicit about this view).

On Sunday 14 September, the Council of Finance Ministers agreed to a 7 per cent devaluation of the lira but this failed to pacify the markets. Weak currencies again came under attack when markets opened on the Monday. On the Tuesday, pressure on the Swedish krona was temporarily relieved by the announcement of a 500 per cent discount rate, but pressure on sterling, the lira and peseta continued.

At the last moment the Bank of England raised its own interest rates from 10 per cent to 15 per cent in two steps on 16 September. The move lacked credibility because it was hard to believe that such rates could be tolerated for long, either in economic or in political terms.

On that evening sterling and the lira were suspended from the ERM. This was an unprecedented move – what would normally have occurred was a realignment (as happened at the same time with a 5 per cent peseta devaluation) rather than the abandonment of the system altogether. It seems logical to attribute suspension to German monetary policy: for Britain (and perhaps Italy) the difficulty with a devaluation within the system was that it would have required them to continue to match German interest rates even at a lower parity, whereas departure gave much more flexibility to domestic monetary policy. The British made use of this increased autonomy to counteract recession by rapid interest rate reductions – down to 7 per cent by the end of the year and 5.4 per cent by the following summer.

Sovereignty regained?

In retrospect it is clear that there were at least two misjudgements in sterling's entry to the ERM: the chosen rate of exchange was too high, incompatible with internal and external balance; and the timing was wrong – Britain at the moment of entry was marked by very severe cyclical strains. It was suggested above that entry in October 1990 was to some extent an opportunistic move. So indeed was suspension in September 1992 – British interest rates had been brought down virtually to German levels (they were a mere 0.2 per cent higher) and further reductions were possible only outside the system (or perhaps through a very large devaluation indeed).

There was also a fundamental difficulty arising from the nature of the British financial system, which was very different from that in continental countries. A change of short-run interest rates in Germany or France bears mostly on the new lending activities of commercial banks: the general impact on other agents is damped by the use of fixed interest contracts and reliance on powerful intermediary organisations. In Britain's more market-oriented system the impact of interest rate changes is both more widespread and, perhaps, less reliable. One factor behind this may be that some long-term debts, such as mortgages, tend to have fixed interest rates on the continent, while in Britain the rates vary with the short-run interest rate so that the debtors concerned are more exposed to changes in monetary policy (Artis and Lewis 1993). Quite big changes may be necessary to have a decisive impact on expenditure; increases are also likely to cause widespread financial difficulties, while reductions may eventually lead to large increases in demand. In other words monetary policy in Britain may require larger and more frequent interest rate alterations than in other ERM countries because, in a more competitive financial environment, monetary policy is a less precise instrument. If this is the case then it would always be difficult to achieve the convergence of British and continental policies required to operate the mechanism. The exaggerated dependence on monetary policy, to the exclusion of fiscal instruments, which developed in Britain over the 1980s certainly tended to aggravate this kind of difficulty.

On the other hand the main source of such incompatibility was not the financial structure, but the excessive tightness of German policy – had German rates been set with more concern for European rather than purely national circumstances then Britain and other ERM countries would have fared much better within the mechanism and might well have preferred simply to realign their rates rather than to suspend participation.

In the debate that followed suspension British Conservative 'Eurosceptics' referred frequently to the issue of sovereignty. The constraints of the ERM were seen as compromising Britain's ability to set monetary policy in a way appropriate to its own situation. Even more would monetary union represent an unacceptable sacrifice of national independence.

There seems to be considerable exaggeration in this view. The measure of genuine autonomy available to Britain is probably quite small under most circumstances. But in 1992 Britain was able to take advantage of the enormous divergence that had developed between two countries large and powerful enough to enjoy substantial sovereignty – that is, Germany and the United States. While the Bundesbank had tightened policy continuously since 1988, the Federal Reserve had with equal determination cut its rates in response both to recession in general and financial fragility in particular. It is an index of the absurdity of the Bundesbank squeeze that it imposed on Europe interest rates some 7 per cent higher than in the US, although nothing in the actual situation of the two trading blocks could conceivably have justified such a differential.

However, for Britain this gap did create an exceptional opportunity. Because the dollar is still an immensely important currency it is open to Britain, which has very important commercial and financial relations with the US, to align its own policies on those of the US rather than Germany. In so doing it would place the stability of the sterling/dollar exchange rate in a more central position than that of the sterling/D-mark rate, but there would still be some measure of exchange rate stability provided the pound offered a certain premium over the dollar. In the period following suspension this allowed for a substantial reduction in interest rates. But it would probably be extremely dangerous for Britain to try to operate interest rates below those of both these powers – such a step would surely run the risk of a colossal flight from sterling and an uncontrolled depreciation.

If this hypothesis is correct than Britain did not so much 'regain its sovereignty' as defect from the European to the American monetary camp. It was certainly very correct to do so, rather than to continue with an extremely damaging credit squeeze, but from this point of view the actual degree of autonomy that was achieved may be quite small. It would depend, essentially, on the gap between US and German interest rates. The closure of this gap in recent years to a much more normal size has, correspondingly, narrowed the scope for British policy.[9] Provided the gap remains narrow and further deflationary adventures are avoided there would probably be little cost, in terms of interest rates, in returning to the ERM; this could therefore once again become a feasible strategy, always provided that the chosen parity is realistic.

The battle of the franc

Britain's brief, unhappy period in the ERM did the system as a whole some damage. In this there are many similarities with Britain's overall relations

Table 6.6 A tale of three interest rates

	US*	Germany†	UK*	
1982	8.5	6.5	10.5	
1983	9.7	6.4	9.3	
1984	8.0	5.8	10.0	
1985	7.1	4.8	11.8	
1986	5.9	4.8	11.2	
1987	5.9	3.7	8.9	
1988 Q1	5.8	3.4	8.6	Germany tightens
1988 Q2	6.8	3.9	9.9	Germany tightens
1988 Q3	7.5	5.0	11.9	Germany tightens
1988 Q4	8.4	5.4	13.2	Germany tightens
1989 Q1	9.3	6.7	13.0	Germany tightens US relaxes
1989 Q2	8.2	7.0	14.0	Germany tightens US relaxes
1989 Q3	8.1	7.4	13.7	Germany tightens US relaxes
1989 Q4	7.9	7.9	15.0	Germany tightens US relaxes
1990 Q1	8.1	8.1	15.2	Germany tightens US relaxes
1990 Q2	8.0	8.2	14.8	Germany tightens US relaxes
1990 Q3	7.4	8.4	14.8	Germany tightens US relaxes Britain joins ERM
1990 Q4	6.6	9.1	13.8	Germany tightens US relaxes
1991 Q1	5.8	9.1	12.9	Germany tightens US relaxes
1991 Q2	5.5	9.1	11.3	Germany tightens US relaxes
1991 Q3	5.8	9.2	10.6	Germany tightens US relaxes
1991 Q4	5.0	9.5	10.2	Germany tightens US relaxes
1992 Q1	3.9	9.6	10.2	Germany tightens US relaxes
1992 Q2	3.7	9.8	9.9	Germany tightens US relaxes Britain quits ERM
1992 Q3	3.1	9.7	9.7	US relaxes
1992 Q4	3.1	8.9	7.0	US relaxes
1993 Q1	3.0	8.3	5.8	US relaxes
1993 Q2	3.0	7.6	5.4	
1993 Q3	3.0	6.6	5.2	

* 3-month treasury bills   † 3-month interbank offer rate
Source: Bank of England

with the Community – participation has often been late, opportunistic and devoid of any real commitment.[10] The inglorious departure of sterling helped to undermine confidence in the system as a whole and made everyone aware of its vulnerability. In consequence, market attacks on the parities of the ERM became more frequent and more determined, leading to a cumulative breakdown.

Late in September 1992, both Ireland and Portugal resorted to capital controls to protect their currencies. Exchange control was rather easier in the case of these less important currencies than it would be for currencies which are more widely traded: in particular, there were no developed forward markets so that it was more difficult for speculators to take a short position – money had to be actually borrowed from the banking system in order to be sold because one could not simply contract to sell at a future date.

The erosion continued in November when Sweden was compelled to float its currency, and the peseta and escudo were devalued. In December, the Norwegian krone was floated; in February 1993 the Irish punt was finally devalued. Increasingly the attention of speculators – now fully persuaded of the system's vulnerability – was drawn to the key relationship in the ERM, the franc/D-mark exchange rate.

The case of the franc seems very different from that of the lira or the pound, in that there was no clear evidence of overvaluation. The French had made a very heavy investment in foreign exchange stability which had been the central plank of their macroeconomic strategy for ten years.[11]

It could be argued that there was no fundamental disequilibrium in the franc/D-mark rate. France had not only brought its rate of inflation into line with that in Germany, it seemed also to have achieved convergence in price levels because the balance of payments did not exhibit a serious deficit. Inflationary pressures were low – even, in the wake of German unification, lower than in Germany itself in 1991 and 1992.

The German monetary squeeze, however, made France's chosen strategy – export-led growth through disinflation and price competitiveness – extremely painful. Policy-makers always stated that external balance took priority over domestic output and employment; they then acted, consistently, in line with these declarations. Nevertheless, it was clear that a high price was being paid for this priority. A change of government in the spring of 1993 could have been regarded as calling policy commitment to the exchange rate into question because the Gaullist component of the new right-of-centre coalition had frequently expressed some impatience with both the Community in general and the new, more assertive, role of Germany in particular. However, leading positions in the new government were taken by figures with strong pro-European credentials and there was no concrete sign of an altered policy stance.

The French position on interest rates seemed well defined. They were ready, reluctantly, to match high German rates even though this meant that real rates were actually higher in France than in Germany. But they saw no good reason to offer a substantial risk premium above German rates because the French record should, it was thought, be enough to demonstrate that France was committed to maintenance of the parity.

The case of France was also of much greater political significance than that of Britain. Franco-German relations have been central to the project of European integration from the very beginning and were still a determining influence over the Maastricht Treaty. The target of monetary unification was above all a French objective – France saw unification as the only realistic alternative to German monetary hegemony. This was another key factor underpinning the exchange rate: the French, following a clear long-term strategy, hoped that a stable franc/D-mark rate would prepare the way for a common currency. French participation would in any case be indispensable for monetary union. There was never much doubt that Germany could establish a union with some of its smaller neighbours – the Netherlands, Benelux, Austria, perhaps Denmark. But without France such a union would be politically impossible as it would institutionalise German domination of European monetary conditions. Thus maintenance of the franc exchange rate was not only a key aspect of French macroeconomic strategy; it was also important to political and institutional progress in the Union and to the survival of the agenda agreed at Maastricht.

Until very late in the day, Germany seemed to recognise the role of the franc. In several episodes market pressure was met by determined intervention by both central banks and, in the case of France, German policy-makers were prepared to give much stronger verbal undertakings than for other countries.

Nevertheless, in the first half of 1993 there were some signs of friction. France was increasingly impatient with the German credit squeeze. The Germans were quite unwilling to alter their domestic policy on European grounds. The fact that many other ERM currencies had been devalued or depreciated increased the pressure on France by reducing its competitiveness *vis-à-vis* countries like Britain, Spain and Italy. The same fact should have given the Germans some scope for relaxation since import costs and export demand were both reduced, thus contributing to disinflation in Germany, but the Bundesbank seemed almost on principle resolved to make no concessions.

In the spring the French expressed their dissatisfaction with German policy by reducing a central bank interest rate very slightly below the corresponding German rate. This was largely a symbolic move, a comment on German hegemony rather than a substantive change of policy, but market reaction was so unfavourable that it had rapidly to be reversed (Mélitz 1994).[12] At the beginning of the summer there occurred a truly astonishing episode. Prior to a regular meeting with his German counterpart, the French minister of finance expressed the intention to raise the issue of interest rates. The German minister promptly cancelled the meeting – surely one of the crassest gestures in the entire history of the Community.[13] Such events may also have indicated to observers that Franco-German economic relations could not simply be summed up as a strong, mutual commitment to the exchange rate. There also seemed to be developing something of a battle of wills.

In July, attention was focused on German policy. Would the Bundesbank council cut interest rates to bring some relief to the French? In fact a very small relaxation was announced – a step in the slow de-escalation which continued over the next three years. However, market expectations were disappointed and the failure to cut rates more decisively seems to have been interpreted as a repudiation of French positions. Over the next two weeks there was enormous selling of the franc. In principle, of course, this could have been met by unlimited Bundesbank intervention but in practice there were always limits to such support. These were reached at the end of July 1993 and a crisis meeting of the Council of Finance Ministers took place.

The move to broad bands

At the Council of Ministers the French refused a simple devaluation such as would have taken place in previous realignments. They argued that their own policies were consistent with a stable exchange rate and that the key problem was the exceptional circumstances that existed in Germany. In fact a compromise was arrived at with the Germans that the D-mark should be temporarily suspended from the ERM. This would have taken the market pressure off the franc and enabled the Germans to pursue their chosen monetary policy unconstrained by EMS obligations, at the same time as giving political recognition to the validity of French policy.

However, the Franco-German compromise proved unacceptable to hard currency countries such as the Netherlands. From their point of view there would have resulted a quite unnecessary depreciation which would undo the work of years spent establishing a firm D-mark value for their currencies.

Thus a different solution was found – the declared parities of the ERM were all left unchanged but the permitted bands of fluctuation were widened. Instead of the previous range of plus or minus 2.25 per cent currencies would now be allowed to vary by 15 per cent up or down from their central parities. In order to protect the position of the Netherlands, which had already achieved virtual monetary integration with Germany, an exception was made by maintaining narrow bands for the guilder.

This reform at once limited market pressure on the system. After the series of devaluations which had already taken place there was no serious danger of currencies being forced out of the new bands; at the same time speculation became more risky as there was now considerable scope for movements in the opposite direction to that assumed by the market operators. However, the new security of the system was obtained at the sacrifice of its fundamental objective – that is, the stabilisation of exchange rates. Many commentators in fact viewed the new arrangements as little more than a fig-leaf covering the actual abandonment of the system by a move to the virtually unconstrained floating of exchange rates. It is certain that the forced move to wide bands was a major political defeat for the EU: the main structure linking economic policy in member states had been weakened by uncontrollable market pressures; and the project of monetary union – the main item on the EU's agenda after Maastricht – now appeared to be unrealistic. It now seems, however, as if this very negative assessment may have been exaggerated. This is because – unlike Britain – France and other countries whose currencies came under pressure in 1993 did not use their new freedom of manoeuvre to break free of the constraints of German policy. Rather, they continued to treat their unchanged exchange rate central values as key economic objectives, while using the wider bands not as scope for currency depreciation but merely as a way of avoiding the need for enormous market intervention.

The most important case is that of France, since Franco-German agreement remains the key element in any reconstruction of monetary arrangements. It was widely assumed that France would accept a substantial depreciation within the new wider bands in order to relax domestic monetary policy and thus stimulate employment. This has not happened. Sticking to the Maastricht agenda the French government introduced legislation to give more independence to the Banque de France. Thus strengthened against domestic political pressures, the central bank is maintaining an unchanged monetary policy – interest rates are aligned on those of Germany while the most important target is the central exchange rate (now unchanged since 1987) against the D-mark. In the summer of 1996 the franc was still within the old, narrow, margins around the central rate (as were other countries).

Paradoxically, relatively precise exchange rate targeting may be easier within the new arrangements because speculators have to consider the possibility of a substantial appreciation of the currency they sell (one economist calls this 'Sword of Damocles' pegging).[14] Of course this effect depends on the central rate being credible in the medium term (that is, consistent with broad internal and external balance under politically feasible policies); if these conditions were not met then a substantial depreciation would easily be brought about under the new arrangements. What is significant is that great efforts are being made to sustain central parities as credible equilibrium rates. The reasons for such an action are fundamentally political. France and other countries are not ready to write off the project of monetary integration, which they see as a way of winning back collectively the economic control which has been eroded at national level.

Meanwhile there were some limited signs of a modification in the German approach to European monetary questions. Although there is no prospect of a formal concession on the question of monetary sovereignty prior to unification itself, there is quite widespread acceptance that policy in the early 1990s paid insufficient attention to Germany's partners. It is likely that, informally, circumstances in other ERM countries will be given more weight in future. In return, Germany policy-makers would like to limit the operational disturbances which ERM has sometimes caused them in the past through the need for very large-scale support interventions which are difficult to sterilise without provoking further inflows. Less extreme policies would themselves contribute to this objective; it seems likely in addition that Germany would look favourably on the use of short-run exchange controls in such countries as Portugal and Ireland as an alternative to massive interventions.[15] In any case the political commitment to monetary integration still seems relatively strong in Germany.[16]

Crisis and recovery?

As with Bretton Woods, so with the latter ERM: discussion simply in terms of fixed versus floating rates, and of whether the chosen parities were compatible with equilibrium, is insufficient. There are, in both cases, two questions to be asked. Firstly, what conditions governed the issue of the dominant, the international, money? Secondly, how did the subordinate currencies relate to this dominant unit? In both cases the first question is primary and the second only becomes meaningful after it has been answered. Bretton Woods broke up because US monetary policy was not appropriate for the industrialised countries as a whole. Generalised floating did not resolve international monetary problems because the dollar continued to be the key world currency and US policy continued to generate instability and uncertainty.

With the ERM, in the form it took after 1987, the key problem, analogously, was German policy, although in this case it was a question of excessive restriction rather than unchecked inflation. It is certainly true that some currencies were misaligned and that correction was inevitable, but the fact that correction involved recession, crisis and a retreat from narrow bands was a consequence of the contractionary pressures which the Bundesbank imposed on Europe as a whole.

In spite of the crisis, reports of the death of EMS, and of monetary integration, are much exaggerated. The project could certainly prove abortive, but outside Britain at least, it retains a great deal of political momentum and continues to guide current policies. This does not mean, however, that monetary unification is necessarily desirable, either in general or in the particular form in which it was conceived at Maastricht. The next chapter begins to look in detail at this unification project.

Further reading

A survey of the EMS crisis is in Cobham (1994). The collection of papers edited by Bordes, Girardin and Mélitz (1995) is mostly devoted to the distressing implications of the crisis for the econometricians but contains a very lucid account by De Grauwe (1995) of the role played by interest rates in the disruption of the ERM. Artis and Lewis (1993) examine the crisis from the point of view of British policy. Collignon (1994) gives an account of the crisis, but this is not complete as regards its later stages (the attack on the franc); similarly, the very interesting papers in Temperton (1993) were given postscripts to deal with the events of summer 1993 itself. Part two of Steinherr (1994) deals with the crisis and its aftermath. The entire literature on the crisis is surveyed in Cobham (1996).

Notes

1. For a full discussion of Italian public debt see European Commission (1993).
2. The present author made a pessimistic assessment of Britain's prospects at the time of entry (see Grahl 1990).
3. A particularly prescient view was taken by Wren-Lewis *et al.* (1991) who made use of the notions of medium-term internal and external balance:

an implication of this method is that the markets themselves could fail to achieve a time-consistent equilibrium.

4. Thus the ECU moved from 1.32 to the dollar in 1985 to 0.78 to the dollar in 1990.

5. Germany had a current account balance of payments surplus equivalent to 4.8 per cent of its GDP just before unification in 1989; by 1991 this had melted away to a persisting deficit of 1.1 per cent of GDP. This is essentially a question of the big difference between East Germany's low level of production and the enormously greater use of resources which it has access to in the Federal Republic.

6. For recent evidence of the Bundesbank's consistent failure to hit monetary targets see OECD (1995) pp41–6. According to Riese (1993) the pursuit of unrealistic monetary targets led continuously to a real undervaluation of the D-mark and thus to pressure on Germany's EMS partners: the correct strategy for a key currency is to lower interest rates when capital flows into the country in order to discourage the flow; the money supply targets of the Bundesbank led to the exact opposite of this.

7. Thus it was no longer possible for weaker currency countries to defend their parities without an increase in *internal* interest rates. See Chapter 9.

8. The economics profession in general certainly did not anticipate events any more accurately than the financial markets and seems to have been subject to the same illusions. The founding of the ERM was greeted with excessive scepticism; by the eve of its breakdown this had given way to widespread euphoria. (Nor is this the only such recent error – an even more striking example is provided by the unbounded, but in retrospect absurd, optimism of professional Western commentators about the problems of economic transformation in the ex-socialist countries. It is a shameless profession which moves rapidly on, with the benefit of a self-serving amnesia, to fresh dogmatic pronouncements and blunders new.) One can mention, as an honourable exception, the judgement of Michel Aglietta (1991, pp329–30):

> Despite its tranquil appearance, this [gradualist] procedure conceals great dangers. For it presupposes that the nature, amplitude and frequency of the disturbances which the EMS will have to absorb will only develop slowly, at the same pace as the more accurate and constraining macro adjustments which governments will decide to implement. Nothing justifies this *a priori* . . . A high degree of capital mobility, in a regime which doesn't guarantee the equivalence of currencies in the expectations of private dealers, releases *balance of payments crises* . . . To maintain fixed exchange rates, the guarantee of gradual convergence according to the specified procedure, through and against all this will probably

require very big changes in interest rates. The heightened volatility of interest rates would aggravate uncertainties, increase the risk premia required by lenders and raise the average level of rates in Europe. Such would be the form taken by the cost of a collective refusal to establish institutions to provide the public good of equivalence among European currencies. Another outcome could be more frequent recourse to realignments . . . In both cases the gradualist procedure would have failed. Besides, if capital mobility becomes total, any expectation of a divergence in monetary policies leads to a speculative attack on the currency which is considered liable to devaluation . . . similarly, unlimited loans and borrowing among central banks would be needed to maintain parities in the face of such a crisis. Otherwise there would be a transition from the EMS to a regime of flexible exchange rates. This would dissolve intra-European relations into a vast global capital market with universally flexible rates.

9. Indeed with US rates above German ones, as has been the case since the beginning of 1995, the Atlanticist orientation of British policy becomes quite costly.

10. National approaches to European integration have changed little over the last fifty years. This is particularly true of Britain, although the immense decline in its world position would perhaps justify a radical reconsideration of policy. The British obsession with (increasingly illusory) sovereignty and its fear of all supranational commitments can be traced back to the time of the Schuman Plan (see Grahl 1993).

11. This is not to say that French policy was well conceived – the social costs of macroeconomic restriction were and remain immense – merely that it was logical and consistent. For a critique of the French strategy of 'competitive disinflation' see Fitoussi *et al.* (1993).

12. Another French tactical error may have been the issue of the 'Balladur Bond' by the new government: this was issued with the guarantee that its market value would not be allowed to drop below par. Since the value of government debt varies inversely with short-run interest rates the signal was given that the government would want to keep the latter low, perhaps implying a relaxation of anti-inflationary rigour.

13. The gesture also seems contrary to the spirit at least of the Treaty of Rome: Article 103 states that member states shall treat their macroeconomic policies as a matter of common concern. 'They shall consult *each other* and the Commission on the measures to be taken . . .' (emphasis added).

14. See Mathes 1994. The notion is that, within broad bands, a currency may have possibilities of appreciation so that it is no longer a one-way bet to speculate against it. Mathes adds, however, that, to secure stability in this way, it is necessary that market agents believe that the wide band

regime is preparing the way for monetary union and will not be followed by a further breakdown in European monetary organisation.

15. This point is argued in Dürkop and Naser 1995.

16. It should be noted, however, that some signs of disquiet exist. Firstly, the German constitutional court in Karlsruhe only gave a qualified verdict in favour of the Maastricht Treaty. Its judgement, which provoked some excitement among European jurists, seems to imply the claim that EU decisions can be made subject to revision by national courts without the whole project of European construction being called into question. Substantively, the court insisted on a strict (that is, monetarily restrictive) interpretation of Maastricht; this implies that the looser interpretation (which is desirable and will almost certainly be necessary if EMU is to take place) might be seen as a serious blow at German interests and could even lead to a juridical challenge to the Treaty itself. (For an analysis of the judgement see Smits 1994.) At the same time there have been critical remarks on EMU within the opposition SPD.

7

Monetary union

The ambitions of Delors

The crisis of the Exchange Rate Mechanism broke out in the autumn of 1992. Six months earlier, member state governments had concluded the Maastricht Treaty which, on the basis of the ERM, made full monetary union the central goal of the European Community (henceforth subsumed in the European Union) for the rest of the century.

It seems clear that the fundamental objectives behind the new goal of EMU (economic and monetary union) were political. The strategy, however, was economic. In this respect, the Commission President, Jacques Delors, was attempting to repeat the sequence of events which had given birth to the Community. From 1945 to 1957 the movement for European integration had failed to make direct progress on political institutions, which seemed to threaten national sovereignty; on the other hand, it had been possible to make important breakthroughs on economic issues – firstly the Schuman Plan for coal and steel, then the Treaty of Rome setting up the European Economic Community itself.[1]

It should be noted, however, that when Delors began his extremely dynamic presidency, the dominant conception of economic advance had changed. Rather than the interventionism of the 1950s, neoliberal views were predominant. Thus the promotion of European integration by economic means now implied a close, but always ambivalent, association between the two projects: European unity and a thoroughgoing restoration of a market economy. The Faustian compact enthusiastically entered into by Delors had the aim of accelerating the integration process by giving it to a great extent a neoliberal content. It is certainly true that this produced a very wide coalition in favour of the new programmes of the Community: free-market conservatives, in particular Mrs Thatcher and her cabinet, endorsed the new trend towards competition, liberalisation and deregulation in European affairs; those with a more interventionist outlook were prepared to accept such measures as a means to the greater goal of a stronger, more federalist, Community.[2]

The first expression of the new approach was the Community's Market Completion Programme, which aimed at the comprehensive removal of remaining non-tariff barriers to trade and to labour and capital mobility in the EC. The deadline of 1992 was set for the passage of the legislation required. It seems in retrospect that the economic effects of this programme are smaller than anticipated. This is because in many areas, particularly manufacturing, the Community was already highly integrated; while in others – such as mobility of qualified labour or tax harmonisation – integration is bound to be a slow and gradual process. However, the 1992 programme certainly gave a new impetus to the Community. (For a critical assessment of the programme see Grahl and Teague 1990.) Some political developments were agreed in the Single European Act which prepared the way for the programme; some others followed, such as the reform of the Community budget in 1988 and the Charter of Employment Rights in 1989.

However, the main initiative launched within the more dynamic Community was a renewed proposal for monetary union. It was suggested that, as *real* economic integration (through trade and movements of resources) proceeded, *monetary* integration became increasingly desirable.

The question of monetary unity was studied by a committee comprising the heads of central banks in the member states and chaired by Delors himself (Committee for the Study of Economic and Monetary Union). Its report, published in 1989, endorsed the project of unification, but specified a very conservative form for the common monetary institutions which would be required: the European Central Bank would be modelled on the German Bundesbank in two key respects – it would be independent of political control and it would have, as its primary, overriding responsibility the elimination of inflation. On these terms member states agreed to explore a new phase of integration. Two intergovernmental conferences met during 1991, one devoted to monetary union, the other to political unity. However, little progress was made on this second issue, so that when the resulting agreements were written into the Maastricht Treaty, by far its most significant component was a commitment to monetary union during the 1990s. The Delors presidency had therefore seen the stagnation of the Community in the early 1980s dispelled and agreement reached on an ambitious agenda; the nature of that agenda, however, remains open to question.

Optimal currency areas

What makes it desirable for a given territory to have a single money? This question was explored in the theory of optimal currency areas which developed in the 1960s. A pioneering contribution by Mundell (1961) suggested that a region which needed to change its prices (and incomes) relative to prices outside, but which had little need to change internal prices relative to each other, might benefit from having its own currency. On the assumption that it is difficult or costly to change prices it might be simpler for the region to change its exchange rate *vis-à-vis* other regions. Thus the criterion proposed is one of industrial specialisation. This cannot, however, be a full discussion as it does not take into account the costs of having several monetary units – if every industry had its own money one would be back in a state of barter.

Subsequent discussion introduced a new criterion: factor mobility, especially labour mobility. The same disturbance – say a switch in the pattern of demand, which necessitated altering one industry's output price relative to that of another – might be best met by transferring labour and other resources between the industries. Where such a transfer was not possible, an exchange rate adjustment would be a useful instrument to maintain employment in the region facing declining demand and to limit inflation in the other.

This second criterion (labour mobility) to some extent conflicts with the first (industrial specialisation). This is because a region with a highly diversified set of industries would have more opportunities of moving labour from one to others and thus adjusting to shocks without a large and difficult change in *internal* prices and wage rates. Hence such a region could use a single currency without excessive problems. The highly specialised region thus would only be an optimal currency area by virtue of its lack of labour mobility. Nevertheless, the theory, as first postulated and subsequently developed, broadly points to labour market adjustment as the central issue. De Grauwe (1996) sums up:

> The central insight of Optimal Currency Area Theory is that countries or regions that experience a high divergence in output or employment trends need a lot of flexibility in their labour markets if they want to form a monetary union, and if they wish to avoid major adjustment problems. The larger is the degree of real divergence the greater is the need for flexibility in the labour markets to make a smoothly functioning monetary union possible.

A critical review of the debate by Kenen (1969) introduced a third, more political criterion: the existence of a common fiscal policy. This is because the industrial adjustments under consideration can be facilitated by government intervention and made less painful by a redistribution of income from the winners to the losers.

The three criteria – industrial specialisation, labour mobility, fiscal policy – still only indicate when it is advantageous to multiply the number of currencies. They need to be balanced by a consideration of when it is costly to do so. The obvious balancing factor is the cost of currency exchange, interpreted widely to cover not just the cost of switching currencies, but all the uncertainties and inconveniences associated with the absence of a single money. This points to the *openness* of the region or country under consideration: the more it is involved in foreign trade and other international exchanges, the more it will gain from monetary integration with its partners (Krugman 1990). We would usually expect small countries to be more open in this way – thus Austria might obtain considerable reduction in such transactions costs by monetary integration with Germany.

Contemporary discussion of monetary integration is still based on these considerations – on the one hand the conditions under which an exchange rate alteration would facilitate adjustment, on the other the extra transactions costs stemming from the existence of several currencies. Can it be suggested in this context that the European Community is an optimal currency area? No one had ever thought so, but the economic service of the EC, responding professionally to the needs of their political masters, would argue that it was not far from being one.

The Commission's case

The general position of the Commission was that monetary integration was a natural continuation and culmination of the market completion process (European Commission 1990). It will be suggested, however, that in many respects, monetary union represents a much more radical step than the 1992 programme, with much more serious implications for output and employment.

The Commission argued that two main benefits would flow from monetary union: the elimination of transactions costs and the control of inflation. It is only the first of these which stems from integration as such; the second was assumed to be a consequence of the conservative nature of the structures which were to be introduced.

The transactions costs arising from foreign exchange transactions were relatively easy to measure. One can look at the charges which banks and other intermediaries make for these services. To the extent that these charges are competitively priced and do not involve the exploitation of customers, they represent the actual costs of switching currencies. Further, there are costs of such transactions which fall on companies – the clerical and administration costs they have in organising currency exchange or in operating in several currencies, which would disappear in a single currency system.

In addition there are costs associated with currency fluctuations (and which go beyond the width of the spread on an exchange). Some of the costs of fluctuations can be measured by the hedging operations taken to avoid them – this would tend to be an underestimate as it is only possible to insure some of these risks.

Whether fluctuations in exchange rates and the resulting uncertainties impose costs much greater than this, by discouraging international trade and investment, is open to question. Many empirical studies have been conducted because this is a key issue dividing the proponents of flexible and of fixed exchange rates. The weight of such evidence seems to be in favour of the flexible rate case: no great loss of trade or international investment seems to have resulted from exchange rate uncertainty. The implication is that price movements can in the medium term compensate for exchange rate movements: for instance, if a company invests to manufacture a product in a country which subsequently devalues it might expect an increase in its foreign currency price to make good the loss of profits, at least over the medium term. However, the fragility of all such econometric evidence should be emphasised. It is not really possible to say what levels of international trade and investment would be today if Bretton Woods had not broken down and a fixed exchange rate system had been maintained on a global basis. All that can be done is to estimate the effect of some additional exchange rate volatility between two countries over time, or to compare trade at the same time within a fixed exchange rate system (such as the EMS) with trade between countries with floating rates.

In spite of these estimation difficulties, the costs of multiple currencies are the easiest element in the whole argument to quantify – since the short-run and direct costs of changing moneys can be priced. The general conclusion is that these costs, while significant, are small. The Commission comes up with a figure between 13 and 19 billion ECUs or 0.3 per cent to 0.4 per cent of Community GDP.[3]

It should be noted that these costs are not evenly distributed – they tend to be higher for small countries (which cannot use their own currencies for foreign trade) and for small companies (since there are important economies of scale in foreign exchange transactions which make them less burdensome for larger companies). Nevertheless, the transactions costs savings on their own are not large enough to justify such an ambitious and dangerous step as monetary unification.

Stopping inflation

At this point the Commission's economists argue that monetary union would produce a second, more important, benefit for member countries: that it would control, or even stop, inflation throughout the Community. What we have here is an alignment of two projects – European construction on the one hand and monetary disinflation on the other. Although the two projects began quite independently of each other, so that monetarism was seen as a prescription for national policy, each is now trying to draw strength from the other. The view taken throughout the present work is that purely monetary disinflation (both in its original, quantity theory, and its revised, independent central bank, forms) is a utopian (unrealisable) and reactionary project, and that therefore the realistic and desirable objective of European construction will only be damaged by the association.

It might be fair to summarise monetarism in the following propositions:

- inflation is a costly economic malfunction;[4]
- inflation can be stopped by restrictive monetary policies;
- it cannot be stopped otherwise;
- the costs of monetary restriction are transient.

Each of these propositions is open to challenge. Specifically one might assert:

- inflation is not particulary damaging in itself but is essentially the symptom of different malfunctions – financial disequilibria, social conflicts, failure to maintain external competitiveness;
- restrictive monetary policies are, beyond a certain point, infeasible because of the financial disorders to which they give rise;
- only an adequate resolution of the underlying problems expressed by inflation offers a guarantee that it will not return;
- the costs of monetary restriction are durable and involve, in particular, very persistent unemployment.

Admittedly, this kind of scepticism remains without influence on most policy-makers, for whom the need for monetary disinflation remains beyond question. However, even monetarists have been forced to recognise certain difficulties with their project, which have led to a certain reformulation. These difficulties are perceived as being of two kinds: on the one hand there are technical problems, in controlling, or even measuring, the money supply and in determining the correct disinflationary stance; on the other hand, the governments which implement monetarist strategies are not to be trusted – electoral considerations always make for compromises on policy and a covert return to the bad old inflationary practices of the past. The first problem aggravates the second since technical difficulties imply that monetary policy cannot be operated by a simple formula – it will always require an element of judgement, of discretion. However, it is just this element of discretion that democratic governments can be expected to abuse, because it makes it possible to operate a populist, inflationary policy while piously claiming to do the opposite.

The notion of an independent central bank responds to both these problems: a space is created for judgement and discretion in the operation of monetary policy; but this space is protected from the malign influence of populist policies by according the central bank a quasi-judicial status, independent of the elected government. This kind of position could be regarded as defining monetarism mark II – and it is this which predominates in the Commission's argument for monetary union (see Chapter 8).

Economies of scale

A further element of the Commission's case was the invocation of economies of scale. Essentially this was an appeal to recent theories of economic growth which place great emphasis on certain *external* economies of scale, in such areas as research, technology diffusion or the development of human resources. These theories are interesting and potentially of great importance in accounting for such phenomena as economic divergence – the ability of richer economies to grow faster than poor ones, even though their wealth itself tends to make labour and other resources more costly for them.

However, the Commission's use of these new growth theories is speculative in the extreme. The argument is that the initial stimulus to EC growth stemming from integration would have continuing beneficial effects because it would generate externalities of the kind mentioned. There are at least three possible objections to this position. Firstly, the immediate consequences of the integration programme might well be negative rather than positive – this is certainly the case if one attributes the recession of the early 1990s in part to the ambition for monetary union. Secondly, it is not clear that the economy of the European Union is sufficiently integrated to make the new growth theories applicable – there are still huge gaps in economic performance among EU countries which testify to significant obstacles to technology diffusion, for example. Finally, the externalities approach may be applicable only to certain, particularly developed, regions within the Union, in which case this line of argument does not necessarily promise faster growth in the EU as a whole but rather threatens further economic divergence.

It is not suggested that economic policy discussions should avoid such difficult themes as dynamic growth effects and stick to issues which can be more easily quantified. On the contrary, it is the dynamic effects which are of the most importance – if even a small increase in economic growth rates results from European integration this is an enormous argument in its favour, since over time this increase will accumulate into a large difference in the level of income. However, it can be suggested that the Commission's appeal to such dynamic factors is, not for the first time, arbitrary and one-sided. (For a survey of the policy implications of the new growth theories see Greenaway 1992; for a critical examination of the Commission's appeal to external economies see Grahl and Thompson 1995.)

Adjusting without exchange rates

So far we have considered the Commission's view of the benefits of a single money: the small, but certain, gains from the elimination of some transactions costs; and the much more debatable effects of a renewed attempt to reduce inflation in the EU by monetary means. We now turn to the possible costs of the exercise. These hinge on the use of exchange rate changes (particularly devaluations) to bring about economic adjustments which would otherwise require slow, difficult and painful changes in prices and wages.

The discussion therefore connects with the classical theory of optimal currency areas. Can the EU as a whole be regarded as such an area? Is it in the course of becoming one? Or on the contrary, do its component countries come nearest to being optimal areas, so that abolishing their individual currencies will be very costly? However, there is a clear distinction between the classical theories and the Commission's argument, namely that the latter is resolutely short run. The Commission economists insist that, whatever the benefits of exchange rate adjustment, they are necessarily transient. In this position they can appeal to much of contemporary macroeconomic analysis which assumes that monetary disturbances have no important effects except in the short run – thus a devaluation of the currency, for example, would be without medium-term effects on output, employment or other real variables.

This approach already minimises the potential costs of monetary union, but the empirical basis for it is not well established. The Commission argues that, in the long run, changes in the nominal exchange rate do not have any effect on the 'real' exchange rate – that is, on the relative price of a country's goods and thus its competitiveness. This proposition is itself questionable – particularly under the Bretton Woods system some countries such as Germany seem to have obtained lasting competitive advantages from low exchange rates (Riese 1994). Even if we take the proposition as valid, however, it does not follow that the use of exchange rate alterations has no long-term consequences. A country which devalues may find that the resulting competitive advantage is gradually eroded by inflation and that it then has to devalue again. It could still be the case that these initial devaluations were necessary to avoid a long-term increase in unemployment, since unemployment might be very persistent.

However, the Commission determinedly situates discussion in the short run, in the use of the exchange rate as a response to 'shocks' which necessitate some adjustment. The argument is that exchange rate alterations within the EU are only useful to the extent that the shocks are *asymmetric* – that is, that they have different implications for different member states. A simple example of an asymmetric shock would be an increase in the price of oil: for most EU countries, which import all their oil, this would be a negative development requiring a reduction in domestic spending and an increase in exports; for Britain on the other hand it might be a net advantage since Britain exports more oil than it imports.[5]

The Commission's case is that asymmetric shocks are less and less a problem, because of the general progress of economic integration. It is argued that real economic convergence makes for a more homogeneous situation in member countries which will to some extent obviate the need for differentiated policies. There are, however, clear limits to such a position, so that it is further argued that alternative adjustment procedures will be enhanced by integration; it is suggested that this is the case for price and wage discipline, for factor mobility, and for public intervention. In these ways, it is suggested, the capacity of individual countries to adapt to disturbances without the need to adjust the exchange rate will be increased.

What is being compared?

A final important point in the Commission's case concerns the actual basis of comparison. What are we using as a standard with which to compare a situation of full monetary union? Two points affect the argument. Firstly, further real integration can be expected as a gradual consequence of the 1992 market completion programme which in the long term will lead to more movement of goods, services and resources within the EU. This tends to strengthen the case for a single money as it makes it likely that there will be more transactions among countries and also a slow tendency towards similarities in economic performance. Secondly, a comparison of the status quo of the early 1990s – the European Monetary System in its second phase – with full monetary unification might be inappropriate as the EMS might become unstable in the absence of further progress towards EMU. And indeed it turned out to be case that the 'strong' EMS broke down in 1992–93. Once again this probably tends to strengthen somewhat the argument for moving to a single currency on the grounds that the real alternative might be a return to more or less free floating among EU currencies.

Criticism of monetary union

For the most part, critical examination of the case for monetary union has identified the question of the exchange rate instrument as the key issue in the debate. Several analyses have been made which have basically the same structure. What is done is to consider all the alternative adjustment mechanisms in turn and to investigate, both theoretically and empirically, how effective they are. Frequently comparisons have been made with the United States – since the US is comparable in size and economic development to the EU, and since it already has a single currency, it gives some indications as to how a single currency would function in Europe. In general the conclusions drawn from such studies have been rather pessimistic – the most plausible view is that the lack of the exchange rate instrument would tend to pose quite severe economic difficulties for some member states. The other measures which might be taken will be looked at in turn. The central example of an adjustment problem is probably where a country suffers a loss of international competitiveness, with some of its important industries losing market shares. The consequence is a balance of payments deficit and a tendency to higher unemployment. One response to this is to devalue – this will encourage exports, discourage imports and, if (as is usual) it is accompanied by relatively restrictive policies, put downward pressure on incomes corresponding to the deterioration of external economic conditions. If devaluation is ruled out by monetary union, what alternative adjustments are possible?

Wage and price flexibility

In principle, any adjustment brought about by a devaluation could be achieved instead by a corresponding reduction of domestic prices and, in particular, wages. If this kind of flexibility actually existed, however, we would be in a rather different world – one where monetary problems would be of no great importance. Indeed, the absence of market-clearing price movements and especially wage movements is not only the starting point for much macroeconomic theory, it is also widely seen as a particularly severe problem in Western Europe – a key aspect of the 'eurosclerosis' that is generally held to have led to high levels of unemployment since the early 1980s (for the most prevalent analysis of European unemployment see Layard, Nickell and Jackman 1994). This standard argument is probably exaggerated: it simplifies both the reasons for higher unemployment and the possible policy responses to it. Nevertheless, in almost every view of the matter adjustments to the general level of wages would be one necessary component of an effective strategy against unemployment. It is just as generally acknowledged that such price and wage flexibility is not easy to bring about. In fact there exist quite opposite strategies by which wage adjustments might be pursued. On the one hand the prevailing direction of policy in most European countries has been towards a decentralisation of wage determination and a reinforcement of competitive mechanisms in labour markets; this is a key aspect of the policy agenda for *labour flexibility*. On the other hand an opposing school of thought has the view that this kind of decentralisation leads to coordination difficulties and that centralised wage bargaining can lead to more efficient outcomes. From either point of view an exchange rate devaluation may be the most effective way of achieving the required wage adjustment. Devaluation adjusts all wages relative to those of other countries instantaneously and by the same percentage – it corresponds to a perfectly coordinated wage reduction across all labour markets.

The difficulty of securing appropriate wage levels is likely to increase with the process of European integration. This is because there will be new pressures towards more *uniform* wages for comparable types of labour as labour markets become more interconnected and, in particular, if the introduction of a common currency makes rewards more easily and directly comparable. At the same time there may actually be a need for more *differentiated* labour market outcomes to compensate for the loss of other policy instruments at national level – above all, exchange rates. Significant reforms in labour markets may be necessary to respond to these increased pressures. At present, however, there is no sign of agreement even on the direction in which such reforms should be moving (on labour flexibility see Grahl and Teague 1989).

Labour mobility

Comparison with the United States indicates that, in practice, labour mobility is likely to be a more important mechanism of economic adjustment in individual countries or regions than is wage flexibility. Although US regions with problems of economic competitiveness do tend to have somewhat lower wage rates, the main process by which they adapt is the out-migration of workers – mobility determined by the availability of work as much as by wage differentials (Eichengreen 1992).

This is hardly an ideal adjustment process – it imposes considerable costs on the workers who move. It may also lead to cumulative patterns of decline in regions which lose a substantial number of workers because economies of scale in the provision of services may be lost, and it can become more difficult in consequence to attract new employment. Even so, in the context of Western Europe this kind of adjustment through mobility seems very difficult to achieve. There is no comparable tradition of geographical mobility within European societies: even *within* individual countries interregional labour movement tends to be less than in the United States. When movements from one country to another are considered there of course arise difficulties of culture and linguistic difference, which are much less marked in the US than they are in Europe.

In fact, labour mobility within Western Europe has been in decline for some time – a decline linked to fundamental changes in economic structure. In the 1960s, rapid industrial growth pulled workers from Mediterranean countries to the factories and building sites of Northern Europe. As semi-skilled operatives, these migrants were often able to begin work right away with a minimal knowledge of the host country language. Today the demand for this kind of labour is very low – and if substantial labour migration resumes within the EU it is likely to involve workers who are far more qualified, with high levels of both professional and linguistic competence. At present, however, such international labour markets hardly exist and it is extremely speculative to regard them as a significant channel for economic adjustment in the near future.[6]

Capital mobility

In principle a country or region might compensate for a loss of export demand by capital mobility rather than labour mobility – that is, it might maintain its level of economic activity by attracting inward investment rather than exporting workers. A critical factor here is the nature and, in particular, the duration of the ensuing disequilibrium.

If the disturbance is temporary it seems certainly to be the case that, within a monetary union, short-term finance should be available to ease adjustment difficulties. The fact that exchange rate risk had been eliminated would make it easier to attract such inflows. Comparison with the US indicates that a region suffering a short-run decline in its exports would be able to obtain credit with a small rise in its interest rates relative to those elsewhere in the Union. This would reduce the immediate impact of the disturbance and allow the region to maintain its previous level of imports and consumption.

However, the same considerations do not apply to a structural problem (what is now often called a persistent shock), where the loss of export markets seems to be long lasting. Interest rate movements in such a case are not helpful – rates tend to fall in a depressed region because of the decline in the local demand for credit consequent on a decline in income. What is needed in such a case is long-term productive investment to generate new employment opportunities. This is unlikely to be forthcoming until there has already been a substantial decline in wage costs relative to other regions. Both European and North American experience suggests that depressed regions can suffer high rates of unemployment for very long periods without attracting substantial capital inflows – in many ways depression itself reduces the attractiveness of an area to external investors so that decline can become self-perpetuating.

Public expenditure

So far the adjustment possibilities which have been discussed concern market processes. But of course public policy can also contribute significantly to industrial adaptation. If private capital flows are inadequate to correct for disturbances to a particular country, then government expenditure, financed by borrowing, might make good the deficiency. The existence of a common currency and of unified, Union-wide, capital markets might make it easier to borrow in this way because weaker countries would no longer have to pay an exchange rate risk premium on debts denominated in their own currencies; they would also have perhaps easier access to common currency credit than they do at present to foreign exchange borrowing.

There are, however, major difficulties with such a policy response to difficulties in export markets. Firstly, a broad trend has developed since 1980 towards a worldwide rise in real interest rates, which has put unprecedented pressure on state budgets. Nearly all EU countries, and certainly all the weaker ones, are experiencing extreme difficulty in financing current levels of public expenditure and it is hard to see how they could easily expand spending in the face of new adverse shocks. The key variable in this context is the rate of interest, in real terms, at which public borrowing is financed. The continuing commitment of the EU to monetary disinflation is likely to keep real interest rates high since the essence of this project is to raise nominal interest rates to begin a slow and painful process of lowering inflation. But lower inflation and higher *nominal* interest rates – that is, interest rates measured simply in money terms – both imply higher *real* rates – that is, corrected for price changes. (See Chapter 10 for a fuller analysis of public finance.)

Secondly, the very process of monetary unification in the way envisaged in the Maastricht Treaty will lead to new constraints on national public finance. Indeed it is intended to do just that, since the unification project was conceived under the influence of the monetarist view that public sector deficits are the main temptation to excessive monetary expansion. Thus the new European Central Bank is specifically excluded from lending directly to government at national or EU level; it is further absolved from any requirement to stabilise the price of public sector debt instruments – government bonds or Treasury bills. In fact the initial proposals of the Delors Report went further than this and suggested that the Community be given the power to set absolute limits to public borrowing at national level. The Maastricht Treaty did not embody this extreme constraint on nation states but it did make clear that neither national governments nor the European Commission could resort to central bank support for a deficit position. As a result public sector budgets in the weaker countries are likely to be too constrained to offer effective responses to adverse shocks or problems of industrial competitiveness.

Transfers within the EU

Finally, one can consider the role of public finance at European Union level. If national governments are unable to cope with adjustment problems, could transfers from other member states through the EU budget make up the gap? The answer is clearly negative. Of course some such transfers do take place already in the Union, largely through its structural funds (Regional Development Fund, Social Fund and the Agricultural Guidance section of the Agricultural Fund) and these have been growing quite rapidly since the mid-1980s. They are regarded as a priority field for expenditure by both the European Commission and the European Parliament. Nevertheless they remain an order of magnitude below what would be required to deal with any severe decline in the industrial performance of member states in the context of monetary union. The sums involved have increasingly been concentrated on Greece, Ireland, Portugal and some regions of Spain and Great Britain. It is only this tight geographical concentration that gives them a certain impact – there is no prospect of major expansion.

The European Council has already, in its Edinburgh meeting in December 1992, established the framework for EU finance in the 1990s.

Although a certain growth in the EU budget was agreed, it will remain around 2 per cent of EU GDP for the foreseeable future because the northern countries – especially Britain – which contribute the bulk of EU revenues, were not prepared to accept a significant expansion. It is generally acknowledged that at this level there is no possibility of EU expenditures with a macroeconomic impact, except for the smaller countries mentioned above. Notions of fiscal federalism have been discussed recently in Europe, but the budget is fixed at a 'pre-Federal' level – that is, it is unable to compensate disadvantaged countries or regions by transfers from the stronger ones. (For a fuller discussion of these issues see Chapter 10.)

A political project

Among economists who have examined the programme for monetary union, there is therefore quite strong agreement. The most obvious cost of a single currency is the loss of exchange rates as a tool of economic adjustment. No plausible alternative for this policy instrument exists and therefore the costs are likely to be very high for weaker countries, far outweighing the somewhat hypothetical benefits. If many commentators are nevertheless prepared to support monetary unification this is explicitly on political grounds: EMU will be a major step towards fuller political unity in the EU and can be defended convincingly only on the basis that much more political unity is desirable. It can be asked, however, whether political unity achieved at the cost of economic stagnation and unemployment for many EU citizens will prove to be durable.

Alternative strategies

The Delors Report not only laid down the objective of monetary unification, but also the path towards it. This was to be through a process of *nominal convergence*, bringing first inflation rates then price levels into compatibility with the requirements of a single currency. Thus what was envisaged was essentially a process of strengthening and hardening the existing exchange rate mechanism, until it became feasible to lock exchange rates irrevocably to each other. Once this was achieved there could be, relatively quickly, the replacement of existing moneys by a single currency (it was decided in 1985 to call this the euro) to be used by the central banking system unified during the process of convergence. This approach corresponded to German views of the need to remove inflationary pressures in the weaker member states before the final steps to unification were taken.

It is important to note that there were other possible paths to unification, with rather different implications for public policy during the course of transition and even thereafter. We can look first at the notion of *competing currencies* briefly put forward by the British government. It is rather difficult to take this proposal seriously. It never commanded much support even in Britain and was seen by Britain's partners almost as a wrecking amendment aimed at undermining the whole project of unification. The idea was – true to the neoliberal ideology of recent British governments – to turn the process of unification over to the free market. Economic agents would be allowed to choose the currency they used for transactions among those used by EC member states. This would avoid introducing immediate new constraints on national governments and national monetary policies, but might be expected over the long term to lead to the selection of one national currency as the monetary unit corresponding most closely to individual preferences. It is difficult to see how this could fail to be the D-mark: the general adoption of the D-mark as a European currency has been frequently advocated by Walters (for example, 1992) although he readily concedes that it is a 'political non-starter'.

There were at least two insuperable difficulties with such a strategy. Firstly, it would lead to growing and finally absolute hegemony of the country whose currency won out in the competitive race. Secondly, this competitive process would itself be extremely unstable: the fact that one money was tending to be used more than another would in itself make it a more useful form of money and could lead to the rapid elimination of its competitors. Similar difficulties apply to extreme free-market proposals for purely private money ('free banking') put forward by Hayek (1976) among others and which may have inspired the British argument.

A second British strategy, rapidly replacing the first which then sank without trace, was more serious. It advanced the notion of a *parallel currency*, issued by the Community, which would be increasingly used in the member states. The process of unification would then amount to the gradual widening of the scope of this common currency. This proposal was tied to the introduction of a 'hard ECU', which is logical since this would facilitate the gradual replacement of national moneys. The present ECU is a basket of EU currencies. The make-up of the basket has been revised from time to time to avoid the stronger currencies dominating it as they are repeatedly revalued against the weaker ones. With a hard ECU there would be no such revisions, so that it would come to be made up predominantly of D-marks, guilders and so on. Currencies with a record of repeated or substantial devaluation would thus eventually cease to make up a significant part of the ECU. This could be expected to reduce fluctuations in the ECU and increase confidence in it as a monetary standard.

The difficulty with the parallel currency proposal can be seen if one asks what functions it would be used for. The obvious division of function would be to use the ECU first for external purposes – that is, it would deployed, both privately and by governments, for transactions among member states. ECUs could be used as a reserve asset, exchange rate standard and intervention vehicle within the ERM; while markets in ECU debt, ECU payments and invoicing in ECUs would be encouraged in the private sector. This strategy, however, would be very difficult if no common policy were defined to stabilise the external (dollar) value of the ECU on a global basis. In other words the parallel currency proposal would lead to a resolution of the $(n - 1)$ problem in European monetary policy through the specification of the terms on which ECUs were issued. In this form it is an attractive strategy because the gradual progress to unification would be multidimensional. A country could try to reduce and eventually eliminate fluctuations of its own currency *vis-à-vis* the strong ECU. But even if this was not possible it could still move forward by widening somewhat the use of ECUs in the national economy, while preserving some degree of internal mobility for its monetary policies.

French economists during the 1980s (Aglietta 1985) argued for exactly such a development but the proposal fell in the face of German resistance to this kind of centralisation of monetary policy prior to a thoroughgoing counter-inflationary process throughout the Community.

Finally, it should be noted that strategy for monetary unification need not be gradualist. A single money could be introduced, not by stabilising and then fixing exchange rates, but by a simple *currency reform*. (The absorbtion of East Germany into the West German monetary system was analogous to this. No effort was made at a prior stabilisation of the Ostmark – it was simply withdrawn from circulation.) Such strategies have mostly been used in the context of hyperinflation, when a discredited currency is withdrawn and a new monetary unit substituted. Although this approach has the advantage of obviating a long, possibly painful, process of nominal convergence, it has the corresponding disadvantage that the new monetary authority inherits what could be an extremely disequilibrated financial situation and has to decide at once how to treat agents, both private and governmental, in serious deficit positions. Weaker countries in the EU might have preferred this route to unification because it would have reduced their own responsibility for establishing national financial and monetary stability, but stronger countries rejected it for the same reason.

The Maastricht decisions

In spite of the existence of alternative, and perhaps more efficient, paths to monetary integration, a compromise along the lines of the Delors Report, requiring nominal convergence, was in place even before negotiations took place on the Maastricht Treaty in 1991. The main reason for this was the widespread acceptance of the project of monetary disinflation throughout Europe. According to these views the convergence process itself – that is, substantial monetary disinflation in the weaker economics – was a desirable direction for monetary policy. This assessment may have been promoted by the real, albeit limited and inadequate, recovery in real economic activity during the late 1980s, which perhaps suggested that the costs of such disinflation would not be excessive. A key determining factor also was German commitment to the lengthy preliminary price stabilisation in other countries which nominal convergence implied. France on the other hand was so committed to the unification project that it was prepared to go ahead even on German conditions. (According to Marsh 1992, President Mitterrand and Chancellor Kohl agreed beforehand on a very strict monetary regime, just to forestall possible Bundesbank objections.)

Thus Maastricht, apart from a few exceptions, wrote the strategy of the Delors Report into the constitution of the now renamed European Union. One important exception was a British opt-out clause, which exempts Britain from the move to a single currency unless there is a new vote to approve this in Parliament. The value of this option could be debated: on the one hand it reduces British commitment to the process; on the other, however, it also reduces British influence on the institutions which will emerge and the policies they adopt. The record of British abstention from the integration process since the Schuman Plan in 1950 does not give grounds for confidence in this minimalist tactic.

Secondly, Maastricht did not adopt the Delors Report suggestion for formal controls over national public spending and taxation policies, although the informal pressures to reduce 'excessive' deficits will be so strong that this is perhaps a secondary issue.

The treaty thus adopts an inflation convergence process, followed by a locking of exchange rates, as the path to a common currency; it lays down both a timetable and a set of targets for nominal convergence. The targets concern five indicators of successful monetary stabilisation: limits on government deficits; limits on accumulated public debt; limits on inflation (defined relative to the countries with lowest inflation rates); limits on long-term interest rates (regarded as reflecting market expectations of future inflation

and once again defined relative to the more successful countries); and requirements for exchange rate stability (adoption of narrow fluctuation bands,
avoidance of devaluation). The timetable is ambitious: phase II, characterised
by close coordination of monetary policy and preparatory work towards a
single central bank, began at the start of 1994 with the establishment of the
European Monetary Institute (EMI), which is to be the forerunner of a
European Central Bank (ECB). Full unification was envisaged as taking place,
at the earliest, at the beginning of 1997, conditional on a majority of member
states meeting the convergence criteria. It was soon recognised that this early
start was impossible. The next date specified is the beginning of 1999; in this
case, however, unification can proceed without a majority of member states
participating. In fact, it is now taken for granted that unification will be a two-
speed, or multi-speed, process, since it is inconceivable that all member states
could meet these targets within this timescale. In practice the participating
group would have to include France and Germany, together with the
Netherlands, Luxembourg, and perhaps Belgium and even Ireland. Even the
minority of countries which lead the way, however, are unlikely to satisfy all
the criteria – those referring to public finance, in particular, will pose problems. The treaty envisages some scope for flexibility in this regard, however.
Thus, even though the full convergence programme has not been completed,
it is likely that exchange rates among participating countries will be frozen at
that date, essentially by fiat, and monetary policy centralised in preparation
for the introduction of the euro.

The grudging ratification

On purely economic grounds there is little case for monetary unification in
the EU: if one attempted to define an optimal currency area the most likely
grouping would include only Germany together with the small, mostly
northern, countries which trade intensively with it – Austria, the
Netherlands, Belgium, Luxembourg and perhaps Denmark – and which
are already close to being on a D-mark standard. Outside this region severe
economic difficulties can be anticipated, both as a consequence of unification and during the process of nominal convergence which is supposed to
lead towards it.

   If, in spite of these obstacles, unification is to be pursued as an important
step towards political unity then a minimum condition for this is that monetary policy in the EU is further relaxed and then maintained in a much more
accommodating stance than has been seen in recent years (see Chapter 10).
Within such a context weaker countries could address the problems of *real*

convergence – the growth of employment and the increased competitiveness which they need to participate in a currency union without very great costs. This amounts to saying that the goals of policy need to be redefined to give much higher priority to lowering unemployment and to modify the exclusive concern with disinflation which has so far determined both the plans for monetary union and the strategy by which it is approached. It was the suspicion that this widening of objectives might not take place which accounts for the grudging way in which European electorates accepted the Maastricht Treaty and came close to rejecting it. In Denmark, a referendum in 1992 actually did reject the treaty; the next year enough voters were persuaded to change their minds to secure ratification but this was achieved only by conceding an opt-out to Denmark, which has declared that it will not participate in the monetary union. Although Britain had been given an opt-out at Maastricht itself, so that the decision whether or not to take part is left to a future parliament, ratification involved serious political problems for the Major administration, confronted by a very hostile group among its own MPs and challenged by the opposition to reverse its negative position on the social dimensions of the EU. In France, although most of the political class endorsed ratification and Jacques Delors even threatened to resign from the Commission presidency if ratification failed, in the referendum of 1992 the majority in favour was tiny. In Germany, ratification was enacted by a large majority in the Bundestag but a legal challenge in the constitutional court led to an insistence on a very strict interpretation of the treaty, which will multiply difficulties for other member states and testifies to growing disquiet about the path of European construction. Ireland perhaps apart, the strongest political support for the unification project exists in Italy, which is unlikely, however, to be an early participant because of continuing financial problems.

Thus the main strategy adopted by the European Union in the 1990s, the project which absorbs nearly all its energy and which demands immense efforts of adaptation on the part of the member countries, is seen by a large part of the EU population as a leap in the dark and seems, increasingly, like an enormous political and economic gamble. Failure would be a huge blow to the integration project as such; even success, however, involves the danger that real economic circumstances for many EU citizens would not be improved and that the often lamented gap between electorates and political leaderships would grow even wider.

Further reading

The economic case for monetary union is in European Commission (1990). It is critically assessed in De Grauwe (1992, second edition 1994) and Eichengreen (1992). De Grauwe (1992) also gives an exposition of optimal currency area theory.

Notes

1. The position taken in the text is the conventional wisdom. A dissenting view is that economic motives as such were particularly important in the foundation of the EEC (see Milward 1992).
2. Delors regarded monetary union and defence cooperation as two motors of European construction. See Delors (1992, p178).
3. The European Commission (1990, p68) gave the following breakdown of savings on intra-EC settlements through the use of a single currency:

Financial transactions costs	8.2 to 10.6 billion ECU
In-house costs	3.6 to 4.8 billion ECU
Reduction of cross-border payments costs	1.3 billion ECU
Total savings	13.1 to 19.2 billion ECU

4. For a survey of the literature on inflation costs see Driffill, Mizon and Alph (1990).
5. The asymmetry in question concerns the differential effects of the shocks, not necessarily different sources.
6. In 1991, less than 2 per cent of EU citizens were resident in member states other than their own. Irish in Britain and Portuguese in Spain made up a large part of this small total; of course these two migrations have little to do with European integration but are rooted in much older historic relationships (European Commission 1993a).

8

The European Central Bank

Maastricht as monetarism mark II

It has already been suggested that the notion of an independent central bank expresses an attempt to reformulate the project of monetary disinflation in ways which cope with the most obvious technical difficulties and political resistances which marked the earlier version of monetarism. The Maastricht Treaty thus inscribed the monetarist project into the EU's agenda for the rest of the present century and beyond.

It will be argued here that this adoption of the monetarist project, while it may have avoided the political danger of a direct clash between the movement for European construction and the currently hegemonic forces of neoliberalism, is in fact full of danger for European integration since it may force the Union into policy positions which seriously aggravate the severe difficulties of economic adaptation facing Western European countries. If this occurs, and the Union is seen as perpetuating high levels of unemployment, it may suffer a loss of legitimacy so damaging as to call integration as such into question. The events of 1992 in Britain already show how this could come about.

Maastricht and the European Central Bank

The Maastricht negotiations essentially confirmed the blueprint for monetary union which was first presented in the Delors Report. Some more detail was added regarding the constitution of the European Central Bank (ECB), which is to be very closely modelled on that of the German Bundesbank. The timetable for unification and the sequence of events was made more clear. Phase I of the process – which was regarded as having begun in July 1990 with the widespread abolition of capital controls in the countries which still made use of them – was to end at the beginning of 1994, and the next phase was indeed formally inaugurated at that date. Phase II, however, will not see any real centralisation of competence for monetary policy. On this issue the view of the national central banks prevailed, that monetary policy is 'indivisible' and that therefore partial or preliminary transfers of control over monetary instruments would lead to possible confusion and would obscure responsibility for policy formulation. Rather, phase

II is to see more intensive efforts at policy coordination among national central banks; they retain, however, full control over national policy. Meanwhile procedures for future coordination in the context of full monetary union are being developed through the European Monetary Institute, a purely transitional organisation which will disappear at the beginning of phase III, to be replaced by the European Central Bank properly so called.[1] Ironically, national central banks will receive unprecedented powers immediately before they are reduced to mere instruments of a common purpose, since during phase II they are to be endowed with political independence – this has already taken place in France and Spain.

The timing of phase III, which involves a full centralisation of monetary policy prior to the issue of a common currency, is made conditional on a complex balance of economic and political factors. The first date for such a move – which required the participation of a majority of member states – was the beginning of 1997. It is now universally agreed that this date is impossible because of continuing divergence in monetary and fiscal conditions. This date having been missed, unification is to go ahead in 1999. Like the earlier date it is conditional on the achievement of a series of *convergence criteria* by the participating countries but it no longer requires these to constitute a majority of member states. At the same time there is a possibility of a certain degree of flexibility even if the prescribed economic conditions are not satisfied to the letter, since the Council of Ministers, in consultation with the European Parliament, will take the final decision as to whether each country has met the conditions. The present situation is that it will be difficult for most potential participants to meet, in particular, the targets laid down for stability in public finance. Nevertheless, many EU states (most significantly, France and Germany) are making enormous efforts at least to approach these targets, so that it seems that the political will for monetary union is still strong, at least within the political class itself.

At the beginning of phase III, the participating national central banks concede their power over monetary policy – in most cases newly won from national governments – to the European Central Bank, of which they become the operating arms. ECB and national central banks together will then make up a unified European System of Central Banks, or ESCB. It is significant, however, that the concept of monetary policy involved in the centralisation to European level is somewhat narrow. Although control over the essential policy instruments of foreign exchange intervention, open market operations and discount policy passes fully to the ECB, this is not the case for the supervision of banks and other financial institutions, where there will be a division of competence between national and EU levels.

The structure of the ECB is modelled explicitly on that of the Bundesbank. The latter is controlled by a Council comprising representatives of the individual German Länder and a centrally appointed directorate, which is, however, in a minority. Exactly the same pattern is adopted for the ECB: an executive board of six members, including the ECB President, will be the core of the Council; the other members will be the heads of national central banks. Council members will each have one vote except on issues concerning the distribution of ECB profits among member states, which will be determined by weighted votes of the national (non-executive) representatives. The tenure of executive board members is to be eight years, nonrenewable – to protect them against political pressures.

The constitution of the ECB has two basic specifications: that it be independent of political control whether by national or EU bodies; and that its primary objective, taking absolute precedence over any other, is to secure price stability. To reinforce its independence it is obliged to avoid the monetary finance of public sector deficits. To reinforce the goal of price stability other internal objectives are explicitly subordinated to it.

It should be noted, however, that the Maastricht Treaty leaves one potentially important lever in the hands of the politicians. Article 109, paragraph 1, gives the Council of Ministers the right, if they act unanimously, to conclude formal agreements with outside countries (the US and Japan are probably the two which might matter in practice) on the exchange rate between the euro and other currencies. In doing so they can override the ECB if they are acting on a recommendation of the European Commission. This hardly seems likely to constrain the ECB in practice since one imagines it could find at least one country (Germany, to offer a plausible example) to veto such an agreement if it seemed to have inflationary implications. Paragraph 2, on the other hand, allows the Council of Ministers to determine 'general orientations' for external exchange rates *by qualified majority vote*. In this case, however, the ECB is not bound to defend the chosen exchange rate if it judges that to do so would compromise price stability. It seems likely that such a judgement would be quickly made if monetary inflows were so large or persistent as to make sterilisation difficult. Now it is widely agreed that an external exchange rate commitment ties the hands of the central bank as regards interest rates or credit expansion, so that a channel exists which could undermine the strategic independence of the ECB, leaving it essentially with only operational autonomy. But the requirement of unanimity in the first case and the possibility of disregarding a politically specified orientation in the second mean that the full independence of the central bank is well protected. It can be assumed therefore that the ECB will normally operate a managed float of the euro against outside currencies and that it will only be ready to adopt exchange rate targets where it regards these as fully compatible with its anti-inflationary mission. These clauses may, in the future, become the site of a battle to subdue the ECB, but they do little to compromise the prerogatives it enjoys under the treaty.

Rarely, in fact, can the abstract propositions of a school of economic thought have received such complete and rapid embodiment in actual institutions as is the case for the notion of central bank independence in the Maastricht Treaty.[2]

Central bank independence

The model of monetary policy most often referred to in the argument for central bank independence was constructed by Rogoff (1985), who in turn drew on the work of Barro and Gordon (1983). Barro and Gordon took as their own starting point two key elements of the 'New Classical' macroeconomics, which continued the basic policy arguments of Friedmanite monetarism while formulating them in a much more analytically and technically sophisticated way. They drew firstly on Robert Lucas' model of monetary policy under rational expectations. The model examines the impact of monetary policy on an economy where flexible prices clear all markets, but where economic agents may for a short period confuse changes in relative prices with changes in the overall price level. Given the assumptions of the Lucas model it was shown that only unanticipated variations in monetary policy can have any impact on real output or employment. If an expansion of monetary policy is anticipated it will merely result in correspondingly higher prices. But since any systematic monetary policy will be understood and anticipated by economic agents this means that there can be no systematic effects of money on employment.

Barro and Gordon's second key source is a discussion by Kydland and Prescott (1977) of the possible time inconsistency of economic policies. There are circumstances, Kydland and Prescott contend, when a rational agent may formulate time-inconsistent plans of action: that is, the agent may rationally decide on a course of action today which will be, with equal rationality, abandoned tomorrow. The same can be true, in particular, for the authorities who decide on economic policy – but in such a case their declared policies are likely to be frustrated by the public, which will anticipate that they will not be sustained.

Using these two building blocks Barro and Gordon model the behaviour of a government which, in order to reduce unemployment, is ready to operate an inflationary monetary policy, even though it is aware that the pay-off to such a policy is transient. Because the private sector is aware of the government's methods and objectives, it will anticipate such policy in setting wage rates and prices; in so doing it will rob the policy of its intended impact on employment. The government might respond by planning an even bigger inflationary stimulus, but of course this too will be anticipated. There will usually be, however, some limit beyond which the government is not prepared to go, some point at which it itself regards the inflation cost of a surprise stimulus to employment as excessive. Barro and Gordon show that it is just this maximum bearable level of inflation which will be both chosen by the government and anticipated by private economic agents. It follows that the interaction between private sector and government leads to an inefficient outcome: inflation will be consistently high although the economy would function just as well in terms of employment at a zero inflation rate. Within the policy game as it is laid out, however, this preferable outcome is not available: governments may promise zero inflation, but, given their known objectives and the known working of their policy instruments, they will not be believed. Rather, the threshold of tolerable inflation will be anticipated: this being the case, governments must generate this expected inflation – were they not to do so, avoidable unemployment would necessarily result.

Such are the basic features of the Barro-Gordon model. What will be stressed here is its extremely *abstract* nature. The models of Lucas and of Kydland and Prescott are important innovations in economic theory and, indeed, move it into new territory – the explicit representation of an economy's information structure, and the formal modelling, rather than the descriptive invocation, of a problem of policy credibility. A key aspect of their originality is to analyse policy choices in a way which makes clear the conflicts which can develop between government and private sector. But these analytical achievements depend on the use of many simplifying assumptions which make it dangerous to apply the models immediately to concrete problems of policy formation. Exhaustive analysis has made this clear for the Lucas model, which makes use of empirically unfounded assumptions – in particular, market clearing. In the real world, where most workers and companies are unable to sell as much as they would choose at existing prices, monetary policy can have a real impact on these demand constraints and this effect will not disappear when it is anticipated. Since the Lucas model is a basic building brick of the Barro-Gordon model, similar considerations apply to the latter. In addition, it could be argued that their representation of government action makes short-sighted policy decisions almost a tautology – in essence the authorities treat each period in isolation and do not consider the impact of today's policy on the constraints which will exist in the future.[3]

Subsequent extensions of the model did deal with some of these limitations. A monetary authority might resolve the problem of its credibility either by investing in its own *reputation* or by finding some device of *precommitment* which guarantees that it cannot renege on its own declared line of action. The seminal paper of Rogoff (1985) argued that a good substitute for precommitment might be to delegate responsibility for monetary policy to a 'moderately conservative' central banker, that is, one with more concern for price stability and less concern for output stability than the government itself. In the policy context of the 1980s both these contributions fed directly into the emerging discourse of central bank independence.

Empirical studies

In addition to the abstract exercises in economic modelling which stemmed from Barro and Gordon, some empirical studies have been carried out which have been held to suggest that central bank independence does in fact lead to lower rates of inflation. Most of this work seems particularly unconvincing. Firstly, independence is not directly observable. Some index may be constructed on the basis of different aspects of a central bank's constitution, but this is bound to be an extremely approximate procedure, if not completely subjective. In any case, the real functioning of an institution need not accord with its formal constitutional position. In most Western countries the judiciary is formally independent of the executive: the substantive degree of judicial independence nevertheless varies both with time and with place and never coincides exactly with the formal position. Secondly, these studies essentially present cross-section data, where the average rate of inflation in countries is correlated with the degree of independence, however 'measured', of their central banks. Because of the limited number of observations it is not possible to control for the multitude of other dimensions – apart from this putative central bank independence – in which the same countries differ from each other, for example their wage-bargaining procedures. (If one takes the model literally it would in fact be wrong to control for other factors because, however important in appearance, these would merely reflect the influence of the central bank – at this point the theory becomes Hegelian: industrial relations systems might look like real things but essentially they are simply *moments* of a reality located elsewhere.) Of course, this is to beg the question by assuming what should be shown, that inflation can be uniquely explained by monetary policy. (For a survey of empirical studies see Alesina and Summers 1993; for a critique of this kind of evidence see Posen 1993.)

The German model

In this context it is worth discussing the case of the German Bundesbank. As is well known the law founding the German central bank in its contemporary form made it independent of the Federal government, and this is often held to be the key reason for Germany's exceptionally low inflation.

There is certainly no doubt about the low inflation. Over thirty years (1960–89) consumer price inflation in the industrialised countries as a whole averaged 6.3 per cent per annum. In the Federal Republic of Germany the rate was 3.5 per cent. No other major industrial producer came near to this figure; only in Switzerland (also with a very conservative tradition in the monetary field) was a similar record achieved.

However, other interpretations of German performance are possible. Firstly, one can point to the *anachronism* of the argument: until 1972–73 Germany, like all industrial countries, operated fixed exchange rates against the US dollar. Both the weight of the evidence and the widely accepted Mundell-Fleming model of medium-term exchange rate movements indicate that there is little that monetary policy can do to stabilise prices in such a regime. Indeed, monetary restriction is likely to be a perverse method of attacking inflation under such circumstances as it tends, as both theory and German experience confirm, merely to attract overseas deposits into the domestic banking system and thus to increase the supply of credit (this happened in 1992, for example; see also Kindleberger 1978, p206).

It can be suggested, next, that the Bundesbank was singularly fortunate in that the pressures for it to operate expansionary policies were much less than elsewhere. What circumstances might lead a central bank to offer favourable refinance to commercial banks and capital markets, and thus to the economy as a whole? One plausible case is that of social conflict – if a militant trade union movement pushed up wages across a wide section of industry, the monetary authorities might prefer to extend credit to industry and its customers rather than permit a damaging squeeze on profits. German industrial relations, however, while certainly not free from conflict, have been more consensual and more stable than in most industrial countries.

A second temptation to monetary laxity might arise from financial tensions.

If a speculative wave in real estate or other assets, followed by a sudden collapse of their prices, weakens the balance sheets of banks or other financial intermediaries, it might be considered expedient to provide them with new funds on easy terms rather than to risk a disruption of the credit mechanism. But Germany of course is characterised by strong and stable private finance – dominated by powerful commercial banks rather than competitive and speculative credit markets. It is significant, in this respect, that the Bundesbank does not take primary responsibility for the supervision of banks and other financial agents but only for monetary policy in the aggregate. This division of tasks is convenient in Germany just because of the strength and stability of its financial system – it is rare for any disturbance to private finance to be so extensive or severe as to call overall monetary policy into question.[4] As will be argued below this is certainly not the case in other industrial countries; nor is it likely to be so in the European Union as a single-currency area.

A third obvious temptation can arise from financial pressures on the government or the public sector as a whole. This is indeed the most discussed aspect of the environment in which central banks work; although there are plenty of fiscal hardliners who are happy to recommend as much drastic retrenchment as one could possibly wish, there are in practice both political *and* economic limits to the pressures which can be applied to public finance without aggravating the original tensions. Again Germany has very largely escaped such problems – public expenditure has been well controlled and the government has avoided premature or destabilising tax cuts. The exception of reunification – which led to huge deficits – proves the rule. Bundesbank restriction was, in this case, quite unable to prevail over 'Reaganism on the Rhine'.

Finally, a central bank might be led to adopt expansionary measures in the face of a loss of external competitiveness. It may either decide to devalue the currency or be constrained to do so by a loss of foreign exchange reserves. In many circumstances this can be regarded as another form of emergency refinance – in this case, of exporting industry and other producers subject to international competition. Once again the Bundesbank has been, almost uniquely, exempt from such pressures because of the competitive strength of German industry throughout the history of the Federal Republic. In fact it has more often faced exactly the opposite problem – the persistent current account surpluses generated by export industry have sometimes posed problems of monetary control.

Thus it can be suggested that it is arbitrary to attribute Germany's exceptionally low rates of inflation to a single institution – the central bank. A more balanced judgement might be that the Bundesbank was only one element in an array of well-functioning institutions which helped coordinate labour, product and financial markets (compare Soskice 1991). The outcome has been an economy exceptionally well equilibrated in real terms, within which endogenous inflationary pressures were low. The task faced by the Bundesbank was not as difficult as that confronting central banks in other countries. It is often argued that, for historical reasons, the German population is very worried by inflation (though they surely have good reasons also to fear mass unemployment); this 'psychology' is seen as providing legitimacy to the conservative approach of the Bundesbank. One can again suggest, however, that to the extent that such a specific national psychology exists, it would tend to influence many other institutions as well.

Nor is it clear that the Bundesbank has been as single-mindedly devoted to the objective of price stability as its elevation to the status of role model for the new monetarism might suggest. There are indications that the Bundesbank has also been concerned with an aspect of real economic performance, namely, the current account of the balance of payments. This was certainly the case under the Bretton Woods regime, when the Bundesbank was on several occasions reluctant to revalue the D-mark even though this was the only secure defence against imported inflation. The very unusual balance of payments deficits posted by Germany in the early 1980s also seem to have aggravated the conflict between the Bundesbank and the government of Helmut Schmidt, which was the most acute assertion of Bundesbank independence. It is certainly possible that concern over the decline (albeit inevitable) in the balance of payments surplus which followed unification was a factor behind the Bundesbank's persistently restrictive policies in recent years.

Finally, one can question the standard view of the way in which Bundesbank influence is exercised in Germany. The current paradigm of monetary control stresses the ideas of *precommitment* and *reputation*. A central bank in this view maximises its force by announcing preset targets for the supply of its liabilities and sticking to them; if it does this consistently its reputation or credibility is enhanced, and other agents in the economy will increasingly adapt their behaviour to the aggregate monetary constraint that this implies.

Now there is no doubt that the Bundesbank has on occasion exercised an important influence over the behaviour of economic agents. Specifically, it has sometimes been able to persuade Germany's powerful trade unions to moderate their pay demands, by pointing to the danger of inflation and threatening to raise interest rates (Streeck 1996). However, it is not clear that this influence amounts to the kind of pre-emptive capacity represented in recent theories. It always remains open to both unions and government to maintain their position in the face of Bundesbank disapproval; and the Bundesbank may not be able to carry out its threat of restriction. Thus while Bundesbank restriction in the early 1980s helped to bring down the government, neither government nor unions were prepared to accede to Bundesbank demands in the wake of German unification, and it was the central bank which ended by moderating its own policy stand. The 'reputation' acquired over forty years did not in this second case permit a simple veto to be exercised on the behaviour of other agents.[5] It may be more realistic to regard the German central bank as one (powerful) negotiating party among others rather than as the source of a unique, quasi-judicial, authority.

Central bank independence and monetary control

It is necessary to make a clear logical distinction between the two sides of contemporary central bank reform: on the one hand the directly political question of independence as such; on the other, the specification of the objective of monetary policy purely in terms of price stability.[6] Attention here will focus on the second issue. On the first question it will only be suggested that the real difficulty is not the division of power as such (the mere fact that monetary policy is not in the hands of the executive) but the dilution of accountability which may result if the central bank cannot be given instructions by *any* democratic body. This may lead to an inappropriate treatment, as if it were a court of law rather than an instrument of public policy. The 'democratic deficit' of the European Union has been discussed over many years; the problem would hardly be reduced by putting what would be the Union's most powerful institution beyond the control of elected representatives. (For a critique of this *depoliticisation* of monetary policy see Cooper 1994; the undemocratic nature of central bank independence is criticised, in a British context, by Burkitt and Baimbridge 1994.) It is very desirable that the political priorities that guide monetary policy are explicit, while efficiency may then require that operational decisions in pursuit of these political objectives are a clear managerial responsibility of the central bank itself. Some such combination seems to be the goal of Goodhart's (1994) argument for central bank *autonomy* (as opposed to independence).

Here, however, the focus will be on the attempt to specify the objectives of monetary policy uniquely in terms of price stability.[7] It will be argued that the central bank's status as the issuer of high-powered (state) money necessarily gives it a decisive influence over financial stability, which cannot be exercised efficiently if price stabilisation becomes the sole policy criterion. In other words the central bank acts not only to regulate the issue of money and credit by the financial system, it also acts as *lender of last resort* to the same system (Kindleberger 1978). These two functions are closely related so that the attempt to subordinate completely the second to the first may result in a severe crisis. Three bodies of evidence can be used to support this proposition: the conflict between financial stability and monetary control in the very short run; the historical association between the issue of central bank money and the provision of emergency finance; and the actual constraints on monetary disinflation which have arisen in industrial countries in recent years.

Monetary base control

The simplest and most direct monetarist strategy took the form of monetary base control – that is, the imposition of a straightforward limit to the issue of high-powered, central bank money. In practice, the closest approach to such a strategy was reached in the early days of the Volcker and Thatcher experiments in the US and Britain respectively. (It should be noted that Germany, although it was one of the pioneers of 'monetary targets', never pushed this doctrine to the point of attempting to introduce such an absolute limit – the Bundesbank's *short-run* operations have always involved interest rate targets.) The underlying notion was simple or even simplistic. Beyond a predetermined limit, the discount window would be closed and open market purchases of debt would cease. The quantity of central bank money thus having been fixed, the market for it would be cleared by pure price adjustment – that is, by whatever rate of interest was needed to adjust demand to supply.

Now this simplest version of monetary control seems to have been infeasible (for a review of these debates see Goodhart 1995a). No pure implementation of it ever occurred, and every time it was even approached there followed an immense build-up of financial tensions which forced a modification of policy – either a relaxation of the supply of central bank liabilities, or the introduction of substitute forms of finance which lifted the constraints on commercial banks and other intermediaries which the policy implied. It became necessary to redefine the strategy of monetary control to avoid this complete short-term inelasticity in the supply of high-powered money. Rather, accommodation of the demand for central refinance was reinstated, but at relatively high rates of interest which were aimed, over a somewhat longer period of months or even years, to encourage a reduction of this demand.

Economists wedded to the monetarist project have wanted to minimise the import of this switch in strategy so that it is seen as a technical problem – in fact one of the many technical difficulties which are seen as making it desirable to transfer monetary control to a powerful central bank shielded from political pressures. It can be suggested, however, that a much more radical conclusion should be drawn: that there is a fundamental tension between a central bank's role of lender of last resort, guaranteeing financial stability, and its role in regulating the quantity of money and the price level. This tension becomes acute, or even an absolute contradiction, over short time intervals.[8] It will now be suggested that it by no means disappears when longer periods are considered.

The evolution of central banks

Historical evidence also indicates that control over the currency and the lender-of-last resort function are very closely related. In many countries the establishment of a central bank was not a decision by the state but the product of an evolutionary process within the private financial system itself. Just as individuals and companies found it more efficient to rely on accommodation by a commercial bank rather than the maintenance of a large stock of liquid assets, so banks and other financial agents came both to centralise a large part of their reserves at one particular bank and to rely on borrowing beyond their assets at that bank if they came under unexpected pressure to redeem their own debts. The centralisation of these functions improved the efficiency of the financial system as a whole by permitting commercial banks and other agents to invest more of their resources in productive activity and less in insuring themselves against illiquidity. This pattern of development occurred both in Britain and in France, where what were initially simply large commercial banks, first among equals, developed a specific stabilisation role. Further evolution required a recognition of the public nature of this role since it created problems of competition: the central bank could not simply behave as another commercial bank because it had a different kind of balance sheet – for example it might have to hold a larger quantity of gold and other liquid assets with a low yield.

It was the emergence of this new role also which forced central banks to concern themselves with the nature and conditions of system-wide stability. It was gradually discovered that the best defence of the system when a large number of agents had problems of liquidity might be the opposite of what would be logical for an individual company or even an individual bank. Faced with a sudden need for money an individual will immediately put pressure on his own debtors to meet their obligations. Central banks learned that to follow this apparently rational procedure would make things worse for them, by increasing the number of agents requiring accommodation (Goodhart 1988; Aglietta 1992). Control over the supply of money as a whole – more correctly, control over the extent and the conditions of credit expansion – was certainly one aspect of this emerging public role. If this was carried beyond the potential for profitable trade and investment in the economy then the quality of debts would decline and the financial system be imperilled. But an equally important aspect was the recognition of a limit to such control: in a fragile economic climate, or an open financial crisis, failure to extend new credit facilities to private financial institutions could lead to widespread and cumulative defaults. Also this kind of central bank necessarily acquired an important supervisory function. Its ability to regulate finance and credit as a whole was enhanced if it could identify individual institutions with particularly risky balance sheets or whose activities were otherwise unsound. Both the formulation of rules for credit institutions and the surveillance required to enforce these rules thus became integral parts of central bank activity. In other words, bankers themselves acted collectively to respond to gradually recognised externalities in their own decision-making; central banks, as evolving but still private institutions, amended their credit policies as a result.

It must be stressed that financial systems evolve and that the emergencies which can arise, while recurrent, are never simply repetitive. Today's institutions behave differently from those of five years ago, never mind those of the last century. It is important to see that the risks to which individual institutions and markets are exposed are ceaselessly changing, as does the possibility of the contagious spread of individual disturbances within the financial system. This factor may lead to *macroeconomic* disruption and may thus call for a modification of monetary policy as a whole.

There are tendencies towards greater stability as well as towards new system-wide dangers. On the one hand, the very scale and speed of modern financial processes reduce certain dangers: particular parts of the financial system are less isolated and may in consequence be more able to deal with shocks; the wider and more rapid availability of information may prevent some of the panic phenomena so obvious in the financial crises in history. But nothing justifies the dogmatic assertion that we are dealing with efficient, self-equilibrating processes which permit an easy separation of 'real' and 'monetary' aspects.

At the same time, the form of system-wide risks is changing rapidly. The bank runs of the past may not be as serious a threat today, partly because of the widespread *disintermediation* of many banking operations (see Chapter 9)

and partly because official intervention in such cases is usually fast and res-
olute. However, this does not mean that there are no system-wide risks; in
fact, the very speed of financial innovation is itself a potential risk factor
because financial agents are always working in a new and imperfectly understood environment. Aglietta, Brender and Coudert (1990, Chapter 5) distinguish system-wide risks today from the financial crises of the past and
suggest the following categories: *breakdowns* are disturbances arising endoge-
nously within the financial sector as a result of imperfect information or
inadequate decision-making (they instance the New York stock market crash
of 1987 as well as potential dangers to electronic payments systems); *accidents*
are financial disturbances provoked by shocks to particular productive sectors when the corresponding risks are imperfectly diversified (for example,
the impact of agricultural distress on some parts of the US banking system in
the 1980s); finally, *drifts* are serious economic distortions which can be produced, especially in a climate of financial deregulation, by the impact of the
financial system on other economic sectors even when credit risks are accurately assessed and efficiently diversified (thus the explosion of consumer
credit in many countries in the 1980s, although it was carried out efficiently
from the point of view of the intermediaries involved, nevertheless gave rise
to significant problems for economic policy). These authors insist on the
potential macroeconomic consequences of such disturbances and on the limited capacity of national authorities to control the situation in a context of
increasingly internationalised financial relations. (For another survey of
system-wide financial risks in an international context see Portes and
Swoboda 1987.)

Central banks in many of the older nation states can thus be seen as the
product of a long sequence of financial development and innovation. In the
light of this, current proposals to remove central bank responsibility for general financial stability and to replace this with a narrow remit for price stability seem particularly voluntarist. One danger might be the outbreak of
open financial crisis if counter-inflationary rigour is taken too far. The short
history of monetarism already offers several examples of such an outcome. A
more insidious danger could also be that the supply of credit is kept excessively tight over an extended period, as this would become the only means
open to a central bank which no longer regulated and intervened in financial
relations to avoid the possible build-up of exposed positions.

It is an irony that the defenders of 'free banking', such as Hayek (1976), are
led to deny their own theories of the self-organisation of the market economy
when they reject the supervisory role of the central bank over modern credit
and banking systems, because the historical role shows that central banks are

the product of just such an evolutionary process by which market dynamics can lead to forms of collective rationality (Aglietta 1992).

Recent lender-of-last-resort operations

A third body of evidence for the importance of financial stabilisation to monetary policy is offered by recent monetary history. The prevailing view some fifteen years ago was that the lender-of-last resort function could be combined with monetary disinflation because the stabilisation problems that occurred were essentially microeconomic – they concerned individual banks or other large companies which might need emergency refinance, and such operations could be carried out without compromising general monetary policy. In retrospect this view can be seen to have been predicated on two conditions of the Keynesian era which no longer apply: firstly, that aggregate monetary policy would be relatively accommodating; secondly, that real economic development would be stable and continuous. In the turbulent economic climate of the 1980s and 1990s, and in the context of thoroughgoing attempts at monetary disinflation, it was no longer always possible to identify and isolate individual companies or banks with potential financial difficulties and take action to contain the problem at a microeconomic level. As a result, changes in general monetary policy have been made with a view to financial stability which have compromised targets for growth of the money stock and the objective of price stabilisation in a narrow sense. One key example was the retreat from doctrinaire monetarism by the Federal Reserve Board in the United States in the late summer of 1982. By that time, recession, high interest rates and a rising dollar had brought a large number of important debtors to the brink of insolvency, thus jeopardising also the intermediaries and creditors who had financed them. This was the case for Mexico and other Latin American countries: the persisting crisis of third world debt may not have been caused only by the Volcker shock, but there is no doubt that this was the precipitating factor. There were also actual and impending bankruptcies on an ominous scale within the United States, particularly in the agricultural sector, which could not live with an overvalued dollar. By the time US policy altered it was a case of recognising the inevitable – credit would necessarily have to be extended to a wide range of economic agents, and further delay would only increase their number and the intensity of their distress. Similar considerations may have been one factor behind the retreat from strict monetary targeting in Britain around the same time: one ironic aspect of the British situation was that the Bank of England actually encouraged the use of substitute forms of credit for firms denied access to bank overdrafts – it helped organise a revived market in bank accep-tances, that is, commercial credit endorsed by the banks, thus effectively undermining its own key indicator for monetary policy. Again in the early 1990s, the urgency with which monetary policy was relaxed in both Britain and the US was related to financial distress – particularly in housebuilding, other construction and property development. The same kind of develop-ment led to the emergency refinance of huge parts of the banking sector by the authorities in Sweden and elsewhere in Scandinavia.

Examples could be multiplied. One particularly dramatic case concerns the collapse of international stock markets in October 1987. This does not in fact seem to have led to widespread financial distress, but central banks were certainly alarmed, and in response the US authorities led a widespread move to lower interest rates. Perhaps future years may see fewer such emer-gencies – although 1995 brought us both a major international rescue of the Mexican peso and the astonishing relaxation of Japanese monetary policy to essentially zero interest rates in a climate of financial confusion in that country. The pace of financial innovation may slow down; the authorities have learned more of these dangers and are responding with closer super-vision and less ambitious exercises in restriction. But there remain major uncertainties in the pattern of real economic development as well as sub-stantial experimentation in national and international forms of credit. In such circumstances a sudden and widespread need for the central refinance of economic agents surely cannot be ruled out.

A fiscal alternative?

One response to the kind of point made above is to argue that, in modern economies, the lender-of-last-resort function should be seen as involving not monetary but fiscal policy, and as the responsibility not of the central bank but of the executive. There is a lot of truth in this. The refinance of finan-cially distressed agents, to the extent that they cannot successfully reorganise their activities, can be seen as a *socialisation* of losses: the citizenry in general, either through subsidies or credit guarantees, comes to the aid of private agents whose failure is considered unacceptable on economic, social or polit-ical grounds. Such an allocation of responsibility seems appropriate in modern democracies – intervention and its costs are inevitably political issues and it is better that they are clearly seen to be so. Minsky (1986, Chapter 2), whose writings on financial disturbance have proved to be very prescient, has argued that 'big government' has altered both the scale and the nature of stabilisation problems. But there are at least two limits to this politicisation of the question. The first concerns *speed*: the need for rapid action will often dictate that it be handled by the monetary authorities – continuously present in financial markets – rather than by much slower executive and legislative means. Secondly, of course, the government itself faces monetary constraints: fiscal interventions may be extremely costly or even counterproductive if the government itself is deprived of emergency refinance or if its own debt is not supported in credit markets. In fact, the independence of the central bank can be seen as threatening coordination between monetary and fiscal policy in general as well as in the case of emergency refinance (Doyle and Weale 1994). Contemporary commentators too often call for ever greater financial constraints to be imposed on supposedly profligate national governments; if the latter are assigned very important stabilisation functions then this implies that monetary policy should take these responsibilities into account. Thus while the classical dilemma of financial stabilisation and monetary control has been profoundly modified by the growth of national government, it has certainly not been eliminated. The acute financial pressure on the executive, which has developed in recent years as economies become more open, also suggests that there may be tight limits to the 'fiscalisation' of the stability issue.

The basis of central control

It can even be suggested that the radical separation of the lender-of-last-resort function from control over the money supply would logically tend to undermine the latter itself. Increasingly it is recognised, in discussions of monetary policy, that central banks largely derive their fundamental influence over the creation of money from their own activities on credit markets – from the fact that they borrow and lend (Dow and Saville 1990, Chapter 4). What would happen if these activities ceased, or were subjected to a strict numerical ceiling? The first consequence, as has been pointed out above, would most likely be quite acute financial distress and costly dislocations in the private sector; but over a longer time period the outcome could well be a tendency to demonetise central bank liabilities, by the evolution of substitutes within the private sector.

The way this could occur is suggested by Hicks' (1974) distinction between an 'overdraft' and a 'reserve' economy. Individual economic agents may come to rely on being able to borrow freely from banks to meet any sudden need for liquidity. In such a situation (an 'overdraft' economy) they will not themselves hold substantial money balances and, in fact, the size of the balances they do hold will lose some of its economic significance as it will not be a binding constraint on expenditure. But if accommodation by the banks is called into question, say because commercial banks themselves are liquidity-constrained, there would be a move to a 'reserve' economy where agents would routinely hold much larger stocks of cash or other liquid claims.

Exactly the same reasoning applies to banks and other intermediaries themselves. If they can be sure of accommodation by the central bank, they will hold much lower reserves of central bank money; they will hold instead higher-yielding assets which they will sell, or present for discount, to the central bank in case of need. If they cannot rely on this source of liquidity they will create others: a first step might be to hold much bigger reserves on their own account, to be deployed in emergencies; a second step could then be the emergence of a private alternative to the central bank which would provide the same refinancing services which the central bank is restricting. At both the level of commercial banks and that of non-financial agents, wide use would probably be made of substitute assets (for example, claims on very large and important private commercial banks or other giant companies) as the key form of liquidity in the system. Even if such assets were, for legal and historical reasons, denominated in units of state money, they would tend to reduce the significance of central bank liabilities, which would come to play an economic role similar to that of gold under Bretton Woods – that is, it would continue to be the official denominator of the system but would lose its other monetary functions. This kind of development is by no means a pure exercise of the imagination: aspects of it – the development of substitute transactions media and the accumulation of private cash reserves – have actually been observed during the most ambitious phases of monetarist rigour. Only the modification of public policy prevented things from going further in this direction. Of course, the outcome of such a process would be not the strengthening of central bank control, but its attenuation. The advocates of pure private money ('free banking') might be happy to see this happen, but their confidence in the stability of purely private economic relations is not widely shared.[9]

There is something abstract and potentially misleading about many models of monetary control. The supply of central bank liabilities and the demand for them is represented as if we were dealing with the supply and demand of an ordinary commodity on a centralised, Walrasian, market with the short-term interest rate being the price which brings about market-clearing. For many purposes this may be an adequate description, but if the analogy is taken too far the *monetary* nature of the process is neglected: money is a device which permits decentralised, non-Walrasian markets to function precisely by relaxing the requirements for a complete and continuous balance between supply and demand in real terms. Absolute monetary restriction impairs, and may even render impossible, the functioning of the decentralised economy.

Financial and real stability

The argument so far has counterposed two objectives of monetary policy: on the one hand price stabilisation and the control of inflation; on the other, financial stability and the avoidance of disruption in the credit system. It has been suggested that modern central banks must necessarily pursue both objectives. It remains to argue that financial stability in these terms is not a separate issue any more than is monetary stability itself; rather, finance is indissociable from the overall functioning of a decentralised production economy, so that financial stability depends on the performance of the productive system as a whole. Thus, to be concerned with financial stability necessarily implies a concern with the course of real economic development. The lender-of-last-resort function is not a technical addendum; it expresses the interaction of 'real' (above all, financial) and monetary factors throughout the economy.[10]

The point can be made by considering the debts incurred by enterprises in the course of the production and marketing of the goods and services they produce. In a fully equilibrated economy these debts are cleared by the successful sale of the product; in such a situation all debts are equivalent to money in that the distinction between money and credit disappears. When, however, an enterprise is for any reason unable to produce the expected output, or to sell it at the anticipated price, there is a financial difficulty and the relation between privately issued debt and more generally acceptable money may be called into question.

In such a situation the creditors of the enterprise, often its bankers, face a dilemma. They have to decide whether to refinance the company, in the hope that its problems are temporary, or to refuse further assistance. This is a dilemma because it involves radical uncertainty (were debtor and creditor to agree even on the risks involved the problem would be virtually solved) and because there is usually no half-way house: if refinance is the correct decision then new funds should be made available promptly and on a sufficient scale to enable the debtor enterprise to continue its operations; if, however, credit is cut off, it is usually best to do so at once and completely. In the latter case, however, creditors face the risk that their own actions may push the enterprise into failure, where much of the value of its assets may be lost. In essence the creditor has to choose between two risky projects: the company's own plans for restructuring and recovery, or a transfer of property to new agents who may achieve better results.

When we next consider the hierarchy of credit relations which exists in modern economies, the dilemma persists but in a somewhat different form. A large commercial bank for example has many debtors whose situation is to some extent interdependent. Pushing one into liquidation may weaken the position of others; alternatively it may put pressure on the bank's own creditors who will then press the bank for repayment. In such circumstances the decision to refinance a group of debtors has a *centralising* aspect: it makes possible the continuation of existing economic relations among customers, suppliers and employees. To cut off credit is a more decentralised process: agents are left to fend for themselves, on the basis of transfers of assets to creditors which may disrupt productive activity. Either process may be successful; either may fail. If refinance is attempted but companies are unable to restructure there will be some inflationary pressure because the bank will have issued money against assets with no real value; in the opposite case contraction may follow as companies have to cease activity and resources go unused.

The central bank is at the top of this complex hierarchy of credit relations based on the activities of real production and consumption. It faces similar dilemmas: a centralising and potentially inflationary refinance of banks and other intermediaries, which preserves the links between economic agents; or a decentralising refusal of accommodation, which exposes debtors to creditors and may tend to paralyse real economic activity. Simple *a priori* policy rules are not applicable in this situation, which always occurs in the context of new phases of economic development and original projects for economic restructuring. It is certainly the case that a strategy of abundant and reliable (and, even more so, automatic and invariable) refinance is infeasible, even self-contradictory. Many commentators have pointed out that automatic monetary accommodation by the lender of last resort presents insuperable problems of moral hazard: debtors have no incentive to avoid losses. An example of the kind of malfunction that can result is given by US savings banks in the 1980s: many of them were close to insolvency or actually insolvent, but because their debts were guaranteed by the authorities they were often able to go on borrowing – often for extremely risky projects. Continuation along this road leads to the 'soft budget constraints' which characterised the old socialist economies (Kornai 1982); not only does inflationary pressure build up but money gradually loses its regulatory function.[11]

On the other hand pure decentralising strategies, that is, the refusal of all accommodation beyond a preset limit, are equally infeasible in modern economies with their dense and vulnerable networks of interdependence. There are immense, and unacceptable, risks of a deflationary contraction of economic activity, while in the long run the private sector itself will create centralised agencies for refinance if the state refuses this role.

The point of this characterisation of financial relations is to indicate that the issue of central bank money is inextricably entangled with ongoing processes of real economic adaptation. Banking systems have to pursue complex strategies, giving as much accommodation as seems possible, but on terms which discourage the accumulation of financial tensions. To lay down in advance a strict target for price disinflation is to risk eliminating the essential room for manoeuvre which the economy requires.

It should be pointed out, finally, that in a rapidly changing economy there are many possible sources of financial distress. Recent economic discussion has tended to concentrate on only one of these – the labour market. It certainly is (or was) true that the initial pressure on company balance sheets may well result from militant trade unionism and rising labour costs. But it is an oversimplification to look only at labour markets. Disturbances and miscalculations in markets for goods and services, in the deployment of technologies and in the allocation of investment are all equally capable of giving rise to financial tensions which will require consideration of general, centralised, refinance.

Maastricht and the lender of last resort

The argument so far has been that an effective central bank necessarily combines two inseparable functions: on the one hand control over the issue of state money and the search for price stability, on the other the preservation of financial stability and, in consequence, the stability of the real economy. It is not possible in reality to isolate the first task, although it can seem possible within highly abstract economic models which assume that the second is always taken care of by the self-equilibrating properties of the free market. Now, the Maastricht Treaty has written just such an abstract speculation into the founding document of the European Union. The European Central Bank's methods of operation are narrowly specified in the Treaty: they give complete priority to the control of inflation and leave very little scope for the pursuit of financial stability.

Firstly, the ECB has not been given clear powers to supervise commercial banks or other private financial companies. In accordance with the fashionable, but speculative, doctrines of the moment, the supervision of private finance is left to national authorities. Now if this is seen as a *delegation* of operational power to national level it is simply a sensible application of the principle of subsidiarity. The national authorities, on the scene, will have good information on the markets and agents concerned. But if it amounts to a refusal of responsibility for financial stability then it conflicts with a long tradition of central banking which sees such supervision as closely related to monetary control, since it can help to reduce the possibility of a sudden demand for the emergency issue of state money. Delegation of supervisory responsibilities may be logical when the financial problems which have to be dealt with are confined to particular companies or banks and can be successfully localised without calling into question the general orientation of European monetary policy. But if there is widespread financial distress or if an originally small-scale problem widens rapidly (perhaps across national frontiers) through panic or financial linkages, only an energetic response, centralised at the level of the Union, may prove adequate to restore confidence.[12]

Secondly, the response of the ECB to such an emergency is narrowly circumscribed. The ECB will be able to deal on private credit markets – thus it has the operational freedom to respond to a sudden need for liquidity in the private sector. But the rules imposed on the ECB do not explicitly provide for a lender-of-last-resort function because they give absolute priority to price stability, and this may conflict with centralised refinance on the required scale. Although such refinance may prevent a downward spiral of default and decline in economic activity it almost inevitably involves the extension of credit to some agents who will, in any case, fail and be unable to repay: to this extent lender-of-last-resort operations socialise losses by creating high-powered money to which there is no real counterpart; they have an inescapably inflationary character. In principle, therefore, they seem to be ruled out by the Maastricht specification of the ECB's role.

What will happen if (one is tempted to say 'when') there is a serious episode of financial instability in the European economy and a large number of private agents are on the brink of failure? The doctrines which inspired Maastricht simply assume that this will not occur, that such financial distress can be identified and isolated at a stage when only a few agents are in distress and can be dealt with by measures of purely microeconomic significance. But the whole history of Western financial relations points, rather, to the inevitability of such disturbances, particularly in periods marked, like the present, by major structural changes and uncertainties.

Three scenarios can be put forward for such a case. In the first, the rules of the ECB are altered to permit it to play a stabilising role. This is likely in the long run simply because the present rules are unworkable. But it will not be easy because such a change will require the unanimous consent of the fifteen member states of the union – not something which can be organised in a hurry.

A second possibility is that the ECB will interpret its own rules in a 'flexible' way, in effect assuming the responsibility for emergency refinance which it was not given in the letter of the Treaty. One way this could be done is to widen the definition of 'price stability' to embrace the prices of financial assets and the value of debts. Thus a collapse of property prices, bank failures, company liquidations and so on would be treated as the *deflationary* phenomena they undoubtedly represent (correspondingly it would be recognised that asset price inflation is just that – inflation; see Goodhart and Schoenmaker 1995a, who argue for such a shift of definitions). Such a reinterpretation would go a long way to remove the most objectionable aspects of the ECB rules and to encourage a prudent engagement with the workings of the financial system. However, the prevalence of simplistic anti-inflationary doctrines and the quite unambiguous nature of the priorities laid down in the Maastricht Treaty may work against any smooth alteration of the ECB's role.

For this reason we have to contemplate a third, alarming, scenario in which a serious financial crisis or liquidity shock is met by official inaction or by refinancing measures which are delayed and on an inadequate scale. The result would be escalating damage to the real economy and to employment as defaults and liquidations proliferate and confidence is undermined.

Such an assessment of the potential consequences of the European Central Bank may seem overly pessimistic. But it should be remembered firstly that the kind of financial emergencies which have been invoked are not the exception but the rule in Western economies. (The fact that Germany has by and large been immune to them is not a basis for optimism, since the ECB will not be dealing with the German economy but with the European economy as a whole – indeed it is the projection of an essentially German institution into a European context where it is quite inappropriate which forms the core of the discussion above.[13]) Secondly, it is clear that excessively restrictive monetary policies, at the beginning of the 1980s and again at the start of the 1990s, were associated with massive increases in unemployment in Western Europe which have tended to persist and to raise the social and budgetary costs of subsequent economic adjustment.

It is a strength of the movement for European integration that it has recurrently been able to redefine its own content in accordance with the changing economic and political priorities of the times. This adaptability has led to a very close association between EU strategies and contemporary concerns with mastering inflation and giving wider scope to market forces. But this strength can become a weakness if it ties the integration project too closely to a particular policy agenda with a limited capacity to resolve emerging problems of economic development and democratic control. The monetary provisions of the Maastricht Treaty seem to involve exactly this weakness: they embody a one-sided, abstract and doctrinaire conception of the relation between monetary systems and the general process of economic development. The consequences could be damaging for the citizens of the EU and for the integration project itself.

Further reading

The collection of papers in Goodhart (1995) provide a comprehensive view of relations between monetary policy and the financial system. Mourmouras (1997, Chapter 6) is a full survey of the macroeconomic models which have inspired the contemporary proposals for central bank independence. Cuikerman (1992) is a technically difficult but very thorough study of the issue from the standpoint of 'new classical' macroeconomics. Posen (1993) is a widely cited critique of the empirical case for independence.

Notes

1. The EMI has its seat at Frankfurt. The ECB will now, almost inevitably, be located in the same place. The originally good prospects of siting this institution in London, the most important financial centre in Europe, were destroyed by Britain's refusal to commit itself to the monetary integration project. If the project succeeds, the City of London could lose a lot of business to France and Germany.

2 The British Bank Charter Act of 1844, however, which wrote into law tight quantitative limits to monetary expansion by the Bank of England, provides an interesting, but not encouraging, precedent. Suspension of the Act, in order to cope with economic crises, became almost routine in the nineteenth century.

3. This assumption – that political decision-makers are chronically short-sighted, concerned only with the next election – is justified by an appeal to the notion of a *political business cycle*, in which macroeconomic policy follows the rhythm of general elections. The empirical evidence for such a view is again weak. It can be added that the view one takes of *planning horizons* is today a clear marker of ideological tendencies: proponents of the unfettered market refer to the time-myopia of the political class; but the business class does not escape the analogous accusation of *short-termism*.

4. German unification would seem to be the exception which proves the rule. In a lengthy conflict between the Bundesbank and the Federal government the outcome was that a much higher degree of inflation and much more generous emergency refinance of the East German economy than the central bankers would have preferred had, in the end, to be accepted.

5. Filc (1994) argues that Bundesbank policy in the face of unification rapidly lost all credibility at least so far as the money markets were concerned: the sign of a credible anti-inflationary squeeze would be that short-run interest rates rise to curtail expenditures while longer-run rates are stable or even fall because less inflation is expected in the future; the upward movement of long rates that actually occurred, however, indicates that inflationary expectations were hard to alter while the uncertainty associated with recession tended to raise real credit costs.

6. There is a contrast here between the Bundesbank and the US central bank, the Federal Reserve. Both are politically independent but the latter enjoys much more freedom in its choice of strategy because it is not constrained to concern itself only with the stability of the currency, to the exclusion of other economic objectives. From the point of view of European construction there seems to be a missed opportunity: institutions modelled on the Federal Reserve might have been much more appropriate, in both political and financial terms, for the guidance of European monetary policy, than the German model which was in fact adopted.

7. It is ironic that Rogoff (1985) did not go so far – his independent central banker was to be only *moderately* conservative, that is, a little less concerned with output and employment stability than the population in general. The Maastricht enthronement of price stability as the absolute policy objective is in this sense more Catholic than the Pope.

8. Even Cuikerman (1992, Chapter 2), one of the most committed proponents of monetary disinflation, has acknowledged the necessity of this kind of short-run smoothing of interest rates.

9. The debate on purely private money (suggested, in particular, by Hayek 1976) competes with central bank independence as a response to the disappointments of early experiments in monetary disinflation. It will not be further examined here, as enough has been said to indicate that from the point of view of the writer (and many others) it is a totally utopian project (for a recent discussion see Selgin 1994).

10. The discussion in this section draws very heavily on Aglietta and Orléan

(1982). The writer's admiration for the economic analysis of this work does not extend to its eschatological aspects.

11. Hence Kindleberger's (1978, p12) paradoxical but by no means frivolous formula: 'The lender of last resort should exist but his presence should be doubted.'

12. The point here concerns the *functional*, not necessarily the *institutional* link between monetary and financial control; Goodhart and Schoenmaker (1995) show that the institutional organisation of these functions is extremely variable.

13. To see how closely the design of the ECB agreed at Maastricht follows the recommendations of the Bundesbank, one can compare the proposals of future Bundesbank president Tietmeyer (1991) with the actual outcome. German central bankers seem to have subscribed to the scholastic doctrine that, in order to secure the immortality of the soul, it is necessary to resurrect the body – certainly the ECB could hardly be closer than it is to a physical replication of the Bundesbank.

9

Money and financial integration

The need for European control

In modern economies, money is created by the process of bank lending. Thus the issue of money is a part of the overall credit system, whose function is to allocate savings among potential users of financial resources. In consequence, developments in the credit system affect the operation of monetary policy. Today in Western Europe financial systems are in rapid evolution due to the increasing internationalisation of credit relations and related changes in the public regulation of borrowing and lending.

Discussion of financial systems often distinguishes the two polar cases of market-based and bank-based credit relations, although in practice only various mixed forms are observed, and there are other important dimensions along which differences in financial systems can be measured. In this chapter, however, this distinction will be used to give a broad descriptive account of financial change in Western Europe, which is, in general, from a bank-based towards a market-based system. It will be argued that this pattern of development raises questions about both the stability and the efficiency of the financial system in an integrated Europe. As a result, the financial environment in which European monetary policy operates may become increasingly adverse in macroeconomic terms. Although there is no easy solution to these problems there is a case for much closer supervision and control over credit relations within the EU. Beyond the issue of supervision of private finance there is also a case for a much more active public presence in borrowing and lending activities, on grounds of both efficiency and stability.

Internationalisation

The emergence over the last three decades of a globalised financial system can be regarded as the result of the internationalisation and deregulation of the US financial system, which is characterised by very high degrees of competition among large numbers of financial agents. During that time, internationalisation and deregulation reinforced each other because moving credit relations abroad was an important way in which the constraints of regulation within the US could be avoided, while the development of external credit relations further undermined an inefficient and obsolete domestic regulatory structure.

In the 1930s the New Deal administration introduced a comprehensive system of control over banks and other financial agents. There were many restrictions on the organisation of financial institutions, on the uses they could make of credit, on the scope of their activities and on the rates of interest they could pay for funds. For instance banks were not allowed to pay interest on current accounts ('sight deposits'); the famous regulation Q also restricted the rates they could pay on deposits ('savings' accounts); banks were restricted geographically from establishing nationwide branch networks; credit for the purposes of stock exchange investment was closely controlled; and so on. This detailed control resulted from the view that unrestricted financial activity had been a major factor in the onset of the Wall Street crash of 1929 and the ensuing Great Depression.

As early as the 1950s, however, the system of control began to crumble. One important factor, at least as a catalyst, was inflation itself. Regulated rates of interest for lenders did not sufficiently compensate for inflation, which reduced real interest rates. As a result banks began to search for new sources of funds, not subject to such restrictions. Thus began what became known as *liability management*: instead of passively accepting such funds as ordinary, depositors brought them and attempting merely to on-lend these funds in the most advantageous way, banks began to concentrate on borrowing as much as possible to take advantage of practically unlimited opportunities for lending. For instance they began to sell commercial debt (Certificates of Deposit, or CD) to their larger customers to whom they could thereby pay higher rates of interest. This was an early example of *financial innovation*, the introduction of new forms of borrowing and lending (new debt instruments) to exploit perceived gaps in the financial structure. The same example illustrates the growing *marketisation* of credit relations. Although the holder of a CD did not have a right to immediate repayment by the bank which issued it, he could sell the CD (which was negotiable) on a well-organised market established by the banks themselves. To the extent that such a sale was easy and cheap, the CD had in practice some of the characteristics of a deposit account, in terms of liquidity.

While inflation tended to persist, and with a large number of borrowers unable to find accommodation at existing interest rates, non-financial corporations and individuals began to look for new ways to maximise the return on their savings. A classical example of this process was the emergence of money market funds (MMFs). In this case new financial institutions started to compete with the banks, forcing the latter to imitate them. The funds were borrowed from the public for investment in secure forms of government debt. Although they were not officially banks, and hence not restricted in the interest rates they could pay, their creditors were essentially in the same position as bank depositors – ways were found to enable them to make withdrawals and payments out of their MMF accounts. The example illustrates the increasing sophistication of private wealth holders, both companies and householders, who began to take quick advantage of such innovations.

In general the US authorities had no easy answer to these ways of getting round their restrictions. On the one hand overall monetary policy, which attempted to keep interest rates low while accommodating inflation, produced large numbers of such opportunities for arbitrage as there was always a huge unsatisfied market for credit. On the other hand the regulatory structure itself was increasingly seen as an obstacle to competition and as distorting the allocation of investment resources.

Another important trend was *disintermediation*. Large borrowers, in whose solvency there was strong public confidence, began increasingly to bypass banks and instead sell securities (debt) directly to lenders. This bypassed the investment banks and got round the restrictions to which they were subjected, such as having to hold capital reserves against possible default by their debtors. In response the investment banks themselves engaged in *securitisation* – rather than matching deposits and loans on their own books they sold these loans in the form of securities to the public on organised financial markets, such as the bond market. This meant that they became, to an increasing extent, credit brokers, relying on commissions and promotion profits, rather than intermediaries between borrowers and lenders.

Although this increasing use of markets to allocate credit introduced a new factor of uncertainty into financial relations, as the prices of assets traded on credit markets fluctuated, the response, ironically, was a further wave of innovation. To deal with this, and other sources of instability, increasingly sophisticated markets in *derivatives* developed, which allowed wealth holders to hedge against variations in the price of financial assets. An example is financial futures – contracts to buy or sell a financial asset at a specified date in the future at a price fixed today. *Options* played a similar role. They permit an agent to buy (with a 'put-option', to sell) a specified security, at a price fixed now, at some date, or during a stated time-interval, in the future.

The internationalisation of US finance both reflected and accelerated these tendencies to deregulation and more intense competition. Euro-dollar markets began when banks operating outside the US began to accept dollar deposits, subject to much less restriction and control than the deposits of the domestic banking system. (Although, as the term 'Euro' suggests, this began in Europe, it led to a worldwide network of external banking.) The credit system thus established widened to include non-bank finance – Euro-bond markets – and dealings in other currencies (Euro-marks, Euro-francs and so on) as well as organised markets for the exchange of the various currencies against each other, either spot or through an increasingly complex array of other transactions. At this point the critical role of computing and telecommunications in facilitating these developments should be stressed. Information technology began to make it continuously easier and cheaper to obtain price and other information across a wide rage of markets in different locations, to conduct financial transactions and to make payment.

Because large companies, large banks and wealthy individuals could, if they chose, make use of these offshore financial networks, the previously established system of domestic control and supervision was further weakened, making the objective of stringent regulation, on a national basis, increasingly utopian. We can characterise the broad trend involved as a switch from passive to highly active financial behaviour. In stylised terms, in the initial situation wealth holders either made long-term investments in equities and real estate or held deposits at a bank at very low rates of interest. The banks sought to lend such funds as flowed in to them in safe and remunerative ways. The end of the deregulatory process has all agents concerned – borrowers, lenders and intermediaries – engaged in an active and never-ending search for more advantageous new markets whenever this seemed to open up better opportunities. Since there were always very large numbers of lenders, borrowers and intermediaries in the US system, and their number tended to grow, these new credit market relations were thoroughly *competitive*. (For the development of finance in the US see, for example, Knodell 1994 and Wray 1994.)

Standard assessments of financial innovation essentially stress the benefits of this competition. In principle lenders and borrowers should benefit from higher and lower interest rates respectively as it became impossible to set a monopoly spread for putting the two into contact, or to exploit the inability of either party to find alternatives. Within the financial sector itself, competition should keep costs and profits low, except for transient profits when a valuable innovation is introduced. The higher degree of interconnectedness of markets should make for a more efficient allocation of savings. Such assessments are logical and to a great extent well founded. They do not, however, exhaust discussion on the financial revolution.

Stable markets?

The paradigmatic account of organised financial markets is the rational expectations (RE) market-clearing model. (Foreign exchange markets are also seen as a particular case of the same general theory.) Organised financial markets – in stocks, bonds or their derivatives, for example – seem in fact to be the field where this theory would most directly apply since, firstly, prices are very flexible and, secondly, information can be assumed to flow rapidly among all participants. In fact the RE model itself evolved out of the *efficient markets hypothesis* first put forward for financial assets.

According to this hypothesis, the value of a security today will be based upon the best available estimate of its future yield – for example, of the dividends that will be paid on the shares issued by a company. Any discrepancy between the actual price and the future value of an asset will create opportunities for profitable arbitrage, which, it is argued, well-informed market agents will immediately exploit. It follows that markets will be efficient, in that all advantageous transactions will take place. They will also be stable – the only force making for discontinuities in price will be exogenous: the arrival of new information altering market assessments of a security's fundamental value. Hence follows the standard view that price changes on such markets are unpredictable – any predictable change in yields will already be incorporated into today's price.

Two rather different discussions bear on the validity of these views. We can ask, firstly, whether this is a good account of how credit markets operate, taking as given the use that will be made of the funds that are used. This is to ask, so to speak, whether RE models accurately describe the game that is played on securities markets. Secondly, there are questions as to how the use of funds – in particular, the process of industrial investment – is affected by the way in which finance is raised. This concerns above all the problem of *asymmetric information* between borrowers and lenders. The first question will be taken up in this section.

Firstly, an important limitation on the scope of the efficient markets hypothesis should be recognised. The proponents of this view themselves acknowledge that markets may well make systematic pricing errors when the general context of market operations is changing: the idea of RE is applicable only when the regime which governs transactions is stable and well understood. This is significant because many of today's financial markets have developed only recently. It could then be expected that a learning process would have to take place before the conditions for unbiased pricing decisions were established.

Secondly, there is some scope for instability even within the structure of RE models. This instability takes the form of self-fulfilling expectations or so-called rational bubbles: a sustained departure of prices from the levels consistent with fundamental yields of assets may be possible if this departure is foreseen by market agents. However, most such phenomena can reasonably be excluded on the grounds that they would eventually lead to some unsustainable increase or decrease of prices; since this situation can, according to the theory, be foreseen, it will be avoided by the agents concerned.

However, there is a widespread view that fluctuations in organised financial markets are generally so wide, and so frequent, as to call into question the adequacy of the simple efficient markets hypothesis. The claim has been advanced that these markets display *excess volatility* – a degree of instability which is too great to be accounted for by changes in the underlying fundamentals. The problem with this challenge to the standard RE position is that it is difficult to specify how much volatility well-functioning markets would display (see Shiller 1989 for some of the most influential work in this field). Nevertheless it is easy to identify episodes – such as the worldwide stock market crash of October 1987 – which call into question the more optimistic accounts of efficient price-setting.

Further, several studies of financial markets, including foreign exchange markets and bond markets, have shown that empirical pricing data is incompatible with the standard RE account unless risk premia are taken into account. This is because patterns of arbitrage over time (between bonds of different maturities, or between currency transactions at different dates) do not follow the paths implied by the standard theory. To preserve the latter one has to suppose that prices depend not only on the mean expected returns on the assets concerned but also, in quite complicated ways, on the scatter of possible returns around this mean value. This is a very important qualification of the standard view, since the more optimistic accounts of financial markets suggest that they make it possible, through the diversification of portfolios, to eliminate many of the risks associated with investment. It is clear that this cannot be the case: either financial markets do not diversify risks as efficiently as has been supposed or there exist important non-diversifiable – that is, *systemic* – risks, which cannot easily be spread because they affect a very wide range of assets. (The capital asset pricing model, widely used for microeconomic analysis, in fact assumes that individual assets can be placed in well-defined risk categories but does not explain why such risks cannot be spread by portfolio diversification.)

It is significant that the risk premia which have to be introduced to make RE models empirically valid are complex and vary over time. This establishes a link with more Keynesian views of finance, according to which the perceived liquidity of a capital asset may rest on fragile conventions – shared views as to the possible future of the economy as a whole – which tend to stabilise individual market behaviour but which are vulnerable to broad changes in sentiment.

Similar difficulties with the RE paradigm have led some economists to criticise the informational assumptions on which it rests: it can be doubted whether all market agents have equal access to information on the likely returns from assets, and whether the market itself rapidly disseminates all such relevant information. One interesting theme introduced in this context is *mimetic contagion*: it can be rational for those investors with doubts about how accurate and complete their own information is to base their own behaviour on that of other market agents whom they may consider to be better informed. This imitative process seems to be double-edged: on the one hand when fundamental conditions are stable it may in fact lead to an efficient market equilibrium; on the other it can lead to cumulative, self-reinforcing, departures from equilibrium if imitative behaviour amplifies the effect of some informational error or disturbance (see Topol 1991 for a highly technical account which draws on the work of Orléan 1986).

Systemic risks

The discussion above indicates that there are three types of process which lead to non-diversifiable, system-wide risks on financial markets. Firstly, the fundamental values of wide classes of asset may all be affected by the same macroeconomic disturbances – for instance by a policy change in an important country. Secondly, there are a large number of financial linkages which may spread disturbances from one asset market to another, and from one investor to another. For instance an asset may be used as collateral for a loan in a different credit market; if the price of the first asset falls, repayment of the loan on which it is based may be jeopardised. In a study of financial fragility in the international context, Eichengreen and Portes (1987) have pointed to interactions among three components of the financial sector – foreign exchange markets, securities markets, and banks – as the key channels through which financial disruption can spread and accumulate. Thirdly, where information is imperfect, market agents may not be able to distinguish clearly the causes and limits of a disturbance so that default on one loan, or a decline in the price of one asset, may call into question a whole class of similar positions. For example, if one company is unable to meet interest payments on its debt, investors may seek to divest themselves of all their commercial paper. This could bring about just the situation which was 'wrongly' feared, because companies will then have unanticipated difficulties in borrowing and this can lead to further disturbance.

System-wide risks on financial markets are a clear case of externality: the transactions of one investor have implications for the safety of others, but there is no reason for these effects to be taken into account by private agents. Hence there is a clear case for public intervention to avoid the build-up of these risks.

Standard accounts see such intervention as essentially a question of supervision and regulation. Financial agents are supervised to ensure that they do not adopt positions which carry a large risk of default and that they make public important information affecting their solvency and liquidity. Regulation has as one important objective to ensure that agents have capital resources commensurate with the risks they run, so that they can absorb a decline in the value of their assets without transmitting pressure to their own creditors. However, on occasion regulation has also placed constraints on the overall behaviour of markets – an interesting example is the 'circuit-breakers' introduced on the New York stock exchange after the crash of 1987, which address 'contagion' effects by slowing down transactions when there are big price movements. The assumption here is that destabilising imitative behaviour is highly likely in such circumstances.

International regulation has been developed in the framework of the Bank for International Settlements, beginning in response to a number of international bank failures in the mid-1970s. The 'Cooke Committee' has promulgated minimum standards for holdings of capital and for the presentation of accounts and the transparency of links among banks; it has also attempted to clarify the division of responsibility for supervision of international financial activities. Many of these regulatory standards were written into EU law during the late 1980s.

High real interest rates and financial deregulation

The argument above has been that competitive financial markets may display high degrees of volatility. This point would be widely, if not universally, accepted. Indeed the 1980s have displayed many examples of such instability. Key examples are the wide fluctuation of exchange rates, particularly for the dollar; the stock market crash of 1987; a boom in real estate values in Britain, the US and many other countries followed by a dramatic slump at the end of the decade; very large numbers of failures in the US savings bank system; the boom and bust in US bank corporate debt ('junk bonds'); and, linked to the speculation in real estate, financial distress and even insolvency in commercial banks, for example in Scandinavia. Of course the most serious disturbance has been the crisis of third world debt – which remains unresolved more than a decade after it broke out in the early 1980s.

A more contentious argument is that financial liberalisation may also have contributed to the marked rise in real interest rates since 1980. According to the standard view this should not occur; rather, more intense competition should narrow the spreads in financial markets so that borrowers, as a whole, would pay lower interest rates and lenders, as a whole, receive higher rates. However, there is certainly still considerable obscurity about the origins of higher rates. It can be argued that financial deregulation, given that it was associated with greater instability in credit markets, may have been a contributory factor. In general we can distinguish three groups of hypotheses:

- *Purely 'real' explanations.* In this view the real rate of interest is high because of non-monetary factors – a decline in savings rates and an increase in borrowing. Often attention focuses on the consequences of large public sector deficits, particularly in the US, which are seen as absorbing a large proportion of the available funds and thus raising the cost of credit to private borrowers. One limitation on such accounts is that they may reverse cause and effect – both the decline in savings and the widening of public sector deficits are as much effects of economic malaise as they are its causes.

- *Monetary policy.* It is generally accepted that any attempt at monetary disinflation raises the real rate of interest on short-term loans. On the one hand these policies work by higher nominal rates of interest in order to discourage expenditures; on the other hand, to the extent that they are successful, they lower inflation rates. Both effects raise the real rate of interest – that is, the rate of interest corrected for inflation. Standard accounts, however, see this situation as a transient, disequilibrium, phenomenon. When inflation and inflationary expectations have been lowered, the economy should return to a real equilibrium with lower nominal and real rates. However, in practice, the period of high interest rates has tended to be much more persistent than such accounts suggest. The difficulty of controlling inflation by these means has meant that the supposedly exceptional period during which nominal rates are kept high has been much longer than was first expected, because only very substantial declines in expenditures, maintained over long periods, produce the required reduction in inflationary pressure. The long drawn-out process of disinflation also means that long-term interest rates will tend to rise, because rates on long loans must to some extent reflect the short rates which are expected to prevail over a long period. These depend to a great extent on expectations of future inflation which have proved remarkably stubborn in the face of restrictive policies. It should be noted also that recessions arising from monetarist strategy are also at least partly responsible for the low levels of savings which are often advanced as a 'real' source of higher interest rates.

- *Financial deregulation.* The French economist Michel Aglietta (1992a) has argued, further, that financial innovation and liberalisation has put pressure on real interest rates. He identifies three mechanisms by which this could have happened:

  1. *Higher risk premia on long-term loans.* The volatility of short-run interest rates, inflation rates and asset prices increases the risk of any long-term credit and thus tends to raise its cost. This must be the main factor in Aglietta's account. It comes close to an appeal to Keynesian liquidity preference theory – system-wide uncertainties, themselves aggravated by financial deregulation, raise the cost of long-term capital. (For a modern restatement of this kind of argument offering a precise definition of uncertainty, see Makowski 1989.) The other processes discussed are more contingent –

  2. *Real estate appreciation.* The deregulation of finance has led to sharp increases in the price of property in many countries at the same time as it became easier to finance consumer loans on the basis of housing. In consequence savings rates declined, at least temporarily, again tending to raise the cost of credit.

  3. *Pressure on banks.* In a deregulated climate banks have had to pay more for funds. Although some large companies have been able to bypass the banking system and sell securities direct to the public, this is not possible for the mass of smaller companies who still have no effective alternative but to borrow from the banks, at higher rates of interest than in the past. This is to argue that the monopoly rents associated with the less competitive banking structures of the past were shared with industrial borrowers rather than being completely appropriated by intermediaries.

It seems likely that, overall, the process of financial liberalisation has not reduced the cost of capital for productive investment. Recently companies have had to compete harder with consumers for investible resources; more fundamentally, risk premia on illiquid loans may have increased, given both the inability of competitive finance market to spread risks completely and the existence of system-wide risks, which the financial revolution itself may have intensified.

Europe and globalised finance

It has been suggested that the emergence of a deregulated, competitive financial system operating at a world level has arisen from the internationalisation of the US financial sector at the same time as its regulatory structure was to a large extent dismantled. In Western European countries the process worked the other way: competitive pressures from outside have transformed their financial sectors, which are now much more based on markets and much less dominated than in the past by powerful intermediaries. These pressures arise generally from the increased openness of European economies – their growing involvement in international trade and investment. However, the European Community has accelerated this process through its own drive for financial integration. This received a strong impetus from the 1992 market completion programme which laid particular emphasis on the financial sector (see Annexe to this chapter). Integration was pursued firstly by removing restrictions on the mobility of capital among member states. Since some countries, such as Britain and Germany, already permitted full capital mobility with the outside world, and since there was never any question of reintroducing restrictions in these countries, the outcome was both internal and external liberalisation – mobility of capital within the EU involves equally mobility of capital between the EU and other countries. Secondly, the 1992 programme made it easier for banks and financial institutions based in one member state to establish themselves in others. This legislation also had a certain deregulatory tendency in that it installed the principle of *home country control*. A financial company which operates in another member state will not need to acquire a second licence, not will it be subjected to extra supervision by the host country. Except for liquidity and other issues tied immediately to monetary policy, the host country will recognise the regulatory competence of the home country authorities. This may not, as is sometimes feared, lead to a downward spiral of competitive deregulation as countries try to attract financial business by relaxing regulatory requirements: in some cases there will be consumer resistance to such a process – for example depositors may prefer to put their savings in more secure, more tightly supervised banks. However, the principle of mutual recognition does, and is intended to, produce a certain degree of competition among regulatory structures. To prevent excessive deregulation, certain minimum standards have been promulgated at EU level – these concern accounting procedures, minimum risk diversification (that is, banks may not lend too much of their funds to a single borrower), and capital adequacy (banks and finance houses must be able to absorb substantial losses before placing their own depositors at risk). In general, however, this EU-wide regulation merely repeats the minimum standards agreed on by the major industrialised countries within the Bank for International Settlements. The philosophy behind this regulation is to reduce risks of individual default, while accepting the general case for competitive financial markets. It will depend for its success on the effectiveness of supervision (which remains a national responsibility) and offers no direct protection against system-wide risks once a large number of credit institutions have been jeopardised.

Thus the recent strategies of European integration have endorsed and perhaps reinforced the strong pressures from the global economy towards liberalised, competitive financial structures in European countries. As argued above, however, there are reasonable grounds for arguing that these structures involve social costs – in terms of instability and perhaps also pressure on the rate of interest – which are not taken into account by the private agents who operate within them. Thus the huge volume of transactions which are undertaken on today's financial markets may be well in excess of what is socially efficient. It is now necessary to look at the actual credit systems which have evolved within European countries themselves.

Strong intermediaries

To present the contrast in a stylised way, it could be argued that whereas in the US, borrowers and lenders are put into contact through competitive financial markets, in Western Europe the same contact has often been established through powerful intermediary institutions. (Of course, this is an extremely schematic statement – there have long been credit markets of many kinds in all Western European countries. The most important such exception is without doubt Britain, which has an extremely large and active stock exchange and has historically been the location of important international markets. In this sense Britain comes much closer to the US model than do the continental European countries – one serious source of the frequent divergence between Britain and its partners on financial and monetary questions.)

The strength of the intermediary institutions – large banks and other, more specialised, financial companies – has had two main sources: on the one hand, non-competitive forms of organisation such as monopoly or oligopoly; on the other, the support of the state, through subsidies or legally conferred privileges. Both sources of power are of course suspect in the free-market climate which prevails today, but the functionality of these inherited European structures needs to be examined, rather than dismissed on *a priori* grounds. It is by no means obvious that either savers or investing companies in the US, for example, have been better served over the long run by competitive financial structures than their European counterparts have been by their more intermediated system.

The working of the European intermediaries changes the nature of credit transactions for both borrowers and lenders. For creditors the liquidity and security of their assets depend, not on being able to sell them rapidly on an open market, but on the reputation and reliability of the institution to which they are entrusted. For debtors, including often business enterprises as long-term debtors, funds can be obtained only from a few, or even a single source, rather than by the issue of marketable debt on a wide market.

The structure of intermediation varies widely according to national tradition and the degree of active state involvement. The best example of a highly interventionist regime was perhaps France, where, until recently, the authorities were able to control the allocation of available credit to broad sectors of the economy: housing, agriculture, export industries and so on. The restrictions (*encadrement de credit*) on which this intervention rested, however, were dismantled during the 1980s, largely because they were seen as impairing the international competitiveness of the financial sector. In Germany the oligopolistic structure of commercial banking has given the three largest banks a particularly significant role in several financial sectors – including long-run industrial finance. As in France, the internationalisation of credit relations has tended to weaken domestic structures.

The most obvious danger of dominant intermediaries is that they will use their powerful positions to increase the spread between the rates they pay savers and those they charge to borrowers; that they will, in other words, extract a monopoly rent which raises the cost of capital. Conversely, there may be certain advantages in terms of stability – huge institutions, with very widely dispersed assets and strong balance sheets, may be less exposed to contagious disturbances in competitive credit markets and also able to take into account ('internalise') what would be external effects to smaller businesses. Thus, in terms of a first consideration, we seem to face a trade-off between efficiency (dependent on competition) and stability (related to scale). However, it is important to note that recent discussion has also called into question the efficiency of market-dominated finance. In order to address this question, it is necessary to look at recent developments in the understanding of the intermediation process.

Asymmetric information and credit rationing

Why should we observe financial intermediaries at all? Why do not the ultimate users of funds simply borrow them directly from the original lenders? Traditional answers to this question produced a theory of financial intermediation as rather analogous to the wholesale and retail distribution of consumer goods. There are economies of scale, in that small financial transactions are expensive. Given this fact, portfolio diversification and risk-spreading are best achieved by intermediaries. A unit trust, for example, makes it possible for small savers to hold, indirectly, a highly diversified portfolio of equities.

However, some economic theorists have recently developed more complex accounts of intermediation, based on asymmetry of information between lender and borrower – that is, the fact that the borrower will often have much better information than the lender about how the borrowed funds will be used, what risks are involved, and how probable is a default on the loan. This asymmetry makes it difficult to equilibrate supply and demand in the credit market by price movements in the standard way. Lenders may fail to raise interest rates beyond a certain level, even though there is still excess demand for credit at that point. The reason is that the quality of the loans may deteriorate: high rates of interest may deter low-risk more than high-risk borrowing, because the latter have a higher probability of failure – thus the chance of actually having to make the extra interest payment is lower. If this effect works among different borrowers, discouraging those with more solid projects, it is called *adverse selection*; if it alters the behaviour of the same borrower, impelling him towards a riskier use of the credit he obtains, it is an example of *moral hazard*. In both cases, raising the rate of interest becomes a double-edged weapon for a lender who cannot discriminate well between good and bad risks. It is taken as confirming this view of credit markets that there are often signs of credit rationing – where only a part of potential borrowings are met, even though the projects rejected are similar to those accepted (for the seminal account see Stiglitz and Weiss 1981). In one view, this market failure may be an additional source of financial instability – in some cases a reduction in the supply of credit may have discontinuous effects because a whole class of borrowers is rationed out of the market. The important point here, however, concerns efficiency: the existence of these information asymmetries suggests another rationale for financial intermediation, that intermediaries may be able, partially, to correct the market failure which arises from information asymmetries by monitoring the performance of debtors. (Of course there may be other solutions – for example monitoring may become the task of specialised agents who do not themselves make loans, such as the credit rating companies who monitor consumers. However, there do seem to be *economies of scope* whereby the gathering of information on an investment project and its finance could usefully be associated. The economies of scale which make it preferable to have a single monitor, rather than a large number, are obvious.) It is suggested, in particular, that such monitoring functions are an important aspect of *banks*.

The nature of banking

It is of interest that recent theories of financial intermediation have not yet led to an agreed understanding of the specific role of banks, in spite of their centrality to both the financial sector and the operation of monetary policy. One difficulty has been the evolution of banks themselves. For example, a considerable amount of theoretical attention was once given to the fact that the most liquid forms of money – including a large fraction of bank deposits – did not bear any interest. But this has simply ceased to be the case in most countries because either interest has been paid on current accounts ('sight deposits') or it has become possible to draw cheques on previously interest-bearing accounts. Thus the non-interest-bearing nature of some money comes to seem contingent on historical factors rather than intrinsic in any way to monetary exchange.

The specificity of banks is sometimes seen in the payments system, since it is the banks which effect most actual transfers of money among individuals and companies. It is certainly the case that payments systems are key components of modern economies. With the recent growth of financial activity and financial transactions, huge payments have to be made over short periods of time so that the security, as well as the efficiency, of monetary transfers are questions of concern. Nevertheless, technology seems to be separating payments from other banking functions, since it is becoming easier for economic agents of all kinds to have direct access to the electronic systems in question.

Thus the specific role of banks is more probably to be sought in their role as *credit* intermediaries. Emphasis is sometimes placed on the unique liquidity (acceptability for transactions) of bank deposits. This in itself can also be a source of instability if a bank's ability to meet its deposit liabilities in central bank money or by transferring its claims on other very strong private banks is called into question. The guarantee of deposit liquidity only works smoothly if depositors do not all seek to take advantage of it at the same time; hence central banks operate or supervise deposit insurance schemes. However, in this field also there is probably a diminishing gap between banks and other financial institutions – whose liabilities have increasingly acquired the characteristics of bank money.

Rather, it is more convincing to see the unique role of banks in the conjunction of these liquid liabilities with highly illiquid, essentially nonmarketable, assets. That is to say that the bulk of bank loans – to individuals or companies smaller than multinational giants – are made in circumstances where information problems would rule out a well-functioning, competitive credit market. The bank's key role is to mitigate the information asymmetry between debtor and creditor by gathering information and monitoring the use of borrowed funds. According to Goodhart, the nature of bank loans explains a significant institutional feature of banks: the fact that their deposits have a fixed nominal value, rather than rising or falling with the value of the underlying assets – as in, for example, a unit trust. This happens because there is no market to put a clear value on a bank's assets, which have therefore to be measured by the fixed nominal sum committed. Given assets denominated in this way, it becomes desirable to fix also the money value of liabilities, to avoid mismatch between them (Goodhart 1988).

The same combination of liquid liabilities and illiquid assets explains the unique vulnerability of banks to crises of confidence: faced with a rapid decline in deposits it will not in general be possible for them to sell off their assets, since other agents will be unable to value them accurately; nor will it be easy in a short period of time to call back loans from debtors. Access to centralised refinance becomes, therefore, a strategic question.

These developing views of bank intermediation, therefore, place information issues in the centre of the analysis. There are implications for the comparison and assessment of different financial structures – those based on strong intermediaries as against those based on competitive financial markets. The comparison concerns both the working of monetary policy and, perhaps more importantly, industrial investment.

Information and industrial finance

For over two decades economic theory insisted on the separability of investment and finance. The classical statement of this position was made by Miller and Modigliani (1958), who showed that the value of an investment project was independent of the techniques by which it was financed. Increased gearing (use of debt finance instead of equity), the balance between internal and external finance, or the degree of dependence on bank credit should not affect the value of a company (as an assembly of investments) nor change what is a profitable project with one financial technique into an unprofitable one with another. Miller and Modigliani's own analogy conveys the underlying logic of their theorem. A dairy farm may sell its milk whole (analogously, a firm distributes all the profit to shareholders); alternatively it may separate the milk into cream and skim in various proportions (use some profit to service debt and distribute the rest); some milk may be used on the farm itself (retained earnings). In each case the marketing (financing) technique chosen should not have influence on the profitability or value of the dairy farm as such; were this not the case there would exist possibilities for arbitrage which would soon be exploited by rational agents. Correspondingly, if a company's value could be altered by a mere reassignment of its profits to different creditors, one would expect financial markets to take rapid advantage. A company might have reasons to choose one financing pattern rather than another, but the optimal financial plan will be independent of the optimal choice of investments.

Information asymmetries subvert this separability proposition, to the extent that different financial techniques imply different degrees of knowledge of the investment by the agent who finances it. (An obvious implication, for example, is the advantage of self-finance, since this is the only case in which there will be no asymmetry.) The arbitrage between valuations in different financial markets is only effective to the extent that they possess equivalent information of the project concerned. It follows that the nature and number of investment projects undertaken may, contrary to the full-information case explored by Miller and Modigliani, become a function of the channels of finance which are used. This concerns in particular the *time-horizon* and pay-back period of investment projects.

The debate around this issue has focused not on banks as such, but on the role which banks may have in relatively long-run investment. Thus a specific form of long-term monitoring of industrial debtors is involved, which depends not on the use of banking intermediation as such, but on the time periods over which banks are involved with industrial companies, the closeness of the relationships which are formed and their density – the number of different links which exist. (It is such characteristics which distinguish US and European banking structures.)

One key issue arising from information asymmetry is the balance between long-run and short-run profitability. It has been argued that where the supply of long-term finance is provided by a competitive market, with none of the agents active on the market having a big enough stake in a company to justify close investigations of its performance, companies may have difficulty in demonstrating their strength and reliability to those who finance them. One signal of quality that is available is current profitability – a company can indicate its strength and creditworthiness by earning and distributing large profits. However, the use of this signal may impose costs – in order to maintain current earnings it may be necessary to forgo projects with a long-term pay-off, even though it would otherwise be advantageous to undertake them.

A similar question, raised by Mayer (1988), concerns the possibility of long-term commitments between companies and their sources of finance. Short of a complete recapitalisation and transfer of ownership there may be difficulties for a company in a highly competitive environment which wants to engage in a long-term relationship with a particular bank; in return for immediate – perhaps emergency – funding, a company wants to promise that its bank will share in future success, that it will, for example, be used to hold the company's deposits in the future or be given a good share of its other financial business. In a highly competitive financial environment it may be impossible, or extremely costly, to reach such an agreement contractually because of the high degree of uncertainty about future developments. More oligopolistic financial relations, where companies are tied, in a stable way, to one or a few banks, may render such a long-term undertaking much more credible. (Economies of scope seem to arise at the same time, in that long-term relations are easier when a company obtains several financial services from the same bank.) The policy implications here are more marked than those implied by the general argument about intermediation and monitoring: often one could expect competitive processes themselves to gradually select efficient institutions but, if Mayer is correct, competition itself may lead to inefficient systems of corporate financial control.

Signalling, long-term commitments, and other aspects of transactions costs under imperfect information have been held by some commentators to explain sustained high levels of investment in countries, such as Japan and Germany, characterised by strong structures of intermediation rather than by atomistic competition on organised financial markets. It is certainly the case that companies in these countries make much more use of external finance than their counterparts in Britain or the US (Corbett 1987). The empirical questions raised are tricky; as usual in the social sciences it is not easy to disentangle cause and effect. The alternative explanation runs in the opposite direction: it is the magnitude and profitability of investment in Japan or Germany which explains the more frequent recourse to external finance and not the reverse. Not only is this alternative plausible, it is bound to be valid to some extent because there are established factors other than finance behind Japanese and German industrial success: for example, their industrial relations systems. However, it is not so easy to dismiss the argument against financial structures of the Anglo-American type. A key empirical issue would be the behaviour of highly profitable, fast-growing companies and sectors in the US or Britain; do they enjoy access to long-term external finance comparable to Japanese companies or are they more like slower-growing companies in their own countries? The first result would support the explanation of financial patterns by investment performance but the second, which Mayer claims to have observed in some cases, would point to financial structures as a constraint on investment.

The most intensive debate around financial issues concerns the *market for corporate control* – that is, the use of open, competitive equity markets to take over companies which are seen as suffering from managerial failure and the imposition, through merger or otherwise, of new management. In most cases this is a question of hostile takeover – that is, one which is rejected by the existing managers. The proponents of this process argue that it provides an indispensable control over managements which might otherwise place their own interests above those of the company's owners. Transfers of company control in this way have become perhaps the most developed rationale for the existence of competitive equity markets (as well they might, since the actual contribution of these markets to new industrial investment is nugatory, and in many years, actually negative. For a clear summary of the arguments on both sides see Krugman 1994, Chapter 13).

The issue in theoretical debate is not the need for a sanction on ineffective management, but whether hostile takeovers are an efficient mechanism of control. The argument again turns on information asymmetries and signalling. It is suggested that, in order to defend themselves against 'predatory' takeovers, companies focus too much on short-term performance, in sustaining the flow of dividends and the current price of their shares. The financial institutions, such as pension funds, which invest through the markets and do not in general have close relations with industrial companies, are said to focus on short-run performance for the same reasons – that this is the only signal on which they can rely. We have here the vexed question of *short-termism* in the financial sector.

Although it is sometimes argued that the best reform would simply be to ban hostile takeovers, or make them much more difficult, this might sharpen the conflict of interest (the 'principal/agent' problem) between companies and investors. But strong intermediaries might provide an alternative, and even more efficient, mechanism of control. In Germany, for example, the large commercial banks effectively represent creditor interests through their long-term relations with companies, the concentrated voting power which arises from large equity stakes, and the presence of bank officials on company boards. This close involvement may be a more efficient response to the problem of managerial control because it reduces to a minimum the underlying asymmetries of information.

From the point of view of industrial investment, therefore, the financial transition of Western European countries from strongly intermediated to competitive, market-based systems is highly ambivalent. On the one hand, the allocation of funds may become more flexible and the yield spreads absorbed by the financial sector itself may come under competitive pressure. On the other, there are obvious problems of stability related to externalities – the interdependence of individual transactions – while, to the extent that information asymmetries impair the assessment of investment projects, there may also be problems of efficiency involving the volume and the time-horizon of investment.

Monetary policy and competitive finance

The extent to which the financial revolution affects the working of monetary policy depends very largely on the view one takes of the latter. In spite of some denials by its more committed proponents, it seems likely that any narrow quantitative monetarist position has been ruined by the new possibilities for asset substitution that have been brought about by financial innovation; certainly attempts to use specific aggregates, such as M3, as control variables for total expenditures now face almost insuperable difficulties – any measures to make one type of asset relatively scarce will provoke a rapid switch into cheaper substitutes. This is sometimes known as *Goodhart's Law* – any aggregate used for control loses its established relationship to economic activity. At the most, particular variables may be used as *indicators*, as signs that expenditure will shortly rise or fall. Even this diminished version of quantity analysis becomes precarious given the rapid evolution of financial institutions and practices.

From a more Keynesian point of view there may seem at first sight to be no corresponding problem. In this tradition it is short-run rates of interest which are the key control variable of monetary policy: the authorities, as major actors in credit markets, and as monopoly providers of the most acceptable form of asset – state money – seem to retain their power to constrain the workings of the financial system in spite of the changes in its structure. However, the new theories of information asymmetry in credit relations suggest that this judgement may require some modification. Ironically, these theories indicate that there is an important quantitative element to monetary policy, even when this is conceived as working primarily through the rate of interest. Certainly, the supply of monetary assets in quantitative terms has little meaning in this context: quantitative restriction of monetary assets is futile when close substitutes exist; it can be dangerous when they do not – as with the central refinance of important banks when they come under pressure. In any case, Keynesians expect there to be important shifts in the demand for monetary assets, related to changing liquidity preference, which have to be accommodated if they are not to destabilise the financial sector and the real economy.

But the new stress on credit rationing forces us to look at the ultimate effects of monetary policy in a new way. Although the instruments of policy are looked at in price terms, that is, in terms of changes in interest rates, these changes affect borrowers – individuals and companies – not only by changing the terms on which credit is available, but, very significantly, by influencing the amount of credit that is available. In other words, they affect the scale and intensity of credit rationing. Confronted with imperfect information, banks and financial markets will not simply pass on higher interest rates to debtors – because this may have undesirable effects on the quality of their loans. They will also respond by stricter rationing to limit the problems of adverse selection and moral hazard which higher interest rates induce among borrowers of uncertain creditworthiness.

Now, when this quantitative dimension is taken into account it may well be the case that the efficiency of monetary policy depends on the financial structure and the nature of intermediation, because they will have a determining influence on credit rationing procedures.

There are two, closely related, aspects to this question. Firstly, if powerful banks can mitigate information asymmetries in the way discussed above, they may reduce the amount of credit rationing that is implied by a given increase in the rates of interest they themselves have to pay for deposit – one might hope, especially, that drastic discontinuities which suddenly ration a whole group of borrowers out of the market can be avoided. Secondly, powerful intermediary institutions can manage and focus the impact of changes in monetary policy, concentrating its most adverse effect on sectors and enterprises least vulnerable to financial stress. Competitive financial markets, on the other hand, diffuse and generalise the pressure of monetary policy. Particularly in volatile environments, where much debt is at variable rates, the effects of higher interest rates will be felt by virtually all agents in the economy. This might be desirable if there were no problems of information, but in a context of uncertainty it may provoke widespread and unpredictable credit shortages as rationing is intensified.

The point can be made in terms of the classical distinction between two sides of interest rate policy. Historically, *open market operations* – which affect the price of credit in general through the working of financial markets – have been contrasted with *discount policy* – that is, the terms on which commercial banks in particular receive centralised refinance. Disintermediation and the thorough marketisation of credit relations alter the balance between these two channels of policy. In strongly intermediated systems discount policy is dominant: monetary policy bears most strongly on the powerful banks, which transmit its effects, in a managed way, to their customers by altering the terms and availability of their own loans. In such systems, open market operations have a supportive role – their main objective may be only to make sure that the banks themselves must have recourse to central bank discount facilities and thus to make discount policy effective (see Hawtrey 1932 for a classical discussion of this process). In a deregulated, competitive financial system on the other hand, it is the price of credit on open markets which is the key channel of monetary policy – discount policy, bearing in particular on commercial banks, becomes less significant, and it may even be dangerous to make great use of it because the competitive position of the banks *vis-à-vis* other financial agents may be impaired.

There are reasons to believe, therefore, that financial liberalisation may have an important influence on monetary policy even when this is conceived in Keynesian terms as working primarily through interest rates. Recent experience of the deregulated structures of both the US and Britain seems to bear this out: monetary policy becomes a rather blunt instrument since small changes in interest rates may have little impact on the flow of consumption and investment expenditures, while large changes can induce sudden discontinuities and uncontrolled rationing effects which certainly have a major impact on spending but at the cost of considerable financial instability and dislocation.

The significance of financial transformation

Both market forces, linked to the accelerating internationalisation of economic life, and policy changes, in the context of European integration, are working to transform financial relations in Western Europe. Simply expressed, the changes involved can be characterised as the undermining of an oligopolistic, often state-sponsored, structure based on powerful intermediaries and the introduction of highly competitive credit relations based on organised markets which are subject to minimal regulation. It would be wrong to deny the advantages of this fundamental structural change. Many economic agents, both savers and investing companies, now enjoy a much wider spectrum of financial possibilities: many distortions in the allocation of credit are being removed and there is pressure to reduce unnecessarily high spreads between interest charges to borrowers and payments to lenders.

But the disadvantages of the process have, in the prevailing climate of free market euphoria, been seriously underestimated. The strongly intermediated systems which have developed historically in European countries had major advantages, in terms of both stability and efficiency. Strong intermediaries stabilised both monetary circulation and financial activity by acting as a strong buffer between wealth holders (who relied on institutions rather than volatile markets to secure the liquidity of their assets) and companies (who were assured of a stable supply of investment finance available for long-run projects).

It would be dangerously nostalgic to argue that no financial changes are needed, or that the old structures can be preserved unchanged. As with many of the most successful institutions in Western Europe, the old financial structures were essentially national: they depended to a large extent, perhaps decisively, on the existence of strong, close social relations among the economic agents of the same nation state. More anonymous, competitive, credit relations, replacing informal networks, are perhaps a necessary aspect of European integration. Indeed, one interpretation of strong intermediaries sees them as an increasingly obsolescent historical form: in this view they are regarded as performing a transitional role in industrial societies which have not yet developed complex, market-based, financial systems (Gerschenkron 1962, cited by Hellwig 1991). But a balanced view of financial transformation requires us to consider aspects of credit which are neglected by the mechanical reiteration of the merits of competition – the externalities which can shorten investment planning horizons and lead to dysfunctional credit rationing effects.

Three conclusions seem justified by the foregoing discussion. Firstly, public control and intervention in the financial sector has an important role, particularly as a means to address shortages of information and the credit market failures to which they can lead. At the very least there is a need for concerted, EU level, policies on supervision and regulation within increasingly integrated financial structures, rather than the almost complete devolution of these responsibilities to national governments which is now the case. Beyond this, public intervention in credit may well be justified to compensate for serious gaps in the provision of investment credit left by the market, and to offer secure forms of savings to the most vulnerable, least well-informed households.

Secondly, it would be wrong to give complete priority to competition in the assessment of financial structures. Very large, and correspondingly strong, financial companies – perhaps on the model of the big German universal banks – may to some extent impair competition but offer compensating advantages of stability and control. (See Steinherr and Huveneers 1992 and Benston 1994 for pessimistic and optimistic accounts respectively of universal banking.)

Finally, the financial revolution has important implications for monetary policy which have not been taken sufficiently into account in the project for monetary unification. Within a continent-wide system of financial markets, marked by strong competitive pressures and rapid innovation, a European monetary policy may prove to be a very blunt instrument indeed, unable on its own to secure either the stability of investment or overall control over aggregate demand. The ambitious project of rapid monetary disinflation within a unified Europe needs urgently to be reassessed in this context.

ANNEXE

Financial integration in the EC

In the context of the 1992 market completion programme, a large body of legislation was promulgated by the European Community in order to promote the integration of the financial sector. However, two key directives laid out the basic rules and established the framework for the other legislation.

1. *Capital liberalisation* (Directive of 24 June 1988 on implementation of article 67 of the Treaty of Rome). This replaced a previous more limited directive on capital mobility by a complete liberalisation of all capital movements in the EC. It set a deadline for implementation of 1 July 1990, with an extension until 31 December 1992 for Spain, Portugal, Ireland and Greece. It is important that safeguard clauses in the Treaty of Rome – which permit capital controls to deal with balance of payments problems and capital market disturbances – were *not* repealed; in fact a new safeguard clause was introduced which permits controls to deal with foreign exchange crises. These controls may last a maximum of six months and require the permission of the Commission, whose decision can only be changed by the Council of Ministers.

2. *Second Banking Directive* (Directive of 15 December 1989 on Coordination of Laws, Regulations and Administrative Provisions relating to Credit

Institutions). This confirmed the right of the banks of one member state to operate in others, but facilitated such establishment by introducing the principle of *home country control* – that is, a bank does not need a new licence to operate in another member state and continues to be regulated by the authorities of the country in which it is based, rather than being subjected to double supervision. This implies that countries eventually recognise each other's supervisory procedures. To make this possible other legislation laid down minimum standards for accounting, capital funds and so on. In general these standards are the same as those agreed by the major industrial countries through the Cooke Committee (Committee on Banking Regulation) of the BIS. An important limitation to the home country control principle is that host countries will continue, for the time being, to control the liquidity ratios (reserves) of incoming banks, in order to be able to operate national monetary policy. Host countries can also apply other measures which they use to implement monetary policy on their own territories. However, the EU intends to harmonise liquidity ratios in the context of Maastricht and monetary unification.

Separate legislation was introduced to promote integration of the insurance sector and to guarantee access to stock markets and other organised security markets. For a detailed account of this legislation see Benink (1993).

Further reading

European finance is surveyed in Steinherr (1992) and Henderson (1993). For commercial banking see Mullineux (1992). Many of the key theoretical issues are examined in Giovannini and Mayer (1991). Once again one can refer to Goodhart (1995) for a comprehensive survey of the interface between private finance and the central bank.

10

Monetary unification and fiscal policy

Monetary policy and fiscal policy

The economic agenda adopted at Maastricht commits EU member states, at least in principle, to a restrictive monetary policy over a long period, as the introduction of a common currency and the construction of common monetary institutions become the occasion for a renewed attempt at monetary disinflation. In view of the continuing, very high, levels of EU unemployment and of persistent macroeconomic instability, this makes the deployment of other policy instruments all the more important. At a macroeconomic level this raises the question of fiscal policy – the use of public expenditure and taxation to affect overall economic activity. (Of course, these aggregate policy tools comprise a host of different instruments; the composition of government spending and revenues is just as important as their totals in influencing the behaviour of the private sector.)

However, several important forces have discouraged the active use of fiscal policy to promote employment. In fact, European public finance is now in such disarray that a major fiscal expansion is undesirable. The future use of fiscal policy as a powerful stabilisation tool requires a lengthy period of consolidation to make governments more creditworthy. However, the consolidation process will take time, and progress depends critically on good rates of economic growth and on interest rates being as low as possible. The working of the Maastricht Treaty is in conflict with these conditions. It has led to member states pursuing impossible fiscal targets over a short time period in a mutually damaging way. Meanwhile monetary conditions continue to be dominated by German policy and are still too restrictive to ease the move to stable public finance during the transition to a single currency. The EU's project for higher employment has fallen victim to these chaotic macroeconomic strategies – a fact full of political and economic dangers for the Union.

Deficit spending in theory and practice

Although the period of high growth in Western Europe to the early 1970s is usually seen as a 'Keynesian' era – in the narrow sense that fiscal activism was seen as the key method of macroeconomic control and monetary policy played a much more passive role – in fact there was very little recourse to *deficit* spending as such by national governments until the slowdown of the 1970s when there were efforts to maintain growth and employment by increased public spending.[1] The disappointing results of these latter exercises helped create a climate in which the efficacy of such expenditure was called into question. It should be noted, however, that at that time the full dimensions of the slowdown had not been realised. Thus expenditure programmes were seen as responding to a cyclical problem, rather than as a mobilisation for structural change and adaptation. This limitation of perspective, as much as the choice of fiscal instruments themselves, explains the failure of policy, which was unable to improve general economic performance and thus to correct the emerging fiscal imbalances through increased revenues and a more dynamic private sector.

The theoretical attack on active fiscal policy (that is, the use of government spending to influence output and employment) developed alongside monetarist theories in the 1970s. We can put on one side the notion that discretionary fiscal policy is unnecessary – this would be plausible only if employment were much higher and more stable than is, in fact, the case. The argument that fiscal policy was *ineffective* centred on the notion of 'crowding out' – that is, the view that public spending displaced private expenditures rather than adding to them. We should distinguish real and financial crowding out. The first would mean that government spending pre-empts resources, reducing those available for other forms of activity. This must be the case to some extent, but its importance depends on how fully resources are being used; if there are large reserves of unemployed or underemployed factors of production, then some of them can be put into use by public spending without preventing the growth of private expenditures. Financial crowding out refers to the working of the credit system: if the state borrows to finance increased spending this might put pressure on private expenditures, for example by raising the rate of interest. Presumably, with a well-functioning economy and credit system, the second type of constraint would reflect the first – expenditures would become more difficult to finance as the real resources available to produce more goods and services became more scarce.

Now in the actual macroeconomic development of Western Europe no such correspondence is to be found. The decisive event which put financial pressure on European governments was the Volcker shock and the very high interest rates to which it led (see Chapter 5). This reversed the dynamics of public borrowing: in the inflationary 1970s borrowing had not led to persistent burdens of public debt because interest rates were low and inflation itself rapidly reduced the real burden of repayment; now interest rates were high while inflation slowed. In the 1980s, debt service very rapidly became the fastest growing component of public expenditure as today's deficits mortgaged future revenues.[2] Regardless of the ideological shift against state spending, direct financial pressure compelled European governments towards retrenchment. Restrictive monetary policies, at first imposed by US policy, later more voluntarily adopted by European governments, were thus themselves a major factor limiting the deployment of active fiscal policies. This period, however, certainly did not involve any increased pressure of aggregate demand on scarce productive resources; on the contrary, it was marked by slowing inflation, stagnation and unprecedented unemployment.

Thus it was an external factor, US monetary policy, which was the first decisive constraint on active fiscal policy. A second factor also had to do with the increasing openness of European economies – this openness meant that any attempt to expand the economy spilled over into its trading partners, thus reducing its domestic impact and tightening balance of payments constraints in the country which initiated the expansion. Strictly speaking, however, these spillovers do not amount to a straightforward limit on fiscal activism; rather, they constitute an externality, requiring the coordination of fiscal measures among nation states.[3] The two factors, interdependence and financial pressures, interacted, in that fiscal deficits now led to a greater need for *external* finance which was only available at high interest rates on the Euro-currency markets.

In spite of these constraints, the 1980s did provide evidence that fiscal policy had not lost its potency. Expansion of public spending in large countries, less vulnerable to external pressures, continued to be an effective way of stimulating activity. This was shown both by the Reagan boom of the mid-1980s, linked to widening public deficits, and by German unification, where public expenditures for the reconstruction and modernisation of the Eastern Länder produced very high rates of growth in Germany as a whole until they were blocked by the restrictive stance of the Bundesbank. Even in these countries, however, it was clear that the *financial* constraints on deficit spending were much tighter than heretofore and that a narrowing of the deficits would be necessary in the medium term to prevent them becoming unsustainable.

The most radical critique of deficit spending (not of public spending as such) was developed by Barro (1974; more accessibly, 1989) who introduced the expression 'Ricardian equivalence'. The basic argument here is that the impact of public spending will be no greater when it is deficit spending, financed by borrowing, than when it is immediately financed by additional tax revenues. This would be the case because economic agents would recognise that public deficits today imply higher taxes, to finance debt service, in the future. The implied loss of private wealth, as a result of these future tax liabilities, will tend to reduce public spending in a way that is essentially equivalent to an immediate tax increase.

At a descriptive level there is a great deal of truth in this argument. In an active financial environment, the balance sheet of the public sector is very closely scrutinised and any signs of weakness, of the necessity for future policy changes, can promote an immediate sanction in the financial markets. Government debt becomes harder to sell and long-term interest rates tend to rise; any sign of balance of payments pressure, as a result either of the need for external borrowing or of an increased import bill, puts pressure on the exchange rate. At this level the notion of Ricardian equivalence encapsulates the new, more immediate and intense, financial constraints on government which have already been discussed.

Where Barro's theory seems much more speculative and open to question is in its presentation of these financial pressures as the reflection of a very long-term calculation, which is seen as adjusting estimates of private wealth to expectations over a very long time-horizon. (For formal critiques of Barro see Blanchard 1985, Buiter 1988.) Little is known, in theoretical terms, about the determination of planning and investment horizons by economic agents, although the whole issue is of immense practical importance for policy decisions. Empirically, pervasive indications of myopia ('short-termism') clash with the standard theoretical postulate of unbounded individual rationality. There is still enormous scope for the reassertion of Keynesian insights – that the precise formulation of long-run expectations lies beyond the scope of individual calculation; that, on the contrary, individual expectations rest on a more or less definite, *conventional*, picture of the broad pattern of future economic development; and that these conventions arise from social (and political) processes and are then transposed into the assessments which guide individual decision-making. From this point of view, the mechanical translation of present fiscal policy into future tax liabilities is not particularly relevant. Everything depends on the prevailing perception of the logic and direction of public policy – on whether it is regarded merely as a series of short-run expedients without a guiding strategy or whether, on the other hand, it is seen as helping to form the general and institutional framework of future individual economic activity. It is, ironically, evidence for this latter position that, for a while, the extreme neoliberal governments of Margaret Thatcher and Ronald Reagan were able to operate in very favourable financial climates. While these administrations were perceived by the business community as successfully transforming the economic structures of their countries, high degrees of confidence prevailed and financial constraints were relaxed on both domestic and external markets. When, however, the inconsistencies and inadequacies of their programmes became more obvious, the markets turned decisively against the governments concerned. The discussion is relevant to the notion of the *credibility* of public policy: what makes a government credible is not the rigidity with which it maintains a given policy stance, but its ability to convince market agents of the validity of its strategic approach and to win them to its own view of future developments.

From the discussion so far it might be concluded that fiscal policy has not become ineffective in an absolute sense, but that it is subject to narrower limits. These derive firstly from monetary policy itself – restrictive monetary policies make it much harder to finance public spending – secondly from the increased power of deregulated and internationalised financial markets, and thirdly from the need to coordinate fiscal policies across countries. Finally, the failure to present a clear and convincing developmental strategy, in which current fiscal policies find their logical place, intensifies uncertainties and invites the sanction of the markets on government spending. In all these dimensions of the problem, European integration is of great significance. In principle, common action by EU member states could relax all these constraints, improving coordination and providing a more stable and supportive external environment. In practice, however, these advantages have not, as yet, been realised. Rather, the reverse has happened – both the EMS and the Maastricht Treaty have tended towards destabilisation of public finance and of macroeconomic conditions in general.

A new fiscal crisis

In fact, the actual process of European integration had the effect, at the beginning of the 1990s, of aggravating the problem of public finance in member states. Government finance, just like that of the private sector, is extremely dependent on macroeconomic conditions. A recession, or a rise in unemployment, automatically boosts expenditures and cuts revenues, while a rise in real interest rates increases the burden of servicing existing debt. (Progress in reducing inflation actually becomes an adverse factor in this context if it is not accompanied by lower nominal interest rates – thus, once again, the disinflation associated with the latter EMS was illusory to the extent that it aggravated financial problems in a way that is highly likely to lead to inflationary pressures in the future, or at least to raise the costs of keeping inflation down.) Now we have seen (Chapter 6) that the working of the EMS from the late 1980s onwards, had both these effects: it drove up real interest rates in all countries and was the main cause of a general recession. The result was to destabilise the public budgets which had been slowly and painfully brought nearer to balance over the previous five or six years (Table 10.1).

Table 10.1 Government deficit (–) or surplus (+) as percentage of GDP

	1983	1989	1993
Belgium	–11.9	–6.5	–7.0
Denmark	–7.2	–0.5	–4.6
France	–3.2	–1.3	–5.7
Germany	–2.6	+0.1	–3.3
Italy	–10.6	–9.9	–9.5
Netherlands	–6.4	–4.7	–2.9
Spain	–4.7	–2.8	–7.3
UK	–3.4	–0.1	–7.7

Source: Italianer and Ohly (1994)

In most cases the recession itself wiped out the efforts of national governments to make further progress in stabilisation. Thus it is calculated that *discretionary* tightening of fiscal policy took place between 1990 and 1993 in Greece, Belgium, the Netherlands, Italy and possibly also Spain, Portugal and Ireland, even though such measures intensified unemployment and social distress during the recession. The *automatic* effects of the recession, however, were so great as to lead, nevertheless, to a deterioration in public finances (de Kam, Sterks and de Haan 1994).

The weakening of public budgets

Besides the financial pressures described above, the general pattern of economic reform over the last decade has also tended to reduce the capacity for fiscal policy with a macroeconomic effect. The size of the public sector was reduced almost everywhere in the 1980s, although in most continental countries this has not been as dramatic as in Britain (Table 10.2). This is important because a large public sector has a stabilising effect on expenditure and economic activity. Further, the expansionary effect of public spending

Table 10.2 Public spending as percentage of GDP

	1983	*1989*
Austria	50.4	49.0
Belgium	63.8	54.9
Denmark	61.6	59.6
France	51.4	49.1
Germany	47.8	44.8
Greece	37.9	44.0
Ireland	53.0	40.6
Italy	48.7	51.3
Netherlands	59.7	53.9
Portugal	45.6	38.4
Spain	37.7	40.9
Sweden	64.5	58.3
UK	44.7	37.5

Source: OECD

does not depend completely on it being deficit spending – public investment can have stimulating effect even if it is financed by current taxes. On the other hand, balanced reductions in taxes and expenditures may have a net contractionary effect if private expenditure is inhibited by uncertainties. In fact, extensive use has been made of fiscal instruments to influence macroeconomic conditions even after the widespread turn to monetarist strategies. But the pattern has been to reduce taxes when a stimulus to private spending was desired and to reduce public spending when more restrictive policies were felt to be necessary. Cumulatively, this pattern reduces the weight of the public sector and makes it more difficult to control overall developments through changes in fiscal stance. Changes to the pattern of expenditures have also worked to reduce the capacity to mobilise the private sector: public investment has been hardest hit although this is most likely to improve both the environment in which the private sector invests and to create a growth-oriented climate of opinion; meanwhile social security expenditures have had to rise in total, simply to cope with the most damaging consequences of the rise in unemployment.

Taxation and the problem of mobile factors

Reforms to the tax structure have, in addition, limited the capacity for fiscal stimulus. Taxation systems have become less progressive – marginal tax rates on higher incomes or large wealth-holdings have been brought down; taxes on companies and direct taxation of incomes have been reduced while more use has been made of expenditure taxes. As a result government revenue has probably become less dynamic, since rising private sector incomes generate less tax payments. Privatisation, whatever its other merits, has also probably weakened public sector balance sheets because state assets have been sold cheaply, at prices which do not compensate for the loss of future revenue from nationalised companies and public services.

A convincing argument for some of these tax reforms is that, in economies facing high unemployment, the taxes on employment itself should be reduced (and there are ecological grounds for increasing taxes on pollution and on the consumption of fossil fuels). However, this is an argument for the reduction of the tax burden on ordinary employment; the reduction of direct taxation on very well-paid jobs cannot be justified in this way. In fact it would be helpful to create fiscal incentives to replace very high cost, elite managerial posts, by a larger number of jobs with more modest remuneration. The 'incentive' arguments for reducing taxes on high incomes in particular always were, and remain, shaky.

Continuing internationalisation of economic life, including European integration, however, makes for a loss of autonomy in fiscal structure by putting nations and regions into increasingly competitive relations with each other. This has led to another, more plausible, rationale for reducing tax burdens on higher incomes – the fear that mobile factors of production will move away from high tax areas and concentrate in countries offering a more favourable fiscal regime. This is said to be the case for highly qualified workers (a version of the 'brain drain' argument) but it applies most seriously to profits and interest on capital. As it becomes easier for capital to move to other countries, the imposition of high rates of tax on these resources becomes problematic: if higher taxes stimulate capital flight then the revenue gains on this kind of tax fall while economic activity may be adversely affected.

The taxation of mobile factors therefore involves external effects within the area in which the factors move. The alternative is to tax immobile factors. Classically, land and real estate would be the key case of an immobile, and therefore taxable, resource, but if land forms part of a package of inward investment it may not be easy to subject it to high rates of taxation. Recently the immobility of relatively less qualified labour has led to ordinary workers being perceived as a reliable source of tax revenue. Thus even if an individual government deplores the distributional consequences of switching the tax burden onto lower-income groups, it may be under competitive pressures to do so in order to attract external investment and avoid the delocalisation of firms.

Some degree of centralisation is the best way to deal with this competitive distortion of the tax base. The European Union would seem singularly well placed to act. Companies may be relatively indifferent about where they produce for EU markets, but there are not many of them who could afford to move away from the EU as a whole. The same goes for interest payments on loans – small differences in tax regime may encourage lenders to switch from France to England. To abandon the EU area as a whole would be a much bigger decision. Even if capital movements beyond EU boundaries have to be taken into account, the EU is also well placed to reach reciprocal agreements on tax flows with other major economies, in particular the US and Japan. (According to Giovannini 1989, the US is concerned about the erosion of its own tax base and would welcome such agreement.)

In fact there have been several attempts to introduce a common 'withholding' tax on interest payments in the Union, which would go a long way towards limiting tax avoidance and evasion on the most mobile of productive factors – liquid capital. However, unanimity on such a measure is vital since capital flows will otherwise simply be diverted to countries which do not impose the tax. This difficulty obstructed German efforts to bring its own taxation procedures into line with those in France in 1989. The attempt, in 1994, to formulate Union-wide rules on capital taxation was vetoed in the Council of Finance Ministers by Britain and Luxembourg. The position of these countries is understandable. Luxembourg specialises in international banking and fears that the application of a tax on interest payments would direct international wealth holders to other countries; similarly, Britain fears that investors would desert its own financial markets, thus undermining one of the few remaining competitive advantages of its weakened economy. Nevertheless, to prevent any common tax measures on these grounds is to impose losses on the EU as a whole and to perpetuate the trend towards lighter taxation of higher, and heavier taxation of lower, incomes which is disadvantageous on grounds of both equity and tax efficiency. Overcoming this obstacle, perhaps with some compensation for the financial sectors most adversely affected, is an important part of the reconstruction of public finance in Western Europe as a whole. At present, however, it is hardly on the EU's agenda, although finance ministers agreed in October 1996 to study the problem of competitive tax erosion (*The Week in Europe* 31 October 1996).

Competitive pressures on the public sector

The difficulty of taxing interest payments exemplifies a general competitive process which will put growing pressure on national public sectors in the EU. Increasingly, countries have to compete to attract foreign investment; if this competition is unconstrained it becomes a negative sum game – all countries are led to offer advantages to investors, whether in terms of subsidies, tax breaks, reduced regulation or special services for business enterprise. Since all countries adopt similar measures none of them in fact derives large competitive advantages, but there is general weakening of public finance and of the capacity for effective public control over economic life. In some areas the EU does limit these negative sum games and the external costs which they generate. Thus the use of investment subsidies is supervised and restricted by the Commission in order to impose common priorities for the location of investment (for details see Swann 1983, Chapter 3). But there are no such constraints on taxation, hence the increasing integration of the EU tends to erode public finance and the public sector. There are related distortions in public spending. Some categories of expenditure, those which provide concrete benefits for business enterprise, may actually be encouraged by the increasing competition for inward investment. Thus countries are impelled to improve the environment, to promote the skills of the workforce and to develop transport and communication infrastructures. Much of this spending may be desirable, and competition here may in some ways become a positive sum game, leading to general improvements in the quality of public services. However, in other areas of public provision concerned with redistribution and social protection, or localities which are not considered the most likely to attract investment, the pressures are all in the other direction – towards expenditure reductions, repeated attempts at retrenchment and further tax cuts for mobile factors. The danger of such a process is that the European public sector as a whole will be reduced to a scale smaller than would be considered desirable by voters and governments taking a collective decision (see van der Ploeg 1991).

The Maastricht rules

Because of the very narrow focus of existing strategies for monetary union, these general difficulties of the public sector were neglected by the Maastricht Treaty. Rather, the emphasis fell exclusively on the potential inflationary threat of excessive public borrowing. The prevailing view was that there will always be political and economic pressure to provide centralised refinance for governments with serious problems of indebtedness and that this could compromise the common monetary policy towards which the EU was moving, with its focus on price stability.

As a result, specific targets for public financial stability were set at Maastricht. These were included in the set of criteria which will be used to indicate whether a country has achieved sufficient price stability to participate in the move to monetary union. The two targets bearing directly on public finance are that the public sector deficit should be less than 3 per cent of national GDP and that the accumulated debt of the public sector should be less than 60 per cent of GDP. The other targets focus directly on price stability: there should have been no devaluation by a country aspiring to join the monetary union within two years; its inflation rate should be within 1.5 per cent of that of the three countries with the lowest inflation rates; similarly its long-term interest rates should be within 2 per cent of those in the same three countries. (Long-term interest rates are taken here as a market assessment of future pressures towards inflation and devaluation.) However, it seems clear that in practice it will be the public finance targets which will be the hardest to achieve for most countries and that it will be failure to meet these criteria which will exclude many countries from early participation in the monetary union.

There has been much discussion as to whether these are appropriate indicators of stable public finance (Buiter, Corsetti and Roubini 1993). For example, public sector debt is not considered in conjunction with public sector assets – a reduction in debt achieved by a massive privatisation, compromising future state revenues, would hardly be a sign of stability. On the other hand, governments have many liabilities, such as the need to honour pension rights, which are not included in standard measures of their indebtedness. (Thus a typical manipulation was the assumption, by the French government, of some company pension obligations in return for a cash sum, providing an immediate, and quite meaningless deficit reduction – *The Guardian*, 13 September 1996.) These figures are, in any case, very sensitive to cyclical change – witness the sudden move of Britain from a public sector surplus to a large deficit at the end of the 1980s.

Beyond measurement issues, the desirability and efficiency of these disciplines on public finance have been debated. The original proposals of the Delors Report were for more centralised control, which would have allowed the EU to require member states to reduce their deficits. This was rejected at Maastricht as too great an infringement of national sovereignty, but quite strong mechanisms of supervision and control remain which could make a country's receipt of EU expenditures and loans conditional on its taking measures to reduce borrowing. Discussion of the possible 'bail-out' of insolvent governments by the EU is sometimes rather abstract. Experience elsewhere, for example in the practice of the IMF, suggests that a simple black or white decision to refinance a government or to refuse accommodation can probably be avoided: the most likely outcome is that successive refinancing packages would be made available, but only with increasing degrees of 'conditionality' which would impose policy changes of increasing severity, culminating in a considerable loss of autonomy as important areas of taxation and expenditure fell under the control of the EU.

For the present argument, what is important is the context of these constraints on public finance. Essentially there is a complete divorce between the issue of price stability and that of economic stability. The question of what structure of public finance – and what changes in taxation and expenditure – would promote real economic adjustment is not even posed. Rather, there is a simple concern to protect the common (restrictive) monetary policy to which the EU hopes to move from any disturbances arising in member state budgets. It is doubtful whether this is an appropriate approach, even from the point of view of price stabilisation. If nominal convergence – that is, the reduction of inflation levels to those of the countries with the most stable prices – is achieved only at the cost of serious economic disequilibria – in public services, in the labour market – then the way is being prepared for a series of shocks to the financial system or the supply side of the economy which will put a disinflationary monetary policy under serious pressure.

From a broader point of view, that of economic policy as a whole, the Maastricht rules in qualitative terms (not the essentially arbitrary numbers) may make sense as a strategy for the medium-term stabilisation of EU public finance. (It is remarkable that Britain has accepted the prescription for fiscal stabilisation even though it is not committed to monetary unity.) But inadequate consideration seems to have been given to the immediate macroeconomic impact of a generalised narrowing of public sector deficits; although some compensating relaxation of fiscal policy in stronger countries occurred in 1990 and 1991 this was because of German unification, not through any effort at coordination, and by 1992 other countries were faced by determined efforts at fiscal stabilisation in Germany. Given the nature of the other pressures on national governments, it seems likely that deficit reduction will take place more through expenditure reductions than revenue increases, which will reinforce the trend towards smaller and weaker public sectors. A key factor is the balance between fiscal and monetary policy: the return to stronger public sector balance sheets creates scope for lower interest rates, which in turn can reduce the cost of interest payments on the public debt and thus make a fiscal correction easier. The fact that the Maastricht process excludes substantial monetary coordination before EMU itself was thus a serious weakness in the convergence strategy.

By 1996 it was clear that the convergence strategy had become a fiasco. In most countries, public debt (Table 10.3) was exploding away from the Maastricht targets – not because no efforts were being made but because interest rates were still too high to offer relief and because recovery from recession was slow and hesitant. This last effect at least was almost certainly being aggravated by the convergence programme itself, which was putting severe downward pressure on employment and expenditure (Artis 1996).

The only response the member states could find in practice was an immense new drive for economies. Increased taxes (but not on privileged, 'mobile factors') were combined with emergency reductions in spending, especially on social security. Thus the *Sparpaket*, announced by the German

Table 10.3 Public debt* (percentage of GDP) in EU countries

	1990	1991	1992	1993	1994	1995
Austria	58.3	58.6	58.3	63.0	65.7	69.2
Belgium	130.9	130.3	131.1	137.5	135.0	134.6
Denmark	59.6	64.6	69.0	80.3	75.4	75.2
Finland	14.5	23.0	41.5	57.3	59.8	66.5
France	35.4	35.8	39.6	45.3	48.3	51.2
Germany	43.8	41.5	44.1	48.2	50.2	58.6
Greece	82.6	85.1	91.5	114.4	113.1	111.6
Ireland	96.5	97.5	95.0	98.1	91.7	87.2
Italy	97.9	101.3	108.4	119.4	125.4	126.0
Netherlands	78.8	78.8	79.6	81.3	78.0	77.7
Portugal	68.6	70.2	62.5	67.3	70.0	70.7
Spain	45.1	45.8	48.4	60.4	63.0	65.7
Sweden	43.5	53.0	67.1	76.2	79.7	81.0
UK	n.a.	35.5	41.8	48.3	50.1	52.5

*according to Maastricht definitions
Source: OECD

government in April 1996, was intended to be the biggest single fiscal retrenchment in the history of the Western world and was to include economies of 50 billion D-marks in 1997 (due to the resistance of the Länder, only some of these measures were agreed). The Spanish 'adjustment policy' announced by the new government of José Maria Aznar included cuts in education, in public employment and subsidies to public enterprises at the same time as reductions in corporation tax and taxes on property income. In Belgium, 1996 brought big cuts in social welfare, public services and public employment. In France there was a freeze on public sector pay from September 1995, with some 25,000 public sector job losses to take place in 1996–97 and more of the same to come (details from de Brie 1996). Driven by the Maastricht agenda, political leaderships further alienate themselves from electorates, disorganise the welfare state and widen social inequalities. The whole process will involve negative spillovers from country to country as A's austerity package makes things more difficult for B. The role of the EU is in practice confined to demanding more of the same.

The chronic deficit countries

It has been argued above that in the 1970s low real interest rates gave artificial support to public finance. Generalised inflation and easy monetary policy – both stemming largely from conditions in the United States – tended to wipe out the real value of accumulated debt at a rapid pace. This was not a sustainable situation over a long period, however, as it encouraged wealth holders to speculate in real estate, primary products and so on rather than holding government debt. Nevertheless it did mean that first attempts to slow inflation by restrictive monetary policy led, as has been suggested, to a marked deterioration of public sector balances.

In some countries, however, governments were much more dependent on inflation as a means of financing public expenditure and had made systematic use of 'inflation taxes' over a long period. The two main mechanisms were the issue of high-powered money to meet public obligations (seigniorage) and the inflationary debt forgiveness which results from the erosion by inflation of outstanding debt, if this is not compensated by high rates of interest. In an open market economy there are narrow limits to both these processes unless external conditions are themselves marked by similar inflation: wealth holders can refuse to lend to their own government and instead purchase foreign securities; provided the inflationary conditions which produce very low or negative real interest rates do not exist elsewhere, they will be able to protect the value of their assets by doing this; seigniorage, which amounts to a tax on money holdings, cannot be absolutely avoided but can be reduced by economising on holdings of the form of money involved. In countries such as Greece or Italy, however, controls ('financial repression') were used to block this kind of avoidance: exchange controls impeded the purchase of foreign securities, and banks were compelled to hold large quantities of central bank money as 'reserves' (for a study of the Italian case see European Commission 1993).

For such countries the disinflation of the 1980s dealt a serious blow to public finance. Essentially, their governments lost the proceeds of an inflationary tax on money holdings and nominal wealth. In principle new taxes should have been introduced to make good this loss as inflation was slowed. This was difficult because of widespread tax avoidance and evasion: those taxpayers who did contribute fully already faced high marginal tax rates; those who escaped the tax net would not be affected by any increases. In consequence, the move towards price stability led to the destabilisation of public finance. In the case of Italy this became an important source of the macroeconomic disequilibria which undermined its position in the ERM. Such effects are an example of the limits to monetary disinflation in a disequilibrated economy. Ironically, Italy avoided such problems in the private industrial sector by ensuring that company balance sheets were healthy before credit was squeezed; in the public sector, however, monetary and fiscal stabilisation can work against each other: the first increases the dimensions of the fiscal adjustment required by putting up interest rates while the second lowers the level of activity and promotes imbalances which will pose tomorrow's inflationary problems – for instance, through devaluation.[4]

A return to the previous pattern is, however, infeasible. Some use of inflation to reduce public sector imbalances is inevitable, and perhaps even desirable. (There is a literature on this issue which discusses the 'optimal rate of inflation'; see the discussion of seigniorage by Grilli 1989.) But the increasing internationalisation of economic life in general, and the Community's market completion programme in particular, exclude any thoroughgoing return to financial controls of the old kind. Meanwhile the single-minded objective of price stability at any cost rules out the most logical European response, which would be to recognise that the EU as a whole has a (non-zero) optimal rate of inflation which should be calculated with a view to the interests of all member states, including those with severe inherited disequilibria in their public finances.[5] In Italy, the election in 1996 of a centre-left government made essentially no difference to the pursuit of austerity policies (cuts in education, health and public services, with a huge retrenchment planned for 1997–99). None of this will, however, move the country even close to meeting the Maastricht criteria.

The countries concerned are those least able to meet the new standards of public financial stability introduced by the Maastricht Treaty. They are almost certain to be excluded from initial participation in monetary union. At the same time their continuing instability threatens either sudden increases in inflation or emergency expenditure cuts on a very large and damaging scale. There are obvious limits to the contribution which the EU as a whole can make towards the resolution of these problems, which will basically remain a national responsibility. However, a more coordinated and more expansionary macroeconomic stance in the EU would certainly provide the most favourable climate for the necessary national reforms.

The rejection of fiscal federalism

Much of the discussion of the central budget of the EU has been by analogy with developed federal states as models of an appropriate division of revenues and expenditures between member states and the centre. The branch of economics concerned, the study of *fiscal federalism*, deals with both micro- and macroeconomic aspects of this division (see for instance Oates 1972). There are often good microeconomic arguments for *decentralisation*: for instance, if a public good benefits a particular region then it may be best to finance the service involved by taxation of that region alone;[6] on the other hand all sorts of externality may arise, even in microeconomic terms, which tell in favour of a division of powers (for a technical, but comprehensive, discussion of these spillover effects see Inman and Rubinfeld 1996). Macroeconomic considerations, however, often point towards a substantial measure of centralisation. One fiscal function which seems to belong to the centre is the response to general macroeconomic conditions – for example, a widespread slowdown in activity throughout the Union. But the centre may also play a major role in dealing with more localised problems. Redistributive patterns of taxation and expenditure can help to stabilise member state economies which are affected by adverse shocks and also, in a longer time-frame, compensate for some persistent economic disadvantages. The short-run aspects, especially, of such redistribution are often regarded as a kind of mutual insurance of each other by member states. (Sachs and Sala-i-Martin 1992, argue, by analogy with the US, that a certain centralisation is needed in the EU; their case is generally supported by Eichengreen 1994a; Allsop, Davies and Vines 1995 appear to be more optimistic about decentralised stabilisation policies.)

However, none of these general or more localised stabilising functions will in practice be within the scope of the central EU budget, because this will remain at a clearly 'pre-Federal' level for the rest of the century. There is no political will among the more powerful member states for a decisive increase in the EU's resources. Some movement has taken place. The European Council of Fontainebleau in 1984 seemed to have sunk any prospect of a larger EC budget (Tugendhat 1987, Chapter 1). The renewed prestige of the Community in the second half of the 1980s permitted President Delors to undo some of this damage in 1988 when it was agreed to finance increased expenditures in such areas as technology policy and regional policy (Delors Package I). Following the conclusion of the Maastricht negotiations, the European Council in Edinburgh at the end of 1992 agreed on some further expansion. However, even after this second Delors Package, the EU budget remains in order of magnitude less than would be required for either general macroeconomic stabilisation or effective insurance against national shocks. The EU's resources will grow slowly over the 1990s but will remain below 2 per cent of EU GDP, and much of its expenditure will continue to be pre-empted by agriculture during that period.

In this situation EU expenditure can have a significant impact on the economic fortunes of the areas in which it is spent only if it is concentrated on a few high-priority regions. Reform of the key EU spending agencies, the structural funds, has recognised and accepted this limitation. Thus expenditures already give important support to the economies of Greece, Portugal and Ireland as well as to some disadvantaged regions in larger countries. The programmes concerned are not insignificant – they make some contribution to the development of the EU's periphery as well as to the goal of social cohesion and the legitimacy of the EU in low-income countries. But the sums involved do not have strategic significance for EU economies in general. What this amounts to is the undermining, by fiscal policy, of the monetary unification which has already been agreed upon: fiscal transfers from the EU to regions or countries experiencing difficulties are a key method of making the Union look a little more like an optimal currency area by compensating for the loss of devaluation as a policy tool. Many commentators (for example Goodhart 1996) assume that, in spite of the lack of progress in this area, a measure of fiscal centralisation is inevitable in an EMU. If this is so, however, it remains a very well-hidden item on the EU's agenda.

Coordination and the White Paper

In principle, any desirable central action by the EU could be replaced by coordination among member states. However, there has been little attempt to coordinate EU fiscal policies since the unsuccessful expansion attempted by Helmut Schmidt and Valery Giscard d'Estaing some fifteen years ago. On the one hand policies have been focused on national price stabilisation rather than the level of activity; on the other hand fiscal policy itself was no longer seen as central to macroeconomic policy. Several plans for coordinated expansion have been put forward by opposition groups within European politics (see for example Kreisky 1989); these have sometimes been stronger on ways of spending public money than on sources of finance, although in some cases they have displayed considerable economic sophistication. In no case, however, have they come close to implementation because the governments of major European countries rejected both the strategy and the underlying political priorities.

However, the EC Commission has recently encouraged member state agreement on a limited programme of spending aimed at generating employment (European Commission 1994). The very preparation of these proposals indicated a certain shift in opinion after a decade in which such initiatives were taboo, but only quite small amounts were agreed upon. It had become clear during the preparatory work that the British government and some others would not accept an ambitious spending programme and the Commission had to scale back its proposals to avoid their rejection.

Nevertheless the Commission's White Paper on employment was designed to signal a transition to the more active use of fiscal instruments in the future. It is noteworthy that Commission arguments attempted to address both the current unemployment emergency and long-run issues of structural economic change and modernisation. They were thus intended to complement the present, purely monetary, agenda of the Union by a commitment to a social project – against unemployment and exclusion – which might narrow the widening gap between political class and citizens. Many of the Commission's proposals did not involve increased spending so much as a systematic attempt to maximise the impact of existing public spending on employment. The 'convergence' programme stemming from Maastricht has already disorganised this ambition. Its very limited expenditure-increasing proposals were aimed at generating employment through public investment in a long-term perspective, primarily by accelerating the development of Europe-wide transport and communication networks. Although member states accepted the proposals in principle, they killed them off in practice at the European Council in Florence in June 1996 by refusing to provide resources. Increasingly the Commission was constrained, as a result, to modify and minimise what were already extremely modest social programmes.[7]

Reconstructing state finance

In the period, following the Second World War, when Keynesian public finance seemed especially potent, the state was in many ways a privileged economic agent. Its solvency was not in question; it had access to abundant and cheap credit; very often public projects for reform and reconstruction established the framework of expenditures which guided individual economic activity. In such circumstances, an increase in public spending could be expected to have a direct and powerful impact on general economic activity.

Today, the conditions for public expenditure are very unfavourable. Governments, unable to impose effective strategies of economic adaptation, seem trapped in a series of short-run, crisis-managing expedients. In an active financial environment their solvency is continuously scrutinised by international credit markets, on which for good measure governments must compete with one another. Credit is tight, interest rates are high and any large deficit threatens to start a vicious cycle in which the costs of debt service feed into new deficits. Increases in public spending are less potent for several reasons, including unmastered spillover effects among different countries.

In spite of these difficulties fiscal policy could become again a powerful instrument for economic control. Three kinds of reform would facilitate this. Firstly, monetary policy should take into account the impact of interest rates on government (and indeed on other agents) rather than being completely directed at price stability. In many cases in the 1980s, governments deflated into crises of public finance, and the Maastricht agenda suggests repetitions of this experience – where one economic instrument is used in a way which undermines another. The programme of fiscal stabilisation agreed at Maastricht can only have any prospects of success if it is carried out in a climate of rapid growth and relatively cheap credit. Provided these monetary conditions were the occasion for fiscal stabilisation and not an excuse for postponing it this would represent the best combination of macroeconomic policies. Inflation rates might be higher during the transition but longer-run inflationary pressures would be reduced by strengthening key sectors of the real economy.

Secondly, some measure of coordination or centralisation is required to internalise the externalities involved in the use of fiscal instruments. Particularly for the smaller member states which trade very intensively with their neighbours, these spillover effects are now so large as to make unilateral decisions on fiscal policy quite inefficient. Although a larger centralised component in public finance, prefiguring a Federal budgetary structure, might be desirable, it can only be a long-run objective: agreement among member states will remain for some time the only basis for such coordination.

Finally, more active use of fiscal policy requires a long-run improvement in public sector balance sheets and thus a faster growth trend in tax revenues. A reconstruction of public finance, guaranteeing the solvency of governments and resolving the fiscal crises of such countries as Greece and Italy, is necessary to create room for manoeuvre: without it, any immediate stimulus will give rise to expectations of tightening in the near future. In this sense, the fiscal direction (not the impossible speed of adjustment) of the Maastricht convergence programme is rational, provided these countries are not simply driven into recession by impossible targets.

It follows from this that there is only limited scope for more deficit spending by EU governments in the near future. They need first to rebuild their financial strength and this implies limiting deficits in the medium term. However, effective public expenditure programmes are still possible on the basis of tax finance, although this requires reversing the persistent drive of the last fifteen years towards smaller public sectors. Two areas of expenditure seem particularly important: firstly, direct job creation – either public employment or support for private sector jobs – remains a particularly effective weapon against unemployment (OECD 1993). In Western Europe at present it is almost the only such weapon. It can be hoped that a more dynamic market sector will eventually generate much more employment but there is by now ample evidence that the forces for recovery within the private sector are too weak and slow-acting to be relied upon in the short run.

Secondly, public expenditure can usefully be directed towards long-run economic adjustment, laying down broad targets for the future of the European economy in such areas as environmental protection, regional development, educational standards, and transport and communications infrastructures; public investment can be used in a deliberate and determined way to work towards these objectives. The value of such investment is not only the direct improvement of public services; it can also help to encourage and orient private investment by reducing uncertainties and guaranteeing the presence of complementary public inputs into private production processes.

The scale of and commitment to such intervention is important, hence the coherence of the spending plans which are developed. As argued above, the European Union is in a position to facilitate such programmes: by coordination, by the pursuit of compatible monetary policies, and by assisting the weakest national governments. A precondition, however, is the adoption of wider and more ambitious economic objectives than those enshrined in the Maastricht Treaty.

Further reading

For a detailed critique of the fiscal rules in the Maastricht Treaty see Buiter, Corsetti and Roubini (1993). For the political battle over centralised expenditure see Coates (1996). Oates (1972) is a classic argument for a division of fiscal authority between centre and member states.

Notes

1. Thus the fifteen present EU member states recorded annual average public deficits of just 0.3 per cent of GDP between 1960 and 1973 – given the high growth rates of these years this implied rapidly *falling* debt ratios. There has been a trend increase in public borrowing since the slowdown for the same countries, with annual deficits of 3.3 per cent in the period 1974–79; 4.3 per cent 1980–89; and 5.0 per cent 1990–94 (OECD 1996).
2. de Kam, Sterks and de Haan (1994) give the following data for public spending in the then twelve member states between 1981 and 1989: transfer payments, other current spending and public investment all declined as a percentage share of GDP – by 0.3 per cent, 1.3 per cent and 0.5 per cent respectively, while the only category to increase, by 1.0 per cent, was interest payments.
3. There were many projects (for example Layard *et al.* 1984) during the 1980s for coordinated fiscal expansions by European countries to 'internalise' such external effects: none of them came to fruition. A key problem was that Germany would be required to undertake most of the spending, and it was reluctant to do this, especially after the change of government in 1982.
4. De Grauwe (1996) calculates that public debt service in Italy is increased to the extent of 3.5 per cent of GDP by the fact that Italian interest rates are nearly 3 per cent higher, in real (inflation-corrected) terms than in Germany in order to offer a risk premium to holders of the lira. The persistence of these premia (which also damages British public finance) is not taken into account in the determination of European monetary policy since German control of monetary policy pays little or no attention to EU conditions in general.
5. An inflation tax is essentially a tax on financial wealth. Integration and

the mobility of financial resources make this increasingly infeasible at member state level, but not within the EU as a whole, where, as a transitional measure, it makes perfect economic and political sense. In distributional terms it would favour those state creditors, in particular pensioners, without a guarantee of their claims and who will be big losers from a precipitate fiscal stabilisation in such countries as Italy (OECD 1995a). In any case, there is no real prospect of repayment in full of existing debt in such countries.

6. See for example Persson and Tabellini 1994. The neoliberal distrust of political processes often leads to a rejection of central spending (because poorer countries or regions which benefit from it might be offered incentives for suboptimal economic performance) and to an insistence on a close territorial match between the provision of public goods and the levy of the corresponding revenues, so that non-taxpayers do not receive rents. In addition, tight central restrictions on decentralised budgets may be advocated to avoid the need for monetary bailouts (see Chapter 8). Such thinking has undoubtedly influenced Council decisions to police national fiscal policies very tightly after EMU. A general objection to this line of thinking is that it assumes a degree of opportunism which would, in practice, render not only political, but also market processes completely inefficient, since most market exchanges also give rise to wide possibilities for dysfunctional behaviour. A more specific objection is that it leads to a kind of fiscal minimalism which eliminates the scope for basic stabilisation (see Eichengreen and Bayoumi 1994).

7. The economic rationale for a Europe-wide growth and employment programme was examined by Drèze and Malinvaud (1994) in work which influenced the White Paper.

11

EMU and the world economy

The global significance of EMU

In the vast range of publications and discussion on the theme of European monetary integration, surprisingly little attention is given to its external effects – the impact that EMU will have on global economic relations. The result is much like a performance of *Hamlet* without the Prince of Denmark, because there can be little doubt that EMU, in its political and historical origins, is essentially a project for world monetary reform. One of its main consequences, perhaps *the* main consequence, will be to bring about a fundamental shift in the balance of international economic forces and to open up new prospects for change in world monetary and financial relations. This chapter emphasises the importance of the external dimension of EMU and discusses the new forms of monetary coordination to which it might lead.

The double hegemony

It should be stressed, to begin with, that EMU is essentially a *French* project. It has certainly been accepted by Germany, the other key player in the development of European integration, but in Germany EMU is typically seen as the price to be paid for a greater measure of *political* integration in Europe, not as necessarily desirable from a national point of view. Hence the excessively detailed and constraining formulae which Germany insisted on writing into the Maastricht Treaty: all these clauses are designed to minimise, almost to eliminate, the discontinuity in German policy which monetary union might bring about. Such a view lies behind the ironic contrast between German and other European anxieties over EMU. The Germans worry that the new currency, to be called the euro, means the replacement of their beloved D-mark; for everyone else the source of concern is that the D-mark and the euro will turn out to be the same thing.

In France, on the other hand, there is a long-standing concern with the functioning of the international monetary system and a desire to move to more symmetric relations in place of the key currency arrangements which require the hegemony of particular states. Resentment of US dominance, and a belief that US policy subordinated common interests to those of the US itself can be traced back to the 1950s (Jeanneney 1994). In the 1960s there were several episodes of friction between the government under De Gaulle and the US over the role of the dollar as, *de facto*, world money. Jacques Rueff (1967), a French economist who advocated a return to a form of gold standard, provided intellectual support for French policy at that time.

The collapse of fixed parities in 1973, contrary to the expectations of the Chicago School, did not represent a full emancipation of national policy from the hegemony of the US. In the international sphere, as within national economies, the need to economise transactions costs tends to promote one or a few assets to the status of money; after the failure of attempts, in the 1970s, to define an effective supranational monetary unit through the IMF, the dollar continued to play a predominant role as an international means of payment and investment medium, to a large extent simply because of the scale on which it was already used (Kindleberger 1981). The fact that this role was now less secure made its continuation increasingly dysfunctional since external monetary relations became harder to predict, but it was still the case that the conditions under which dollars were issued determined the external constraints faced by enterprises and policy-makers in other countries. US policy therefore had major external effects; these tended, increasingly, to be negative as that policy became more erratic and volatile. Episodes of 'benign neglect', when dollar depreciation threatened other countries with sharp losses of competitiveness and/or imported inflation, alternated with sudden turns to restriction equivalent, in global terms, to negative demand shocks. The hypothesis that other countries could insulate themselves from such effects by allowing their own currencies to fluctuate freely proved to be quite analogous to most other propositions about the 'neutrality' of money: it expressed an undeniable truth about the *logic* of an idealised, equilibrated, market system but had no relevance to short- or medium-term developments in actual market economies.

For most European countries, including France, the partial relegation of the dollar only had the effect of complicating, rather than removing, the patterns of domination to which they were subjected (for a French view see Brender *et al*. 1986). Within Europe, the D-mark, which started to rival the dollar in some global monetary functions, had a clear regional pre-eminence which could make German policy the source of intense pressures on other countries; but, partly because the Bundesbank resisted a full global role for the D-mark, this local domination did little to counteract the impact of US policy. Dollar 'imperialism' had mutated into a *double* hegemony – that of the Bundesbank within Western Europe, and of the US on a global scale. The consequences can be illustrated by reference to the two most damaging recessions experienced in the post-Second World War era. The recession of the early 1980s was clearly made in America and was a consequence of the Volcker shock. It might, in principle, have been resisted by the Germans, who in fact transmitted it to the EMS countries by tightening their own policies. The recession of the early 1990s, on the other hand, had much more to do with autonomous German decisions to raise interest rates at a time when they were falling in the US. In neither case did wider European interests enter into the policy equation. In both cases the resulting damage was intense and long-lasting. Now there is no doubt that the French see the EMU project as a challenge to both hegemonies: within Europe the dominance of a single state is to be replaced by supranational decision-making in the interests of the Union as a whole; but, on the basis of a single European currency, EMU will make possible a fundamental challenge to existing world monetary relations and a move towards greater symmetry between Europe and North America. The opportunity for this would be created by the emergence of the euro as an international currency equal in status to the dollar.

Minimising external effects

If what has been said about French strategic ambitions is correct, then the EMU project must be seen as an attempt to recast global monetary relations in a quite radical way. It would be difficult, however, to detect these wider ambitions in the official literature on monetary union, where the external consequences of a single European currency are treated as very much a subordinate theme. This is to be explained by political and diplomatic reticence, rather than by any genuine belief that these issues are unimportant. On the one hand the open expression of such ambitions might alarm the US, as a direct challenge to its established position of leadership; on the other, it would offend the Germans because of the suggestion that European monetary policy might have other objectives besides the sacrosanct aim of price stability. In fact it has been a concern of German policy to *resist* the global use of the D-mark because it is seen as threatening the autonomy of national policy – the fear of additional policy constraints has outweighed any desire to exploit potential global monetary power.

Thus the official discussion concentrates on the implications of EMU for *seigniorage*. This term originally denoted the charge made by the sovereign for minting gold or silver into coin; today it refers to the privilege, enjoyed by the issuer of money, of borrowing at low or zero rates of interest, and for an indefinite period, when money is put into circulation.

Now EMU as such has only limited implications for the amount of seigniorage *within* the Union. All that happens is the transfer of this privilege from national monetary authorities to the ECB (and in fact there will then be a redistribution of the corresponding central bank profits back to the member states). If, in addition, the common currency is less inflationary than the national currencies which are replaced then less seigniorage will be obtained in total – this would correspond to a reduction in the 'inflation tax' levied on EU residents, in particular those in high-inflation countries. In any case, these internal effects are to be regarded as a change in the pattern of internal transfers.

There is, however, a possible external gain for the Union if, as seems likely, the euro is widely used as a reserve asset by countries with important trade and investment links to the EU (for an assessment of the potential use of the euro as an international currency, see Bénassy-Quéré 1996). The purchase of such reserves would constitute a transfer of resources to the ECB to the extent that the latter did not need to hold equivalent reserves of the currencies concerned. This is certainly likely to be the case for many countries – in Eastern Europe, Africa, the Middle East and elsewhere, as well as in those Western European countries who do not immediately participate in the monetary union. If the euro acquires the reputation of a solid store of value then euro reserves will be held more widely – notably in America and East Asia.

In quantitative terms, however, these seigniorage effects are not of great significance. It is estimated that in 1988 some $100 billion worth of claims on the US central bank were held outside the US itself – some of this could be expected to switch to the euro and this could be seen as an interest-free loan to the EU. But the value of such a loan is put by Commission economists at about 0.045 per cent of EU GDP (European Commission 1990, p186).

One can take a wider view of seigniorage, to include money issued by the commercial banking system. If the status of the euro attracts additional deposits from outside Europe into EU banks, this represents a gain to the European economy to the extent that external credit is now available on better terms than before. For at least two reasons, however, such gains are not likely to be large. Firstly, in the contemporary world economy there is no close relation between the currency in which a deposit is denominated and either the national base of the bank which accepts it or the country in which the corresponding bank advance is made. Thus, to the extent that commercial banks do make gains from the use of the euro, these gains will be distributed among world banks as a whole according to their strength and competitiveness; they will not be concentrated exclusively on Europe.

Secondly, there is a point which applies to the whole seigniorage discussion. International wealth holders already make considerable use of EU assets, in particular those denominated in D-marks, so that no large inflow of capital is to be expected unless there is a complete collapse in the international role of the dollar. Such a collapse is not desirable in itself and is certainly not an objective of EU, or even French, policy. It would amount to the replacement of the dollar by the euro as key currency. There is no point in attempting to establish European dominance in this way – the aim should rather be to replace increasingly uncertain and dysfunctional US dominance by a more symmetric and cooperative set of world monetary arrangements.

Now the achievement of EMU and the introduction of the euro do not guarantee any such reform. But they do modify the conditions under which it could be sought. Both in international institutions – such as the IMF – and in coordination forums – in particular the G7 summits of leading industrial countries – the member states of the EU (or at least those participating in the monetary union) would be constrained to speak with a single voice and to express a common interest. Neither has been the case in the past. At the same time the importance of the currency they controlled would give rise to large external effects from European policy decisions and thus make it more important for other countries to reach some sort of accommodation with the Union.

The coordination issue

Most economic discussion of policy coordination issues uses the concepts of game theory (for a critical exposition of this body of theory see Kreps 1990). Players, in this case national policy-makers, are involved in strategic interactions where the choice made by one country can affect the outcome for others. The overall outcome can be examined under various assumptions as to the way the players interact – whether each, for example, takes the policy choices of the others as given or whether procedures exist to avoid mutually damaging combinations of policies. These theoretical devices have limitations – perhaps the most problematic aspect in this context is the standard assumption of full rationality, according to which national decision-makers are responding in their own best interests given the specified pattern of interaction.

Nevertheless, international policy interactions do seem to be a field in which game–theoretical concepts are appropriate. The models do seem to indicate that coordination failures are indeed possible in the absence of procedures to encourage compatibility of decisions; at the same time, conflicts of interest, such as the possibility of exporting adjustment costs onto other countries, may make it difficult to agree on such procedures.

The specification of interdependence is a difficult task. An influential model of strategic independence (Cooper and John 1988) indicates that a coordination failure can occur when one agent's decisions (in this case one nation or bloc's policies) impact not only on the *outcomes* experienced by another, but on the *trade-offs* which are faced, so that A's decision affects the pay-offs to B's decision in a way which modifies B's choice. In such a case it can matter whether decisions are made cooperatively in the attempt to avoid mutually damaging combinations, or whether they are made independently in the sense that each agent treats the other's policy as a given factor.[1]

In the discussion of international coordination two main channels of interdependence have to be taken into account: those arising from trade relations and affecting directly the current accounts of different countries; and those which arise from international capital flows, in particular through the ability of residents of one country to make placements in the banking system or organised credit markets of another.

The nature of policy interactions has been profoundly modified by the increasing mobility of short-term capital. The impact of external policies on total demand, via trade flows, may be less of a problem because it is now often easier to finance current account deficits – in this sense national policy may have become more autonomous. In addition, it can be noted that current expenditure interactions among the major powers and trading blocs – the EU, the NAFTA (US, Canada, Mexico) and Japan – are not in themselves large enough to give rise to colossal interdependence. The external trade of the EU and the NAFTA amounts to little more than 10 per cent of their GDP, and only some of this, of course, is with each other. In broad orders of magnitude, then, a 1 or 2 per cent variation of aggregate demand in the US would provoke a variation of little more than 0.3 per cent in the demand for EU output even if indirect effects – working through third trading partners – are taken into account. Spillovers of this kind among the major trading regions are not as big as those to be expected within each region (see, for example, the rough estimates of such interdependence given by Krugman 1994 p127).

Effects working through short-run capital flows are potentially more important, if, as seems the case in practice, they induce changes in monetary policy, since this will impact on the entirety of domestic expenditure (as well as on domestic costs) and not simply on the export sector. The possibility indicated by Cooper and John is that a shift in monetary conditions in one country will significantly affect the trade-offs governing its use in others, because there would be unacceptable exchange rate effects if monetary policy were not altered.

207

Fiscal policy can be involved in this process, but this is largely because of the way it interacts with monetary policy. For example, the big fiscal deficits run by the Reagan administration were a problem for Europeans largely because, given the objectives of the US central bank, they drove up US interest rates – the direct effect of the US fiscal expansion was probably beneficial to European industry as it tended to expand their export markets. For some years, however, this demand effect was more than outweighed by the induced tightening of European monetary policy in the early 1980s, which narrowed domestic markets for European producers.

A second point should be made. If the key global interdependence among countries and blocs is now centred on international credit markets then the efficiency and stability of these markets becomes a critical question. Standard theories of exchange rates, based on the assumptions of rational expectations and market clearing, would not lead one to expect massive destabilisation of monetary policy in one country as a consequence of a change in conditions elsewhere. A divergence of short-run interest rates would have certain, limited, implications for the evolution of output and relative prices in the two areas over the medium term; these in turn would imply a certain equilibrium exchange rate adjustment; in the short run, exchange rates would perhaps overshoot this adjustment by a margin related to the gap in short-run interest rates, but this effect on its own would not usually be very great, not enough to destabilise monetary policy (see Chapter 2). If such destabilisation does tend to happen – if a change in one country's or group's policy has violent effects elsewhere – then credit markets cannot be functioning in the efficient way specified by standard theories.

If this is the case then global monetary reform has to address two issues. The first is the question of policy settings in the main groups – the spillover effects which monetary and fiscal policies in each of the main regions (the EU, the US and North America, Japan and its neighbours in South-east Asia) have on the others – and whether the effectiveness of policy can be increased by taking these linkages into account in a systematic way.

The second question concerns the functioning of credit markets themselves, through which international capital flows respond to developments in different countries and whether, on the basis of a stronger and more united EU, common measures are possible and desirable to increase control over these vast, and largely unregulated, financial systems.

The first question concerns international policy coordination in the narrow sense; the second goes beyond this to deal with international monetary reform.

Experiments in policy coordination

The growing belief, after the end of the Bretton Woods system, that lack of economic policy coordination among major industrial powers could be damaging has led to the emergence of a loose structure for policy discussion and examination. This involves meetings of representatives from the G7 countries for which the IMF provides some technical support. (The G7 comprises the US, Japan, Germany, France, Italy, Britain and Canada.) These meetings examine economic developments in the countries concerned, make forecasts which focus on economic interactions among them, and may result in agreements on policy changes, although in general these agreements are vague and imply no real additional constraints on national policy formation (Dobson 1991).

In two particular episodes, however, attempts were made to achieve a greater degree of coherence and commitment to joint action. In the late 1970s major countries agreed on a coordinated economic expansion to respond to the stagnation which followed the oil shock of 1973–74. Germany was given particular responsibility for stimulating demand because of the strength of its balance of payments. Coordination was not a failure but it was short-lived – continuing weakness of the US dollar, blamed by other countries on excessively loose monetary policy, and further oil price rises induced German policy-makers (led by the Bundesbank) to feel that the policy agreement had inflationary implications. US monetary policy was soon tightened but this was on a unilateral basis, and the first Reagan administration moved away from international coordination.

The second episode occurred in the mid-1980s and revived the interest of policy-makers and commentators in the possibilities of joint action. Very large imbalances in the global economy had emerged, partly as a result of US policy, partly through the malfunctioning of international capital markets. The Federal government was running very large and increasing fiscal deficits, which the central bank was trying to counter with restrictive credit policies. This policy combination would normally be expected to strengthen the dollar, because, although the government deficit would (and did) lead to a trade deficit, this would tend to be more than covered, in a world of mobile financial resources, by capital inflows to take advantage of higher interest rates. In fact, however, the appreciation of the dollar went well beyond anything that could be explained by policy shifts as such (see Chapter 6). Although a high dollar gave a boost to US incomes it had devastating effects on many industries and, by 1985, led to increasing demands for protection. Other countries, meanwhile, although they found their competitiveness in

US markets improved, had to confront very difficult financial conditions – weak currencies and high international interest rates. (For a full length study of this episode see Funabashi 1989.)

In 1985 international policy coordination came dramatically back into the spotlight when a G7 summit at the Plaza Hotel in New York announced that the dollar was overvalued and that concerted foreign exchange intervention would be used to bring it down to levels more consistent with balance in international trade flows. At the same time countries committed themselves to move towards more stable macroeconomic policies, in particular by reducing the US public sector deficit. In the next two years the desired dollar depreciation did in fact take place (although it had actually begun prior to the Plaza as market agents themselves became aware that the dollar exchange rate was quite out of line with any plausible interpretation of the 'fundamental' factors involved, such as the relative strength of industrial economies). By the G7 meeting at the Louvre in Paris in 1987 concern had switched to stabilising the dollar and avoiding a speculative flight of capital *from* the US. Once again it was announced that concerted intervention would be deployed to this purpose. Later the same year mechanisms of coordination were again used in response to a worldwide stock market collapse – agreement was reached by telephone on a coordinated reduction of interest rates to forestall a possible downturn in expenditures as a result of financial distress (Dobson 1991, p108).

This period of two years in the mid-1980s probably marked a high point of global coordination. The prestige of the G7 was enhanced by very visible, and at least partly successful, action to counter clear financial malfunctions – the overvalued dollar and the stock market crash. In response, the G7's procedures for mutual policy examination were considerably extended. In subsequent years, however, and in the absence of similar dramatic threats to stability, progress was more limited. Discussion had to deal with improving medium-term policy formation in ways that would be mutually beneficial, rather than responding to emergencies. In these debates the main industrial countries were very reluctant to accept international responsibilities that would limit their room for manoeuvre; the policy undertakings they were prepared to give were very vague and imprecise.

A proposed system of coordination

We can measure the actual weakness of global coordination by contrasting it with the best-known plans for organised and continuing policy coordination, those developed by Williamson (for example, Williamson and Miller 1987).

Williamson's proposals can be seen as a way of resolving the $(n - 1)$ problem among a group of n countries. If each country has both internal targets (for the growth of aggregate demand, say) and external targets (say, a desired exchange rate) for monetary policy, and seeks a compromise between the two, then a failure to take into account policy interactions may worsen the trade-off between internal and external objectives for the countries as a group. Overall monetary conditions may tend to become either tighter or looser than countries would desire without this contributing to more acceptable external results for any of them. If we envisage countries attaching complete priority to external targets then these interdependencies may take the extreme form of incompatibility – it becomes impossible for them all to achieve their exchange rate targets, at least one of which has to be renounced, perhaps after a damaging phase of conflict.

In Chapters 3 and 6 we have already described the *asymmetric* solution to the problem which depends on a key currency and the hegemony of a strong country. The latter orients its monetary policy not to the exchange rate but to a general objective such as the short-run interest rate or the growth of some aggregate such as domestic credit or total demand. The other countries accept this general policy setting and devote their own policies to managing their exchange rates against the leading currency. International monetary relations seem to tend spontaneously towards such a structure. Its efficiency, however, depends critically on the quality of leadership exercised: the leading country must be strong enough to command the adherence of the others and responsible enough to set general monetary policy with a view to collective interests.

In the argument put forward by Williamson, the overall or general setting of monetary policy would not be a matter of leadership but of *agreement*, at least among those major countries whose policies can give rise to important spillover effects. A general rate of interest would be set for the international economy in view of the perceived general trade-off between expansion and price stability. Individual countries would address their exchange rate targets by manipulating *not* the rate of interest but the *differential* between their own interest rates and the generally agreed rate. The target exchange rate would be estimated as the rate compatible, over the medium term, with balance of payments stability at an acceptable level of internal production and employment. These targets would be *consistent* as they would be based on agreed views of payments equilibrium and competitiveness.

The Williamson scheme sees exchange rate targets, therefore, as designed to prevent disturbances to international trade and investment. Exchange rates would be aimed at 'real', not price, stability. The trade-off between inflation and unemployment would be a matter for each country to decide for itself by determining what level of demand corresponded to *internal* balance. It would use fiscal policy as the main instrument for internal objectives. Countries with relatively high inflation would accept a corresponding depreciation of their currencies to keep the real exchange rate in line with the agreed view of international balance.

Partly because of the need for such depreciations, Williamson proposed broad bands for exchange rates rather than precise values. In this way, it was hoped, speculative attacks on fixed parities could be avoided. The plan as a whole treated the international money and capital markets as capable of generating destabilising capital flows. The announced exchange rate bands are seen as providing strong signals to the markets and would control such inherent tendencies to instability. For this reason the coordination plan conflicts with widespread views, according to which free capital markets by themselves arrive at efficient assessments of equilibrium and operate as a desirable corrective on misguided or inefficient policies.

The full assessment of this kind of coordination framework raises technical complexities which go beyond the purposes of the present discussion. What will be stressed here is that the degree of coordination required would be greater, by an order of magnitude, than anything that has so far been achieved by the industrial powers. They would be obliged not only to reach agreement on exchange rates (which has sometimes proved possible) but also to come to an understanding on the underlying settings of macroeconomic, especially monetary, policy instruments. The use of interest rate *differentials* implies close and continuous policy concertation. For example, if it were agreed that the external position of the US ought to be strengthened by a rise in interest rates then some other players – say Japan and Germany (in the future, perhaps, the EU) – would have to undertake to *cut* their own rates in order to preserve the agreed *general* setting of policy. If this did not happen one would be moving back to the uncoordinated policy games which have been observed in the past.

On any realistic view the world seems a long way from such a deep form of coordination. The high point of policy agreement in the mid-1980s was perhaps only reached because useful interventions could be identified which did *not* require national control over monetary policy to be diluted. The overvaluation of the dollar in 1985 was so great, and so obviously unsustainable, that the G7 could encourage a correction by largely sterilised forex interventions which did not put national monetary policy at stake; the emergency interest rate cuts of 1987 certainly did involve altering policy settings, but only as a short-run measure – this transient agreement did nothing to prevent the huge *divergence* of US and European monetary policies which developed from early 1988 and which contributed to the disruption of the EMS.

To what extent can EMU change the conditions for global coordination? Nothing is guaranteed – it is at least conceivable that a stronger and more united Europe would simply lead to damaging policy rivalries with the US, for example. However, if, following Williamson, one conceives coordination as resting on an understanding about the general level of interest rates then there are several considerations which suggest that monetary union might help to improve coordination and to avoid inflationary or contractionary games among the main actors.

Firstly, Europe may find it much easier to specify its own *internal* objectives. For nearly thirty years US policies have had both an asymmetric and a divisive impact on the Europeans because every fluctuation of the dollar has given rise to internal tensions in Western Europe. This has meant that US policy was much more important to the Europeans than European policies have been for the US, a circumstance which has made genuine reciprocity in policy discussions very difficult. At the same time the differentiated impact of US policy on the various member states has obstructed the development of common positions. EMU will force the Europeans to speak with a single voice and to adopt a common negotiating position, at least as far as monetary policy is concerned; it will probably have the same effect on fiscal policy if, as is widely expected, European fiscal policies become more centralised after the move to a single currency.

Secondly, EMU will represent a simplification of international monetary relations which may itself render effective coordination more feasible. In the next century new powerful regional economic groupings may emerge in Asia or Latin America, but in the foreseeable future there will only be three centres with substantial autonomy in monetary policy: Europe, the US and Japan, a system involving only two independent exchange rates and three monetary policies. Exchange rate coordination failures, where each party makes policy moves while ignoring the likely reactions of the other two, would surely be almost absurd within such a system.[2]

More pessimistic assessments are certainly possible. Kenen (1995) suggests that, just because the dollar exchange rate will become less important to a monetarily unified Europe, it may be more difficult to reach agreement on exchange rates. However, the argument here is that such agreements are extremely superficial unless they bear on the underlying setting of domestic policy. In the tripolar world that is emerging a key question for policy in each centre will be the response of the other two – whether they match the move, leave their own policies unchanged, or even counter it. Without this kind of assessment the consequences of the policy shift for expenditure and finance will be impossible to calculate. In this more symmetric game among three players the incentives for *deeper* coordination would appear to be stronger.

Structural reforms

It was argued above that, unless one takes an extremely optimistic view of competitive asset markets, then international monetary reform raises not only the issue of coordinated policy setting but also the question of globalised foreign exchange and credit markets, which constitute an increasingly dense network of financial linkages among national economies.

The explosion of international financial activity arising, in the first instance, from the deregulation and globalisation of US finance (see Chapter 9) poses complex and hotly contested issues. The scale of the transactions involved are unimaginable. According to Eichengreen (1994), gross turnover on world foreign exchange markets amounted in 1992 to 1,354 billion dollars *per day*. Clearly the vast majority of these transactions had nothing to do with international trade, which is smaller (by several orders of magnitude) than these figures, and are concerned with borrowing, lending and portfolio adjustments.

At the same time, it would be very wrong to interpret the growth of international finance as representing a simple globalisation of the savings/investment process. The overwhelming weight of evidence indicates that most investment continues to be financed by savings drawn from within the country concerned.[3] When we consider the globalised credit markets we are dealing with massive, continuous arbitrage among *relatively liquid* financial assets – bank deposits, public debt, the debt of very large and well-known companies, and derivative instruments based on these. Information asymmetries and the importance of local data mean that the vast majority of risky, long-term investments continue to be financed by creditors with the special knowledge required, on a national, local or even personal basis. What has happened is that financial agents in all countries now place the temporary surpluses, and finance the temporary deficits, of their still nationally distinct investment activities on globalised credit markets of amazing sophistication and fluency.

The interpretation of these phenomena is therefore in dispute. If one takes a strong view of the efficiency and rationality of the markets involved, then what has taken place is an intensification of competition which should both reduce credit costs to borrowers and raise rates of return to lenders. The ways in which financial processes were partitioned from each other in the past amounted only to so many restrictive practices, swelling the rents extracted by intermediaries from the original sources and final users of financial resources. A more jaundiced view sees globalised finance as both unstable and dysfunctional: the ceaseless migration of funds from one liquid placement to another reduces the relative yield to genuinely risk-taking investments, while threatening productive enterprise with drastic, unpredictable swings in the financial environment.

All that will be done in the present context is to invoke some of the aspects in which EMU might alter the relation between policy-makers and contemporary credit markets. The first point is that simple effects of scale will tend to strengthen the hands of the authorities. Speculation against their individual currencies will obviously become a thing of the past for participating countries. This is no small result in itself as it remains the case, up to the eve of EMU, that every variation in external conditions has provoked damaging internal tensions within Western Europe; thus every weakening of the dollar has led to pressure on the French franc and other currencies *vis-à-vis* the D-mark – tensions which have often aggravated the problems of policy-makers. By the same token, unity will make it much easier to exercise influence on external conditions themselves: the declarations of the authorities are likely to have more credibility when they express a necessarily unified position and, although not even a continent-wide union will be invulnerable to market disturbances, it will clearly require much larger movements of funds to destabilise the Union as a whole than those which, today, can force policy switches in most individual countries. If European policy, in addition, rests on agreements with the US and Japan, then it will be difficult for market operators to challenge interest rate or exchange rate settings unless they have the most convincing reasons for believing that policy is set on an unsustainable course. This kind of ultimate sanction on policy errors may well be desirable and is very different from the swings in sentiment which can, today, force policy changes on individual countries in spite of well-formulated strategies.

Can EMU go beyond these scale effects to alter the functioning of international credit mechanisms? One of the most significant proposals for reform derives from James Tobin (1978). He suggested that transactions costs in the foreign exchange markets may be too low from a social point of view because the aggregate effect of private transactions might be to generate instabilities which individuals have no reason to take into account. The correction he suggested was to raise transactions costs in these markets by imposing a small tax. This would hardly disturb either international trade or long-run capital flows as it would be an order of magnitude too small. But it would tend to discourage short-run, purely speculative, capital movements by creating a hurdle which market operators would have to surmount before they could anticipate a profit from arbitrage between liquid assets denominated in different currencies. A consequence would be to shield national governments against self-fulfilling expectations of a devaluation. In going short of a particular currency one would be forgoing not only any interest rate premium which it offered (this might be quite insignificant if it was intended to close the position within a short period of time) but also the tax payment which would become more onerous the more frequently such shifts were carried out. The classic 'one-way' bet against vulnerable currencies would be harder to find. On the other hand, there would still be a market sanction against policies which were clearly out of line with exchange rates. The objective of the tax could be specified as to make it necessary for market agents to examine long-run 'fundamental' factors very closely before launching an attack on a given parity.

Such a reform might be expected to eliminate a very great proportion of the foreign exchange transactions which take place today. But this could be interpreted as indicating that the value of such transactions is very low – too low, perhaps, to justify the social costs in terms of instability to which they give rise. Where there was a clearly defined benefit to a transaction – the finance of trade, the finance of a long-run portfolio or direct investment or insurance against a clear exchange rate risk arising from either of these, then the tax would be too low, relative to the time periods involved, to constitute a significant barrier.

Objections to the Tobin proposal, and to similar suggestions such as penalising banks which take uncovered foreign exchange positions, have tended to focus on their *feasibility*, rather than their desirability. This itself may indicate that the underlying rationale for such measures is very hard to contest: if the huge volume of foreign exchange deals which is observed today really does generate significant advantages then it would hardly be disturbed; only if transactions are of dubious or marginal benefit could they be deterred in this way.

On the other hand, the issue of implementation does seem formidably difficult. The immense variety of international credit instruments and the existence of multiple markets working in parallel create many possibilities for evading any fiscal controls which were not comprehensive in scope.[4] Individual financial centres are reasonably concerned that any such measure would deal a mortal blow to their competitiveness by driving agents to locations and markets which escape the supervision of the authorities concerned. Although electronic technology and telecommunications may not themselves be an insuperable barrier to such reform they certainly threaten to lower the costs of access to any uncontrolled markets which seek to profit from business diverted by the tax. Paradoxically, it may be the case that some small countries can assert control over financial processes just to the extent that their credit systems are primitive and unsophisticated because agents do not have easy and cheap access to a huge range of credit instruments and a wide variety of intermediaries. A recent example of stabilising controls illustrates the point. On the New York stock exchange, 'circuit-breakers' were introduced in the wake of the crisis of 1987. These slow down trading when overall price movements become very volatile. The measure is possible because of the dominance of this market and its convenience for equity transactions: there are no cheap and easily accessed alternatives to the NYSE for most of the traders concerned; were this not the case then the control would inevitably become much harder to enforce. International credit transactions, on the other hand, are less focused on a single location and a single market.

No definitive judgement will be made here on the feasibility of Tobin's 'sand in the wheels of international finance' proposal because it raises technical questions which the writer is not equipped to handle. (For a recent debate see the symposium edited by Greenaway 1995.) But it can be asserted that EMU will dramatically alter the parameters of the problem. There would be, firstly, an immense simplification of the problem which, in global terms would now only involve three central currencies and three authorities; conflicts of interest among the European countries and their financial centres would not disappear but would necessarily be easier to settle when they were all placed under a single structure of regulation and control; if, in addition, the reform were agreed and implemented jointly by the new G3 – the EU, the US and Japan, each of whom has important interests in exercising more control over globalised finance – the logistic difficulties would be further reduced; in particular, offshore financial centres would find it very difficult to specialise in the provision of loopholes if they were confronted by the concerted opposition of the major powers.

For the purposes of the present discussion it is not necessary to adopt a strong position on this particular proposal. Rather, it is suggested that the consolidation of European interests associated with EMU makes for a fundamental shift in the balance of power between globalised markets and public authorities in ways that offer, for the first time in almost three decades, real possibilities of social control over financial processes. If it is accepted that international credit markets are often a source of both inefficiencies in the allocation of capital and instabilities at the macroeconomic level, then these possibilities are a compelling argument in favour of monetary union.

International liquidity

Recent developments in international monetary relations have given rise to a sharp discontinuity in the way reform is thought about: the theme of international liquidity has virtually disappeared (Williamson 1994). Until the break-up of the Bretton Woods system, discussion frequently focused on the provision of liquidity to the world economy, *conceived as a public function*. It was considered that the supply of the media used in international trade and, especially, the reserves held by individual countries, was subject to public control, exercised by the US as source of the dominant form of money. The availability of liquidity was seen as affecting the trade-offs between adjustment and finance of national balance of payments equilibria, in a way analogous to the impact of domestic monetary policy on the strategies of private agents. According to this view, the time period and the terms on which debtors have to adjust their positions are influenced, within a country, by the availability of central refinance. In the international system, the trade-off between adjustment and (re-)finance was similar: excess liquidity would delay necessary corrections, with, as a result, a build-up of dangerous and possibly inflationary imbalances. Insufficient liquidity, on the other hand, might promote a contractionary downturn in trade and investment if too many countries attempted too rapidly to reduce their imports and capital outflows. Both monetarists and Keynesians adopted this kind of perspective, differing on whether they felt that liquidity should be managed in an active and interventionist manner or, on the contrary, governed by some more or less automatic quantity rule. Towards the end of the Bretton Woods system there was quite intense debate on the replacement of the US by a supranational monetary authority which would assume this role of liquidity creation. Proponents of such a shift argued that it would contribute both to equity and to stability to do this: a better balance between the interests of the US and other countries might be achieved; policy would relate more to general conditions and less to those in a single, dominant country. Some moves were actually made in this direction, through the creation of the Special Drawing Right (SDR), a form of international money issued by the IMF and defined, as with the EC's ECU, as a weighted basket of national currencies. The first expectation after the collapse of Bretton Woods parities was perhaps that an IMF-centred system would emerge, similar to Bretton Woods but governed by a supranational authority rather than the central bank of a leading country. As with the 'institutional phase' of the EMS (see Chapter 5), however, negotiations to this end, at the Jamaica summit of 1977, came to nothing. Countries were unwilling to surrender, at that time, what appeared to be a substantially greater degree of autonomy within a floating exchange rate system. Although it was subsequently learned, by painful experience, that generalised floating was not as liberating for national policy-makers as had been suggested by convinced free marketeers, in the late 1970s low international credit costs, reflecting the easy monetary policy of the US, seemed to offer countries a great deal of control in the management of external constraints: financing a deficit was cheap, while failure to adjust carried limited risks of currency depreciation given the weakness of the dollar.

The fundamental nature of the problem then altered at astonishing speed. The immense growth of private international credit flows meant that governments increasingly borrowed foreign exchange reserves from the markets rather than receiving allocations from other countries or international organisations. It was soon perceived that variations in interest rates and in market sentiment could constrain national policy very tightly indeed, and the first optimistic assessments of floating were revised. But by this time there no longer seemed to be any clear connection between the external financial constraints faced by countries and the actions of any public authority, whether national or international. It was as if, within a national economy, a hierarchical monetary system – focused on the issue of high-powered money by a central bank – had given way to pure 'free banking', where commercial lenders compete among themselves in the issue of deposits without being subject to any constraint of convertibility managed by a central authority. Of course, national policies impact on this global credit-creation process. But the focus of national policy on *domestic* credit-creation, the ability of intermediaries to operate in foreign currencies and the absence of any particular currency enjoying clear supremacy as an international medium all mean that the behaviour of the globalised financial system was everyone's – that is, no one's – responsibility. To all intents and purposes, the creation of international liquidity became a pure market process.

The absence of social control may already have exacted a heavy cost in terms of stability. In the late 1970s a super-liquid debt economy allowed many countries – in the industrialised West, in the socialist bloc and in the developing world – to delay adjustment at the price of widening disequilibria. With the general turn to disinflation in the early 1980s, private credit virtually disappeared for a host of countries. In fact, under the auspices of the World Bank, some collective public intervention did take place which helped to avoid wholesale default by developing countries and preserved the integrity of world financial relations by extending emergency loans to

Latin American governments, for example. (For a recent study of the World Bank see Gilbert *et al*. 1996.) This centralised refinance was made 'conditional' on drastic programmes of retrenchment and austerity which imposed huge, often insupportable, burdens on their populations. But for the world system as a whole the pure private debt economy continued to dictate the cost and conditions of international finance to individual countries.

In such circumstances, the provision of international liquidity ceased to be a meaningful policy issue as the resources flowing onto private markets dwarfed any conceivable volume of official reserve creation. Some econom-ists have described this by saying that nations no longer face a liquidity, but only a solvency, constraint: in other words, what regulated their ability to finance, or need to adjust, debtor positions was no longer any identifiable public policy, but the estimate that market agents made of the sustainability of their positions. But it seems perverse to describe this as the disappearance of liquidity constraints, since the markets concerned are so volatile and so prone to overreaction that no alteration of fundamental conditions is needed to produce a drastic tightening of credit terms – or even the effective refusal of any accommodation – for a country to be perceived to be in difficulties. (For the changing significance of payments balances see Allsop, Jenkinson and O'Shaughnessy 1990.) If the markets had actually concerned themselves with sober calculations of solvency, then governments would have been able to focus their decisions on the long term, in disregard of short-run financial developments. The actual situation was the reverse of this – there was a complete tyranny of the immediate, as the continuous reassurance of financial markets became the first objective of policy-makers, often ruling out the adoption of any stable longer-term strategy.

Nevertheless, it was true that large, creditworthy nations were no longer subjected to any publicly determined limits on their choices as regards adjustment or finance of imbalances. In such a world the introduction of a central, supranational authority providing liquidity to governments could seem a useless fifth wheel on the financial engine. While credit markets continued to escape all effective supervision of their aggregate outcomes, no conceivable institutional innovation could make an appreciable difference to patterns of adaptation in trade or investment relations among countries. It is difficult to see how the SDR, for example, could obtain a decisive superiority, in the eyes of market agents, over other currencies in widespread use; and without such a well-defined liquidity premium the issuer of such a currency would be quite unable to influence market developments in the way a national central bank influences the domestic credit system. When a proposal was made in the late 1980s, typically by a French representative, for the major countries to return to the Jamaica agenda and to create a genuinely international monetary authority, it fell on deaf ears – such suggestions seemed to refer to a world that had completely disappeared.

Whether, and how, international reserve and credit creation might again be brought under some form of social control must remain, at present, very obscure questions. The globalisation of finance, and the consequent competition among very large numbers of agents on international credit markets, are irreversible developments – a comprehensive return to the financial autarchy of the early post-Second World War years would impose large costs on borrowers and lenders alike. For example, demographic differences among countries make it rational for those which will have elderly populations in the future to accumulate claims on those which will have larger active workforces. But the continuation of the present non-system will require a degree of stability that unregulated private finance has not, in general, displayed. Major disturbances may again make necessary the organisation of public rescue operations, and any lender of last resort is compelled by the logic of its own situation to seek to develop control over the financial relations whose breakdown will force it to provide widespread relief. On the other hand, designs of the past for a supranational authority issuing liabilities as the world money *par excellence* may prove outdated – an illegitimate extrapolation of previous experience into an uncertain future.[5]

Once again, it is not necessary for the present argument to adopt highly specific blueprints for the global institutions of the future. It suffices to point out how the monetary unification of Europe will alter many of the most important determinants of the situation. On the one hand, no new powerful institutions at global level may emerge for a very long time. It would still be true that the workings of the international debt economy would be profoundly modified. The weaker member states of the Union would no longer be subjected to dangerous swings in market sentiment – rather, the EU as a whole would be in the position of Germany today, so large and powerful as to command stable and continuous access to external credit. If, at the same time, the EU agreed on basic policy settings with the US and possibly Japan, the mere concertation of these powerful governments might alter the balance of power between authorities and markets, making it possible to regulate financial agents and influence credit flows to an extent that is today impossible. On the other hand, instability and inefficiency in private competitive finance may prove, at some point in the future, so menacing as to militate in favour of more fundamental reform and the construction of new world institutions to replace or control the global markets. In this case too EMU will be of the first importance – as a *precedent*, on a continental scale, for the new forms of organisation that are required and as a consolidation of fragmented national interests necessary to make the new task of construction feasible.

The bifurcation

To conclude this discussion of the (greatly underestimated) external implications of EMU, reference can be made back to De Grauwe's (1989) analysis of international monetary history, mentioned in Chapter 3. National and international credit systems evolve for a long time in parallel, following what seems to be a similar logic in spite of immense differences in scale: from the disorganised issue of different moneys on a competitive basis; to agreement on a common standard (gold); to the promotion of one money issuer to central prominence – the role of the central bank as it evolved within private banking, the role of the US within Bretton Woods; and finally to the gradual supersession of gold by state-issued money. At this point, as the Bretton Woods structure breaks down, there is a bifurcation into two paths of development – whereas national systems develop through explicit political control and the substitution of fiat money for gold, the international system moves to a plurality of monetary units, scrutinised only by a sophisticated set of financial markets. It must be suspected that this divergence has produced an unstable situation. Either national systems of monetary control will gradually give way to the pure market ('free banking') relations which surround them and which tend to erode possibilities of public intervention and control by offering 'exit' options to any agent adversely affected by domestic regulation. Or means will be found to assert closer and more continuous control over the global system, which might then tend to evolve towards a managed structure, centred on a powerful authority, analogous to that which has emerged within national economies.

It is surely difficult to overstate the importance of these issues for the future of industrial societies. The argument of this chapter has been that the success or failure of EMU could be critical to the direction in which international monetary relations as a whole develop. If this is the case then there is a lot more at stake than is suggested by discussions focused on Western European arrangements in themselves.

Further reading

For the official view of the external aspects of EMU see European Commission (1990, Chapter 7). An overview of the practice of international coordination is in Dobson (1991). Literature on international monetary relations is immense; the recent text by Copeland (1994) is a useful introduction.

Notes

1. For a survey of the technical literature on policy coordination, see Currie and Levine (1993, Chapter 2). Kenen (1989) argues that the most active phases of coordination have not been a question of policy optimisation but of system preservation; in this sense they may be regarded as analogous to the lender-of-last-resort interventions discussed in Chapter 8.

2. The discussion in the text neglects the impact of global monetary arrangements on the developing world, and the ways in which countries and regions outside the main industrial groups might influence macroeconomic policies. This is not because the problem in itself is considered unimportant but because it is believed that in practice the direct influence of developing countries is bound to be limited for some time to come.

3. Krugman (1989) reports such observations in a particularly striking way: there is essentially no correlation across countries between the balance of payments and the rate of investment. If the international finance of productive investment were usual, one would expect a significant correlation even if this were less than total.

4. See Garber and Taylor (1995): 'The effectiveness of the ... measures ... depends on their comprehensiveness across borders, institutions and products.'

5. Aglietta (1986) argues that, following the decline of the dollar as a key currency, the most appropriate line of international monetary reform is towards close coordination rather than the development of a supranational currency.

Conclusion – the narrow space

The starting point in any assessment of the current state of European integration is to recognise how closely the project of European construction has become engaged with a very narrow and dogmatic project for monetary stabilisation. This linkage is both damaging and inextricable. On the one hand it is clear that both the 'convergence process' preparing the way for EMU, and its immediate consequences – particularly the inevitable division between insiders and outsiders – will do nothing to resolve, and may well aggravate, the European social crisis which arises from persistent unemployment and insecurity and which expresses itself in a dangerous alienation of populations from political leaderships.

On the other hand, however, it is not possible to undo the Maastricht Treaty or to renegotiate the delicate political compromise on which it rests. No doubt this is to be regretted – one can imagine alternative starting points which would have been more favourable, both in terms of the objectives set for the Union and in terms of the strategies and institutional structures through which they would be pursued. But these alternatives are no longer real. In practice, political perspectives can only be developed if the real circumstances of the Union are recognised: these include an immense commitment of political capital to the achievement of EMU according to the formulae of Maastricht and an increasing momentum towards that goal.

What is called for, therefore, is a precise strategic orientation within a very narrow space. This space is not wide enough to permit the rejection of Maastricht and EMU. The failure of monetary integration is certainly possible, although it is less and less likely. But failure would leave the Union in a political and economic vacuum, in which it would be impossible to formulate a constructive strategy. The loss of authority and prestige of EU institutions, the break-up of existing coordination procedures, the promotion of anti-European political forces which would follow such failure, would all be severe blows to the wider project of European construction as such. In such a context the EU would be reduced to a mere free trade zone, which might be widened to include new member states but in which there would be no possibility of deepening the process of integration. Nor would the disabling of central political structures produce a larger choice of strategies at national level. On the contrary, constraints on national economic policy would be tightened by uncontrolled competition to attract investment and economic activity from one territory to another. The pressures on state budgets arising from the Maastricht convergence process would be perpetuated by efforts to advance national competitiveness in a Dutch auction of welfare cuts, deregulation and tax give-backs.

However, although rejection of Maastricht leads to a strategic dead end, there is no scope for any strategy which merely accepts the Maastricht agenda. The dysfunctionality of the Maastricht project has only become more obvious since the ratification of the treaty. The political resources and energy of the EU are being absorbed by an absurd war on inflation at a time when inflation has ceased to be a serious economic problem in many EU countries. And even in its own terms, as a counter-inflationary exercise, the Maastricht agenda – both convergence criteria and the European Central Bank – may prove self-defeating by inducing financial disequilibria and social tensions which increase rather than reduce inflationary risks. Beyond this exaggerated concern with price stability, it is clear that Maastricht is obstructing the elaboration of effective EU economic policies and narrowing the range of objectives which can be addressed. The most important example is the attenuation of the employment strategy developed by the Commission in 1994: the failure to carry through even these modest measures carries major political dangers for the Union (see Chapter 10). European electorates, in France for instance, can see quite clearly the impact of the Maastricht programme on employment, welfare and social stability; if it becomes impossible to point to other EU programmes which promote security for Union citizens then the already alarming gap between the project of European construction and the populations which the project is meant, in principle, to serve will become a threatening gulf.

This is the narrow space in which any change in strategy must be considered: between a rejection which would strike, effectively or otherwise, at integration as such; and the endorsement of a programme so blinkered and dogmatically conceived that it has already begun to disorganise the political and economic life of the Union. The only feasible approach is to attempt initiatives inserted into the Maastricht agenda itself – into its incoherences, its lacunae, its limitations – with the aim of *strengthening* the advance to EMU, securing the political and economic basis of a common currency, rationalising the process by which it is pursued and enhancing the further objectives of the unified currency area.

The nature of the political forces for change also raises very difficult questions. There can be no doubt that discontent with present developments is both intense and widespread: dissatisfaction is experienced not only by the citizenry of several member states but also by significant elements of the political class, including much of the European Commission itself. But it is not clear that these forces could easily cohere around a common project for an alternative. One possible line of fracture is along national boundaries; another is between forces deeply committed to a different vision of European construction and those fundamentally hostile to integration as such. In these conditions the specification of ambitious immediate objectives may have the effect of fragmenting rather than mobilising the forces for change.

Thus realistic consideration of a more appropriate strategy must be tightly constrained, both by established political arrangements and by economic imbalances which can only be slowly corrected. But it is still the most fruitful approach to avoid a negative, and probably futile, refusal of the realities of the post-Maastricht period, but at the same time to attempt to widen and enrich the Maastricht agenda. In spite of the constraints there are a number of significant strategic opportunities to promote a more positive interaction between developments at national and EU level. The key policy areas include: an alteration of the macroeconomic stance of member states in order to facilitate the transition to EMU; a stronger and more explicit political commitment to limit exclusions from the monetary union and to shorten the period during which major member states will be outside; a relaunch of the employment initiatives which are, indeed, a necessary political and economic complement to the EMU programme; and efforts to valorise the achievement of EMU both internally and externally, through balancing centralised monetary policy with new fiscal powers and through initiatives for global monetary and financial reform. Such proposals may themselves appear excessively ambitious, but they have a practical basis in that they are necessary to secure and stabilise the actual strategy for European construction and to control the political and economic risks which Maastricht has begun to generate.

This concluding chapter aims to assess these risks – the literal interpretation of Maastricht, the excessive and uncoordinated drive for fiscal consolidation, the narrowing of EU economic policies, the alienation of Britain from the integration process. On this basis, some of the most promising initiatives can be sketched – these opportunities exist precisely because they would defend and stabilise the EMU process itself by limiting the costs and enhancing the benefits to which it gives rise. Particular attention will be paid to the case of Britain, whose lack of engagement with the current phase of European construction in itself goes a long way to explain the imbalances and inadequacies of the Maastricht agenda.

Locked in

By the summer of 1996 it had become obvious that the drive for monetary union, intended to be the occasion of a new and deeper phase of European integration, had become almost the opposite – a clear sign of the inadequacy of European institutions. The formulae of the Maastricht Treaty, both as regards the convergence process *before* monetary union and as regards the ways in which a common currency is to be managed *after* it is introduced, were more and more clearly damaging to European economic development in the present and more and more threatening for its future. Yet no political process, no forum for discussion, no strong institutions devoted to general European interests, permitted the adaptation or amendment of these formulae. To touch them would be to jeopardise the EMU itself and rob the Union of the project which has increasingly monopolised its political energy and its strategic capacities; the Inter-Governmental Conference (IGC) of 1996 was designed to examine the workings of the Treaty of Union and to bring about such corrections as were necessary. Yet the IGC, it was decided, would not discuss the monetary aspects of the treaty since the compromise on which these rested was too fragile to admit of any alteration. In particular, the highly qualified endorsement of Maastricht in the German constitutional court (see Chapter 7) seemed to threaten denunciation of the treaty by Germany if any of its monetary clauses were to be amended. EMU was kept off the IGC agenda although the first obvious consequence of the Maastricht formulae would be to exclude the majority of EU member states from early participation in this key project of the Union.

Proposals for a more rational and less costly approach to monetary union were not lacking. They ranged from the daring (De Grauwe's 1995a suggestion of an EMU *without Germany*); through the strategic (the European Parliament's argument that the preparatory process should rest on the closest possible collaboration among core countries – above all France and Germany – likely to be the first participants in EMU – see Collignon 1994); to the modest but eminently practical (allow the weakest countries to make extensive transitional use of capital controls – Dürkop and Naser 1995). Yet realistic commentators were gradually forced to recognise that no substantial deviation from the formulae was politically conceivable because the underlying political compromise was too delicate (Winkler 1996). The most that could, perhaps, be hoped for was to relax, slightly, the criteria for participation in EMU in exchange for even more solid guarantees of counter-inflationary rectitude after it begins (Artis 1996).

Meanwhile the 'convergence process' put EU citizens, in their millions, on the rack. Ferocious expenditure cuts were used to reduce public sector deficits, even though these budgetary retrenchments, applied everywhere, rapidly became a major aggravating factor in the decline of European growth rates and thus of the problems of public finance which they were intended to resolve.

The economics involved is neither complex nor controversial: it is a standard procedure to distinguish structural (trend) deficits from cyclical deficits, arising from the decline in tax revenues and increases in welfare expenditure which take place in a recession. There is no good argument for drastic measures to reduce cyclical deficits, because they constitute a stabilising, counter-cyclical mechanism. But since the Maastricht Treaty does not pay much attention to the distinction, European governments promoted ever more stringent economies in the attempt to narrow the deficits induced, at least in part, by their collective resort to previous measures of the same kind. (For the macroeconomic dangers of this public deficit reduction, see Allsop and Vines 1996.) The political leadership of the EU was quite incapable of preventing, or even moderating, this self-destructive process. Increasingly, the Commission has confined itself to calling for ever more budgetary rigour (European Commission 1994a).

It must be conceded that the drive to restrict public spending does not arise simply from the Maastricht agenda. National governments are to some extent using Maastricht as an alibi for their own projects to establish more restrictive welfare regimes, to intensify market disciplines and to favour particular social strata. Only such motives can explain the tax reductions which, in many cases, accompany expenditure cuts and make the achievement of Maastricht public finance targets more difficult. But the speed and intensity of the adjustments which are being attempted, together with the damaging way in which they are combined with otherwise inexplicable monetary restriction, indicate that macroeconomic policies are very largely driven by the EMU process in reality as well as appearance.

France paralysed

Ironically, it is in France – the source of European strategy and the principal inspirer of the EMU project – that the 'convergence process' has proved most painful and disruptive. The presidential election of 1995 was barely over when Jacques Chirac began to sacrifice his promised programme on the altar of budgetary rigour. The reshuffling of the Juppé government in the autumn of the same year had no other purpose than to focus ministerial efforts on the drive for economies. These provoked a huge protest movement by the end of the year, but this lacked the focus of a clear alternative strategy at least in part because the main opposition grouping, the Socialist Party, was committed to the pursuit of identical ends by identical means. As economic activity stagnated, the room for manoeuvre in economic policy virtually vanished: as each new set of data revealed slower growth and, as a result, wider public sector deficits, the Chirac regime could only put forward more austerity proposals – aggravating the already exceptionally high and persistent unemployment and increasing social tensions which appeared to work only to the benefit of extreme right-wing, anti-EU, political forces.

The only possible source of relief would be a decisive relaxation of monetary policy which would both encourage private expenditures and reduce pressure on state finance. But here France and other member states are closely constrained by German policy. Again following the Maastricht formulae, the EU left monetary policy in the transition phase completely at national level: in practice this was to perpetuate the key currency role of the D-mark. Once again, however, the Bundesbank was reluctant to assume its inescapable international responsibilities – relaxation came at a grudging pace which did not give sufficient stimulus.

In fact, the post-1992 EMS, with very wide fluctuation margins, may even have taken pressure off the Bundesbank to consider the external effects of its policies because it is not obliged to intervene in support of the franc, while the Banque de France continues to hold it close to the old central rate and thus well above the new floor (Thomasberger 1995a).

Employment policy stagnates

The Commission has always tried to claim that monetary union, and the fiscal stabilisation which Maastricht necessitates, do not exhaust its economic strategy and that it also has plans for tackling Europe's persistently high levels of unemployment.

Since 1994 these plans have centred on a strategy of publicly sponsored investment in Europe-wide transport and communications networks. Ambitious proposals were put forward both by the European Parliament and by the Commission (see European Commission 1994). They had already been very much diluted to win the consent of national governments, but then failed to win agreement on finance at the Florence Council of June 1996 (Chapter 10). With the Florence Council, the fig-leaf covering the absence of an effective EU employment strategy was stripped away. All that the proposals could have achieved, in any case, was a mobilisation and coordination of national efforts to stimulate employment; the network programmes were little more than a symbol of the commitment that might be achieved. The reality so far, however, is that national policy is everywhere committed only to budgetary retrenchment and that Commission activity has been reduced to encouraging the latter in line with the dubious formulae of Maastricht. (For the debate on investment initiatives see Coates 1996.)

Towards two-speed Europe

If the *approach* to EMU has become dysfunctional for member state economies, its *implementation* promises little better. How the ECB will function when it begins operations remains obscure: it is doubtful whether it can do what it is designed to do and replicate the performance and procedures of the Bundesbank, since it will not be dealing with the highly coordinated German economy but with a much more complex and much less coherent assembly of economic relations on a continental scale. In this sense, as De Grauwe (1996) points out, the initiation rites imposed by Germany for participation in the EMU were always of doubtful effect – there is no way in which the rigours accepted today can guarantee anti-inflationary probity tomorrow. The Council of Finance Ministers at Dublin in 1996 attempted to introduce a post-EMU system of fiscal discipline which may prove effective, but it cannot, in advance, stabilise the environment in which the ECB will work. (The most rigorous proposals for such fiscal control, the Stabilisation Plan advanced by Germany, met considerable resistance from other member states: they are likely to be accepted in a modified form but it is still unclear how they will work.) Meanwhile the mood in the markets remained sceptical: Holtham (1996) points out that D-mark debts likely to be redeemed in euros carry a substantial interest rate premium. In any case, the aim, endorsed by Maastricht, of projecting a German institution onto the European plane, appears fundamentally misconceived. The ECB will be dealing with such a different, and difficult, situation that only a very wide interpretation of its remit is likely to prevent serious destabilisation.

What can be confidently predicted is that EMU in 1999 will immediately split the EU into two zones, according to whether countries are deemed to have met the convergence criteria. (For a full assessment see Arrowsmith 1995.) This situation itself is dangerous for the EU: frictions between insiders and outsiders may impair both commercial and political relations. Already France has tried to introduce a disciplinary regime to prevent competitive devaluations by outsiders, only to be told by the Commission that this approach was not acceptable. Nevertheless, the exclusion of a large number, probably a majority, of member states from what will be the EU's most powerful structure could turn EMU into a disintegrating strategy: outsiders will be constrained to accept less favourable positions on international credit markets while insiders such as France will fear the loss of market shares and investments to weak currency countries. Only a real relaxation of the fiscal criteria for entry can resolve this problem, since otherwise Italy, in particular, will be left to wrestle with its disequilibrated public finances for a very long time before it qualifies for the EMU club (see for example European Commission 1993).

The two projects

It has always been a strength of the movement for European integration that it has been able to redefine the content of the process of European construction in order to meet the political and economic priorities of the day. The danger of using other projects as vehicles to carry integration forward is that, although it makes Europe relevant to other programmes of reform, it may tie the fate of European institutions very closely to projects with an uncertain future. Thus in the 1990s, two projects became dangerously confused: on the one hand, the strengthening of EU institutions; on the other, the pursuit of monetary disinflation as this is now understood (that is, with the discretionary but restrictive policies of an independent central bank substituted for yesterday's discredited formula of reliance on some simple quantitative rule for the issue of money – see Chapter 8).

In most contemporary discussion, it is the second of these projects which is seen as necessary and practical (who does not believe, today, in a rigorous monetary policy?) while the first, European federalism, has come to seem distinctly old-fashioned (surely the last great scheme for a rational reordering of society to survive into the postmodern twilight). Such judgements may be as precarious as they are fashionable.

Disinflation by means of monetary policy alone, to begin with, rests on very shaky intellectual foundations. The fundamental premise of the argument for it – the separability of real and monetary phenomena – is not well established. All the economic reasoning involved relies on models in which one can specify, at any given point in time, a given set of productive possibilities, formalised as some aggregate production function. But, for short- to medium-term developments, there is no empirical basis for this *a priori*. Few products (except perhaps for leisure in the sense of Robert Lucas – that is to say, unemployment) can be turned out using purely current inputs to satisfy an immediate want. The vast mass of employment depends on some kind of investment activity – that is, it is part of some future-oriented strategy and thus conditioned by the view taken of future economic developments. The coexistence of these heterogeneous employing activities requires both the respect of monetary constraints by all agents and the perpetual recycling of financial resources from surplus to deficit units among them.

The relation between monetary constraints and financial flows is itself variable. In periods when the economy comes close to overall balance and is perceived to be on a stable path of development, a wide range of goods and assets will be treated as having monetary properties and will be acceptable as security for loans.

In such circumstances money, narrowly defined, does tend towards neutrality; monetary constraints do not disappear but they tend to become essentially microeconomic – they play the role of ensuring that weaker agents (such as households or small businesses) observe budget constraints, and of lowering transactions costs in the presence of imperfect information. The financial process of recycling from surplus to deficit units is smooth and unproblematic so that money and finance become relatively independent.

When, on the other hand, disequilibria and system-wide uncertainties call industrial projects and the established asset values which they support into question, the recycling of surpluses ceases to be a matter of routine. Monetary constraints tighten simultaneously for very large numbers of economic agents as wealth holders seek the safety of those assets which are perceived as liquid.

Thus the two conditions – monetary constraints and financial recycling – are now intimately related, so that the expectations which govern financial relations impact not only on the small fraction of economic activity which is usually identified as investment but on the monetary constraints faced by virtually all enterprises. All the experience of modern economies indicates that these constraints have to be *managed* at an aggregate level to avoid severe disruption in function of financial disequilibria and changing conventional views of the future. This creates a need for centralised refinance which places a constraint on monetary policy. The latter can only be safely devoted to price stabilisation in conditions of stability and confidence (see the discussion in Chapter 8).

It follows that the project of monetary disinflation depends on the successful control of real economic imbalances and the construction of a healthy and robust climate for investment; it can only succeed as part of a successful economic strategy with much wider objectives. (For an analysis of monetary policy which makes this argument see Minsky 1982.)

This raises the question of the other project – European construction –

and the contribution it might make to improved real economic performance. The possibilities here have hardly, as yet, been explored, largely because prevailing economic orthodoxies place excessive faith in the power of markets to secure real economic adaptation. Two areas seem of particular importance: the promotion of a favourable environment for long-run investment by the clear specification of developmental priorities – regional, ecological and so on – which can orient market agents; and the stabilisation of external conditions through the deployment of the collective influence of EU countries on a global level. Both ambitions certainly inspired the original drive for monetary integration but both have been submerged by the increasingly narrow and restrictive interpretation of the latter as an exercise in disinflation.

However, the balance between the two projects, in spite of Maastricht, is not fixed for all time. European monetary union itself will create a new situation and bring new priorities into view – above all the problem of persistently high levels of unemployment, for which the Union will no longer be able to escape direct responsibility. It is not only desirable but in fact necessary to begin to enrich the economic objectives of the EU to meet the responsibilities which EMU will place on it. One aspect of this will be the need for policies, beyond mere exhortation, to overcome the exclusion of non-participating states.

Britain without a project

The argument above has stressed the ambivalence of the projects behind the present phase of European construction. It is now necessary to insist that no project whatsoever, no view of economic reconstruction or of social or political renewal, inspires current British policy or the attitude of rejection fostered by 'Eurosceptics'. In fact this political force seems only to express the impasse at which British social and economic development has arrived; it constitutes the demand that British institutions escape the otherwise harsh judgement that might be made of them, and attempts to exculpate irresponsible national leadership by directing popular discontent against EU institutions, which in truth have little to do with either Britain's lamentable economic performance or its increasingly divided society (Grahl 1995). It is symptomatic of the vacuity of contemporary British political life that *non*-participation in EMU is virtually the only clear economic strategy that one can detect. On the right, Euroscepticism covers the exhaustion of a Thatcherite agenda, of which the few remaining elements are pursued simply as a *fuite-en-avant* from the chaotic consequences of the same strategy; while the Euroscepticism of the left has little more to offer than nostalgia for a nationally based economic programme which has been manifestly obsolete for over a decade (certainly since the failure of the experiment carried out in France between 1981 and 1984).

The obfuscation of contemporary British political discourse is so dense that it seems worthwhile to insist on the following clarifications. The logic of each point is direct but none of them is clearly perceived in what has become an unreal debate, concerned with little more than symbols.

Firstly, as argued in Chapter 6, Britain does not enjoy any significant measure of monetary 'sovereignty'. Its departure from the ERM in September 1992 did indeed permit a rapid and substantial relaxation of policy. This, however, was by no means a simple reassertion of national priorities as against external constraints: it was, in fact, only made possible by a unique monetary situation in the global economy. At that time, short-run interest rates in Frankfurt were some six percentage points higher than in New York. Under these exceptional, and probably unrepeatable, circumstances, it was indeed possible for Britain to cut its own rates in disregard of German policy. This was not an expression of 'independence' but merely a reorientation of policy from a European to an Atlanticist setting. Sterling is a weak and dependent currency; while it survives, it will have to be defended by offering a costly risk premium above the interest rates prevailing in the key currency – dollars, D-marks (or, in the future, euros) – which forms the indispensable external reference. The external constraint will always be primary in the formulation of British monetary policy, since a 'clean float' and the primacy of internal objectives is only possible for the very strongest economies – such as Japan – which inspire such confidence in international wealthholders that a depreciation today does not raise fears of a collapse tomorrow. The exceptional (and, from a European point of view, absurd) policy settings of 1990–92 apart, it is probably to Britain's advantage to link sterling to the D-mark rather than the dollar, because this is a more reliable point of reference for a country trading largely within Europe, and because interest rates can generally be expected to be lower with a European than with an American orientation.

Secondly, current heated debate on the question of an EMU referendum is fatuous. Immense industrial, commercial and financial interests are at stake in Britain's adhesion to, or absence from, the single currency. Largely because, until recently, EMU itself has been in doubt, these interests have not yet been expressed in a decisive way, although there are several straws in the wind, for example the increasing anxiety of City banks and financial institutions about lack of access to the euro payments system, TARGET; it seems that access may be limited to participants in EMU in the interests of monetary control (*The Guardian*, 6 October 1996). If a clear position in favour of participation in EMU is adopted by the majority of the corporate players, then the consultation of the electorate becomes meaningless and a foregone political conclusion. Britain is too weak in economic and industrial terms to enjoy the luxury of obstructing private sector strategies on such an issue. It is sometimes observed that the Eurosceptic drift of the Conservative Party has opened up an unprecedented gap between its political rhetoric and the views held in British boardrooms. It is necessary to draw the corollary that such a gap empties Conservative discourse of force and conviction.

Finally, Britain remains deeply, albeit silently, engaged in the Maastricht process. This is, in fact, the real content of the anguished governmental debate on fiscal relaxation versus consolidation. Kenneth Clarke explicitly recognised as Chancellor, some years ago, the claims of the convergence criteria on British public finance (such explicitness seems frequently to have got him into trouble). Although this motive for financial prudence is now unlikely to be stated openly, it remains a key determinant of the direction of British budgetary policy – under any conceivable government – and provides a rationale of such cogency as to constrain, or even override, the electoral logic of tax cuts.

Given these realities of British economic and political life, a negotiating position centred on the rhetoric of 'sovereignty' and on 'opt-outs' constitutes a simple failure to articulate authentic national interests. The modalities of EMU are of great importance to Britain; in spite of British industrial decline, its political status and its centrality to global financial developments guarantee that it can be influential in European financial and industrial affairs; the simplistic and rigid formulae agreed at Maastricht are not appropriate to British economic circumstances; no player can have the same possibilities as Britain to persuade Germany to amend these formulae or to interpret them with more flexibility. In this sense, the re-engagement of British political discourse with European (and domestic) realities has become one of the key conditions for the constructive implementation of the Maastricht programme.

Failure

One can introduce the programmatic section of this discussion by considering the possibility, real but fading, that EMU will not be achieved, that the experience of the 1990s will in the end replicate that of the 1970s and Delors will go the way of Werner.

Although such an outcome would be most welcome in Britain, where it would release several political groupings from a most painful dilemma, it seems clear that it is not in Britain's power to block a process from which it has already distanced itself. Britain, it is widely agreed, will not be among the pioneer members of the currency union; but it cannot, on the other hand, obstruct the formation of a union if France, Germany and their smaller neighbours are determined to achieve it. (Ironically, the minimalism of the Conservative British government may have reinforced that determination since all the other paths to further integration were narrowed or blocked by British representatives at the IGC.)

In fact, EMU seems to reproduce the decision-making conditions of the Schuman Plan. When asked how many participants were necessary, Adenauer replied 'two'. The same two countries control today the fate of the Maastricht agenda: without France the experiment will collapse as it would represent a simple extension of German hegemony – a politically unacceptable threat to the European project rather than a contribution to it; without Germany, the euro would be too weak and dependent on external circumstances to constitute a genuine advance of European construction.

It follows that the contingencies which might block or delay (every delay is dangerous as it could lead to blockage) the move to EMU are easy to specify: social revolt in France, if the population refuse the final heavy instalment of austerity required to place France at the rendezvous of 1999; bad faith in Germany, if political leaderships, having extracted the highest obtainable price for their participation, nevertheless decide that the sacrifice of the D-mark is too great a cost.

Neither contingency can be assigned an objective probability; but neither seems plausible – most of the costs of EMU have already been met; the prize is now only two years away; to retreat at this point would be to devalue vast amounts of political (and financial) capital. Rather than speculate on such an outcome one can insist on its drastic and unavoidable consequences for the EU. No alternative strategy exists with any lodgement in the European political class; no alternative compromise could be constructed when nations have been brought with such difficulty to hazard some elements of their sovereignty; political recrimination, against leaderships which have demanded such substantial sacrifices in an ultimately futile venture, would be comparable only to those which have overthrown governments in the wake of economic or military catastrophe.

No doubt the huge industrial and commercial interests linked to European integration would try to contain the most violent of the centrifugal forces that would be released. But that, surely, would be a question of damage limitation. One can easily develop conceptual alternatives to the Maastricht agenda, many of which might, in abstract terms, be preferable to it. But in the aftermath of such a setback they would remain concepts – no political dynamic would exist capable of bringing them into effect.

Easing the transition

It is appropriate, at this point, to pass from the contemplation of failure to the initiatives which might help to secure and consolidate success. The most concrete and immediate of these is a distinct alteration of macroeconomic stance.

At present, fiscal policy in most EU countries is – largely as a function of Maastricht itself – extremely restrictive. (One can add that immense efforts had already been made in this direction before the recession of 1991–92, induced by the malfunctioning of the EMS, wiped out most of the progress that had been made.) Although one can quarrel with the timing and speed of the fiscal correction which is being attempted, and the failure to coordinate it across the Union, the necessity of the correction is surely beyond dispute. Even if one maintains the widest Keynesian ambitions for fiscal stimulus, such a stimulus requires, as a first condition, that the governments which undertake it are creditworthy. Now it is a matter of arithmetic that public finance in the majority of member states is not sustainable. Thus a medium-term correction to limit deficits and stabilise indebtedness is unavoidable (see Chapter 10).

What can be changed is the monetary context of fiscal policy. The Bundesbank has carried out a significant easing since the climax of its frenzied post-unification squeeze in the summer of 1992 (for a discussion of the Bundesbank's policy errors at that time, see Chapter 6). But the steps taken have been too slow and reluctant. They hardly take into account the 30 per cent appreciation of the D-mark since 1992, which was partly a consequence of the ERM crises German policy triggered at that time. Bundesbank policies can be criticised on several grounds: they continue to focus on internal developments at a time when it is increasingly clear that the D-mark is destined for extinction and monetary policy will be translated to the European plane; they still refer to the invariably misleading monetary aggregates which have long since lost all meaning as intermediate targets, rather than to any objective assessment of inflationary pressures (for example OECD 1995). A consideration of the latter indicates that inflation is subdued in Germany itself, while in France the most sober commentators have begun to measure the risks of a straightforward deflation (Fitoussi 1996). Meanwhile, the consequences of the current fiscal retrenchment have not been drawn – it might be rational to use the threat of monetary restriction to concentrate government attention on the stability of public finance; but such pressure is self-defeating if governments are already committed to the most rapid stabilisation that can be endured. For countries like France and Germany – each with public debt around 50 per cent of annual GDP – a percentage point on interest rates adds half a percent to the PSBR. Likewise a corresponding reduction moves the deficit substantially downwards. These payoffs are even higher for heavily indebted states, such as Italy (De Grauwe 1996).

There are two dimensions to the necessary relaxation. As regards interest rates, Japan offers a good example of the potency of monetary expansion in an essentially stable economy; discount rates have been reduced to near zero for over a year to promote the refinance of both public and private agents in a situation characterised by financial stress but where underlying inflationary pressures are small. Even discount policy understates the extent of the relaxation since open market operations have made cash so cheap that banks have little incentive to make use of discount facilities. No doubt such measures strike the Germans as too colourful; but they indicate that there is substantial room for manoeuvre.

The second dimension is exchange rates. The Banque de France portrays any depreciation of the franc as dangerous to confidence and as likely to be counterproductive in provoking a rise in long-run interest rates or a wider risk premium on short rates. This is almost certainly correct if the depreciation results from unilateral French action. The same logic, however, does not apply to a realignment agreed with Germany and which is jointly declared to be the final readjustment prior to EMU. If a realignment is treated in this way, and followed by a qualitative rise in monetary coordination, eliminating sterilisation of monetary flows between France and Germany in anticipation of 1999, it could relieve pressure both on French unemployment and on German costs. (For the argument in favour of devaluation see Wyplosz 1996.) The dogma of Maastricht is that monetary competence – like God, indivisible – must remain at national level until it is, at one fell swoop, centralised. It would not be necessary to challenge this doctrine explicitly to make room for much closer and more effective monetary coordination.

Some straws in the wind suggest that the logic of this kind of argument is beginning to penetrate even the unimaginative thinking of German monetary authorities. The Bundesbank Council, addicted to announcement effects, chose recently to surprise by the scale of their interest rate cuts rather than by another exercise in immobilism; and Council members have even been quoted as calling for a more proactive approach to the forthcoming currency unification. It is desirable to deepen and accelerate this change of perspective. No doubt, achievements will fall short of what is possible – the optimal decision would be a temporary increase in the 'normative inflation' targets of the German authorities in order to levy an inflation tax on a European scale as the most effective financial preparation for EMU. But already the realities of the European political conjuncture are beginning to shift habitual responses.

Relaunching the employment programmes

The political necessity of an extension of EU employment initiatives was put clearly by the President of the European Parliament: 'More and more people associate the EU with social breakdown and the destruction of jobs. We must link it again with the creation of jobs and social progress. The success of monetary union depends on this' (Klaus Haensch, quoted in *The Guardian*, 19 September 1996). To this case we can add that the same kind of development has a solid economic rationale from any but the most one-sided neoliberal position. As investment, these initiatives can work to lengthen time-horizons and stabilise expectations, on the condition that they reflect a long-term political commitment. If the priorities are clear then private agents will begin to recognise them: for example, they will recognise that full economic integration does constitute the future for unified Germany to the extent that this has become a solid commitment of the Federal German government. At European level, such priorities embrace the development of peripheral and decayed industrial regions, respect for the environment, the adaptation of educational structures and so on. One aspect of this is just to guarantee the availability of complementary public inputs to private investors; more generally, uncertainties can only be limited by such positive action.

The second key economic aspect concerns the impact of active measures on employment itself. There is a strong case for EU-wide coordination to limit forms of labour market competition which would tend to nullify active measures or discourage their application at national level: this is clearly the case for moves on hours of work, the conditions of precarious workers and so on. (For the general argument for regulation see Deakin and Wilkinson 1996; for a discussion in the context of the EU see Alogoskoufis *et al.* 1995.) Without EU sanction one can also expect damaging forms of inter-state competition in such fields as job promotion, training schemes and so on – it is at least rational to exclude such expenditure, a recognised Union priority, from the 'convergence' accounting exercise. In a more positive view, tax reform – to reduce impositions on low-paid labour – is a central part of the strategy laid out in the Commission's employment strategy. Such measures, and the corresponding levy of a carbon tax or other environmental sources of revenue, can become the occasion of a new round of fiscal harmonisation and coordination. Progress without coordination is at present hardly conceivable because many of the benefits of such action will spillover into other member states while the costs remain a charge on domestic economic activity.

A first step in this direction would be to return to the European Commission's (1996) *Pact of Confidence for Employment*, which was refused adequate funding at the Florence Council, and use it as the basis for the promotion of employment issues to the top of the Union's agenda. It can be noted that a change in British policy would be the biggest single contribution to such a development. (For argument in favour of a European 'growth initiative' along lines similar to that proposed by the Commission, see Drèze and Malinvaud 1994.)

Fiscal centralisation

A significant centralisation of fiscal policy follows from EMU itself, in spite of the Maastricht formula, according to which monetary unification can take place while the entirety of public finance remains at national level. One can refer, firstly, to the implications of theory: no one has ever seriously argued that the EU constitutes an optimal currency area, but the development of centralised public finance would certainly move it nearer to being so. The issue of fiscal federalism is intensely disputed: commentators of neoliberal persuasion (Alesina, Perotti and Spolaore 1995) argue that decentralisation remains critical in order to maximise the territorial congruence between contributions and public services received; on the other hand, comparison with other developed federations indicates that mutual insurance among regions is an almost universal characteristic of actual monetary unions. Beyond this, the political theme of cohesion in the EU points to more developed redistributional capacities as a necessary compensation to the losers in the integration process. (A central authority with monetary, but without fiscal, powers might seem alarmingly suggestive of nineteenth-century economic policy – and could be expected to result in nineteenth-century degrees of instability.)

It seems that in this field there are significant opportunities to encourage a disengagement of the project of European construction – even though it is centred on monetary stabilisation – from the general thrust towards deregulation, privatisation and public service economies with which it has become so closely associated over the last ten years. This is because the success of

EMU may well hinge on the emergence of a centralised economic steering capacity within the currency union which only fiscal centralisation will make possible. Even the restrictive approach to public finance stemming from the Maastricht criteria becomes ambivalent in this context: ECOFIN has agreed in principle (September 1996) to tighten the centre's supervisory role over national budgets through the introduction of sanctions to enforce member state fiscal discipline. But such power is likely to attract a measure of responsibility – if weaker nations are prevented, by central rules, from a certain range of expenditures then, at least for those public functions regarded as common priorities, it may become incumbent on the centre to guarantee the appropriate continuity of policy.

Goodhart (1996) has suggested that such a centralisation of public finance is barely hidden behind the EMU project. He points out, in particular, that monetary union will disturb the existing structures of interest groups. At present, these are still very largely national; but when central control over a significant dimension of economic policy has been established, the congruence between national polities and groups concerned with taxation and expenditure issues is likely to become looser, so that fiscal policy at the level of the Union will no longer involve the simple bargaining among member states which is seen today. It will encourage, though, the interaction of increasingly transnational groupings.

It is certainly true that little can be done in this direction while fiscal developments continue to be governed by the outcome of the Edinburgh Council of 1992, because the establishment of the Cohesion Fund placed a ceiling on expenditures for the rest of the decade. Nor should one underestimate the resistance to any centralisation of public finance that was mounted by the last British government. The British attitude was well displayed in its insistence that a windfall underspend on agriculture be returned to member states rather than used to promote the Trans-European Networks which are the most prominent budgetary item arising out of the Commission's employment initiative. But the new British government may be less dogmatic than its predecessor, and the terms of the Edinburgh agreement will soon require renegotiation.

In any case, it is clear that a substantial degree of fiscal centralisation would follow from any recognition of the arguments put forward in the previous section, namely that employment-generating actions are a necessary political and economic complement to the Maastricht agenda established so far. This by no means absolves the EU, taken as a whole, from the need for a medium-term stabilisation of public debt and state deficits, since otherwise the public agencies which attempt to undertake stimulative action will not be creditworthy and their initiatives will lose much of their effectiveness. For this reason there is, at present, little chance of significant deficit-financed expenditure at Union level. But fiscal consolidation can be interpreted as a reconstruction and reinforcement of the active state rather than as another step towards the minimal state of the neoliberals. There are already some signs that this first interpretation finds widespread favour among the European political class – particularly in the readiness of France and Germany, according to recent reports (*The Guardian*, 13 September 1996) to introduce an explicit employment commitment into the IGC negotiations. The simple concern to defend the existing, however narrow, project for EMU can, here again, become a stepping stone to a fuller and more adequate agenda for the EU (Chapter 10).

Two-tier monetary Europe

All the proposals which are put forward here as possible growth points in a post-Maastricht Europe are mutually reinforcing. For instance, the alteration of macroeconomic stance, made necessary by the contractionary effects of 'convergence', would work to accelerate and ease the fiscal correction which, in the medium term, is unavoidable. Again, the relaunch of the EU's employment programme would compensate for these contractionary effects while preparing the way for more active and centralised public finance. The pursuit of fiscal coordination and harmonisation is likely to present opportunities for some budgetary centralisation. The same applies to the most difficult problem which the first achievement of EMU will present to the Union in the next century – that is, the division of member states into insiders and outsiders. This Maastricht-induced division is indeed full of dangers for the EU. In economic terms the outsiders will continue to pay high and variable interest rate premia as long as the exchange rate at which they will enter EMU is in doubt, even if some EMS-like arrangement pegs their currencies to the euro; at the same time the single market will be weakened even if the French nightmare of competitive devaluations by the outsiders is not realised. In political terms it is in the about-to-be-excluded countries, particularly Italy, where the will to achieve EMU is strongest. In Italy, the Europeanisation of policy areas is seen as a solution to intractable national difficulties rather than a source of constraints. If this aspiration is frustrated then the EU will be deprived of the most solid political support that exists at present for European construction.

All these factors imply that the reintegration of the Maastricht-divided Union will have to be given a very high priority in the post-EMU period. Now the conditions which can accelerate and ease the transition of the financially weaker economies are exactly those which have been discussed. An easier monetary stance will further the control of public finance, which is the biggest obstacle for Italy and the Mediterranean countries; while a certain centralisation of public expenditure would shield at least some key functions from the dislocation that fiscal stabilisation will certainly involve. The defence of a newly emerging EMU – even if one reckons narrowly in terms of price stability – requires the adoption of wider objectives, since otherwise the ECB will face major risks of financial or structural imbalances so acute as to necessitate inflationary refinance; and the exclusion of important member states will not avoid but may even accentuate these risks. In this way also, the very commitment of EU leaderships to the Maastricht agenda opens up some possibilities for a wider and more adequate conception of the integration process.

External implications of EMU

In Chapter 11 it was argued that it is impossible to exaggerate the potential implications of EMU for the global financial and monetary environment in which European economies function. What is at stake is the assertion of elements of social control in a sphere where disorganisation and unregulated market forces have given rise to qualitatively greater pressures on individual countries and to their penetration by financial forces which have rendered whole fields of domestic policy increasingly difficult over the last twenty-five years. EMU cannot transform this situation rapidly; but it does introduce a new dynamic into the global economy which can gradually alter external constraints in small and large ways. It is important to emphasise that nothing of the kind is possible for isolated member states, with the partial exception of Germany: the globalisation of economic and financial processes is irreversible; only global intervention and regulation of these processes is conceivable. EMU brings forward a body capable of strategic action at global level.

To avoid suggesting that huge and dramatic change is an early possibility, one can begin with the most modest but most secure example of the kind of developments which can be envisaged. In the territory of the currency union, monetary conditions will be protected from the destabilisation which has followed, over more than twenty-five years, every significant variation in the external value of the US dollar. Invariably, internal exchange rates have been put under pressure by dollar depreciation – a pattern that clearly continues into the summer of 1996. These are not trivial disturbances: to this day they place critical pressures on internal monetary policies and, sometimes, on the working of the internal market. EMU will eliminate them overnight in the countries using the euro – an additional motive for the most determined efforts to extend the single currency to as many member states as possible.

A second significant external theme is the taxation of capital income. As argued in Chapter 10, high degrees of capital mobility have tended to undermine the imposition of mobile, especially financial, resources. Policy reactions are not blocked by US attitudes; on the contrary it is plausibly argued that the US would welcome forceful European measures which could underpin its own fiscal stance, which it is extremely reluctant to dismantle (Chapter 11). The key obstacle in this field has been European disunity, and the failure to define a common position: EMU will not guarantee an effective, unified position but it will make such a position much easier to achieve.

Macroeconomic policy coordination, international financial regulation and world monetary reform were discussed in Chapter 11. It is not necessary to rehearse the details of that discussion, or to adopt an implausibly optimistic view of what might be achieved. It remains the case that the success of EMU would open a path towards more effective international coordination and, in the longer run, reform of the international monetary system. In no other sphere does European integration promise such a critical contribution to the welfare of European populations as is possible through the reassertion of some degree of social control over global credit and money markets.

Conclusion

If we take the danger of European war as remote, the EU is, or should be, about world government. To put the point in a less grandiloquent way, it is about social control over the terms and methods which govern the insertion of the European economies into the global economy. Globalisation is sometimes perceived in an undifferentiated or exaggerated way (Hirst and Thompson 1996 can be read as a necessary correction to apocalyptic views of globalisation even if one rejects their argument that constraints on national economies are qualitatively unchanged; for other views see Boyer and Drache 1996). Nevertheless it is an unavoidable and irreversible process, full of dangers for European populations. The EU can influence this process in two ways: internally, by organising economic life to improve adaptation to external constraints and by redistributing some of the gains and losses that occur; but it can also act externally to modify the constraints themselves, using its immense political, commercial and, in the future, monetary powers to obtain advantageous reforms in the global economy itself through compromises with the other principal actors. Monetary union as such is a logical part of this mission: it eliminates an enfeebling fragmentation of European interests and makes possible a wider, more coordinated and deeper influence in a key dimension of the emerging global economy – financial and monetary relations.

However, the forms and modalities of monetary integration agreed at Maastricht turn away from these responsibilities; under the obsessive, and self-defeating, preoccupation with internal price stability, European institutions were designed in ways that negate the possibilities of enhanced social control that are the only constructive rationale for the EU itself. Influenced by the same worship of spontaneous, market-determined adjustment to all problems that seized the EC during the 1980s, European leaders designed a mechanism that will in fact fail to shield either citizens or member states from the harshest aspects of ever-tightening external constraints.

It is certainly possible for the EU to fail in the only task which gives it meaning – the use of the strength of unity to alter the environment in which its peoples live. In this case European integration will prove, in retrospect, to be a self-liquidating enterprise, a mere moment in the dissolution of its member states into an increasingly uncontrolled global economy. What is not possible is for its present projects – the single market, EMU – to succeed as strategies for internal stabilisation and modernisation in the absence of wider and more far-reaching objectives.

The fragility, and lack of democracy, which characterise EU political relations make it impossible to achieve a comprehensive renegotiation of the Maastricht agreement. But to abandon it would not serve European interests because it would only throw European peoples back on national state structures that are increasingly unable to exert decisive leverage over external conditions, and this in circumstances that would make the external environment more dangerous by promoting damaging forms of rivalry among European countries themselves.

It follows that the least worst strategy, for those concerned with the deteriorating social climate and economic performance of European countries, is to accept the Maastricht agenda while proposing gradualist and, initially, piecemeal strategies for its amendment and transformation in the desired directions: priority to employment, rather than price, stability; interventions, internal and external, which genuinely benefit the most disadvantaged groups and regions of the EU. This strategic orientation has to recognise multiple political, financial and economic limits that cannot as yet be addressed. But it can draw strength from the circumstance that the Maastricht agenda, in its present form, is quite unworkable, the reflection of a damaged, utopian, project for a universal market to which all political instances would be subordinated. Thus the incoherences, inadequacies and gaps of the existing pattern of European advance may provide points of entry for a movement aimed at its enrichment and correction.

However, the modesty of the immediate goals which can be formulated in this way should not be confused with a lack of ambition as regards ultimate objectives. The latter include both the comprehensive modernisation, in a positive way, of internal systems of social protection and a growing contribution to a more stable and equitable world order. Nothing less, in any case, would be compatible with the values which inspired the project of European integration. Only if a wide vision informs the inevitably constrained attempts at immediate amelioration will these attempts have some prospect of success.

Further reading

For a recent account of the problems of monetary union see Arrowsmith and Taylor (1996). For the debate in Britain see the symposium in the *Political Quarterly* (including Palmer, Wolf and Radice, all 1996). An extremely optimistic argument for British participation is made by Johnson (1996); Currie (1995) is more balanced. It is impossible in Britain to avoid the views of the Eurosceptics who had, by late 1996, produced a veritable moral panic; a cool presentation of this point of view is in Minford (1992). MacShane (1996) endeavours to counter the scepticism of the left.

References

Aglietta, M. (ed.) (1985) *L'ECU et la Vielle Dame*, Economica, Paris.

Aglietta, M. (1986) *La Fin des Devises Clés*, La Découverte, Paris.

Aglietta, M. (1991) 'Stabilité dynamique et transformations des régimes monétaires internationales' in Boyer, R., Chavance, B. and Godard, O. (eds) *Les Figures de l'Irréversibilité en Économie*, Éditions de l'École des Haute Études en Sciences Sociales, Paris.

Aglietta, M. (1992) 'Savings, Financial Innovations and Growth' in Steinherr, *op. cit.*

Aglietta, M. (1992a) 'Genèse des banques centrales et légitimité de la monnaie', *Annales*, 3, May–June.

Aglietta, M., Brender, A. and Coudert, V. (1990) *Globalisation Financière: l'aventure obligée*, Economica, Paris.

Aglietta, M. and Orléan, A. (1982) *La Violence de la Monnaie*, PUF, Paris.

Alesina, A., Perotti, R. and Spolaore, E. (1995) 'Together or Separately: Issues on the Costs and Benefits of Political and Fiscal Unions', *European Economic Review*, 39, 3–4.

Alesina, A. and Summers, L. (1993) 'Central Bank Independence and Macroeconomic Performance: some comparative evidence', *Journal of Money, Credit and Banking*, 25.

Allsop, C., Davies, G. and Vines, D. (1995) 'Regional Macroeconomic Policy, Fiscal Federalism and European Integration', *Oxford Review of Economic Policy*, 11, 2.

Allsopp, C., Jenkinson, T. and O'Shaughnessy, T. (1990) 'The Balance of Payments and International Economic Integration', *Oxford Review of Economic Policy*, 6, 3, Autumn.

Allsop, C. and Vines, D. (1996) 'Fiscal Policy and EMU', *National Institute Economic Review*, 158, October.

Alogoskoufis, G. *et al.* (1995) 'Unemployment: choices for Europe', *Monitoring European Integration*, 5, CEPR, London.

Arestis, P. (1996) 'Post-Keynesian Economics: towards coherence', *Cambridge Journal of Economics*, 20, 1, January.

Argy, V. (1994) *International Macroeconomics: theory and policy*, Routledge, London.

Arndt, H. (1994) *Lehrbuch der Wirtschaftsentwicklung*, Duncker und Humblot, Berlin.

Arrow, K. and Hahn, F. (1971) *General Competitive Analysis*, Holden-Day, San Francisco.

Arrowsmith, J. (1995) 'Economic and Monetary Union in a Multi-tier Europe', *National Institute Economic Review*, 152, 2, May.

Arrowsmith, J. and Taylor, C. (1996) 'Moving Towards EMU: the challenges ahead', *National Institute Economic Review*, 158, October.

Artis, M. (1996) 'Alternative Transitions to EMU', *Economic Journal*, 106, 437, July.

Artis, M. and Lewis, M. (1993) 'Après le Déluge: monetary and exchange rate policy in Britain and Europe', *Oxford Review of Economic Policy*, 9, 3, Autumn.

Bank of England (1991) 'The Exchange Rate Mechanism of the European Monetary System: a review of the literature', *Bank of England Quarterly Bulletin*, 31, 1, February.

Bank of England (1992) 'Operation of Monetary Policy', *Bank of England Quarterly Bulletin*, 32, 4, November.

Barro, R. (1974) 'Are Government Bonds Net Wealth?', *Journal of Political Economy*, 82, 6.

Barro, R. (1989) 'The Ricardian Approach to Budget Deficits', *Journal of Economic Perspectives*, 3, 2.

Barro, R. and Gordon, D. (1983) 'A Positive Theory of Monetary Policy in a Natural Rate Model', *Journal of Political Economy*, 91.

Benassy, J.-P. (1986) *Macroeconomics: an introduction to the non-Walrasian approach*, Academic Press, London.

Bénassy-Quéré, A. (1996) 'Potentialities and Opportunities of the Euro as an International Currency', *European Commission: Directorate-General for Economic and Financial Affairs – Economic Papers*, 115, July.

Benetti, C. and Cartelier, J. (1980) *Marchands, Salariat et Capitalistes*, Maspero, Paris.

Benink, H.A. (1993) *Financial Integration in Europe*, Kluwer, Dordrecht.

Benston, G. (1994) 'Universal Banking', *Journal of Economic Perspectives*, 8, 3, Summer.

Black, S. (1985) 'International Money and International Monetary Arrangements' in Jones and Kenen, *op. cit.*

Blackburn, K. and Sola, M. (1993) 'Speculative Currency Attacks and Balance of Payments Crises', *Journal of Economic Surveys*, 7, 2, June.

Blanchard, O. (1985) 'Debts, Deficits and Finite Horizons', *Journal of Political Economy*, 93, 2.

Blanchard, O. and Muet, P.-A. (1993) 'Competitiveness through Disinflation: an assessment of the French macroeconomic strategy', *Economic Policy*, 16, April.

Blinder, A. (1994) 'On Sticky Prices: academic theory meets the real world' in Mankiw, N. (ed.) *Monetary Policy*, NBER, Chicago.

Bordes, C., Girardin, E. and Mélitz, J. (1995) *European Currency Crises and After*, Manchester University Press, Manchester.

Boyer, R. (1990) *The Regulation School: a critical introduction*, Columbia University Press, New York.

Boyer, R., Chavance, B. and Godard, O. (eds) (1991) *Les figures de l'irréversibilité en économie*, Éditions de l'École des Hautes Études en Sciences Sociales, Paris.

Boyer, R. and Drache, D. (eds) *States against Markets: the limits of globalisation*, Routledge, London.

Brender, A., Gaye, P. and Kessler, V. (1986) *L'Après-Dollar*, Economica, Paris.

de Brie, C. (1996) 'Les Européens dans la nasse de l'austerité', *Le Monde Diplomatique*, July.

Britton, A. and Mayes, D. (1992) *Achieving Monetary Union in Europe*, Sage, London.

Brock, W. (1990) 'Overlapping Generations Models with Money and Transactions Costs' in Friedman and Hahn, *op. cit.*

Brunner, K. and Meltzer, A. (1971) 'The Use of Money: money in the theory of an exchange economy', *American Economic Review*, 61; reprinted in Brunner, K. and Meltzer, A. (1989) *Monetary Economics*, Blackwell, Oxford.

Brunner, K. and Meltzer, A. (1990) 'Money Supply' in Friedman and Hahn, *op. cit.*

Buiter, W. (1988) 'Death, Birth, Productivity Growth and Debt Neutrality', *Economic Journal*, 98, 391, June.

Buiter, W., Corsetti, G. and Roubini, N. (1993) 'Excessive Deficits: sense and nonsense in the Treaty of Maastricht', *Economic Policy*, 16, April.

Burkitt, B. and Baimbridge, M. (1994) *An Independent Central Bank: an end to democratic economic policies?*, Full Employment Forum, London.

de Cecco, M. (1984) *The International Gold Standard: money and empire*, 2nd edition, Pinter, London.

Central Banking (1995) 'Symposium on the Bundesbank', *Central Banking*, 6, 1, Summer.

Chamberlin, E. (1933) *The Theory of Monopolistic Competition*, Harvard University Press, Cambridge, Mass.

Clower, R. (1965) 'The Keynesian Counter-Revolution: a theoretical appraisal' in Hahn, F. and Brechling, F. (eds) *The Theory of Interest Rates*, Macmillan, London; reprinted in Clower (1969) *op. cit.*

Clower, R. (1967) 'Foundations of Monetary Theory', *Western Economic Journal*, 6; reprinted in Clower (1969), *op. cit.*

Clower, R. (ed.) (1969) *Monetary Theory*, Penguin, Harmondsworth.

Coase, R. (1988) *The Firm, the Market and the Law*, University of Chicago Press, Chicago.

Coates, K. (1996) *Dear Commissioner: an exchange of letters*, Spokesman, Nottingham.

Cobham, D. (ed.) (1994) *Europe's Monetary Upheavals*, Manchester University Press, Manchester.

Cobham, D. (1996) 'Causes and Effects of the European Monetary Crises of 1992–93', *Journal of Common Market Studies*, 34, 4, December.

Cohen, B. (1978) *Organising the World's Money: the political economy of international monetary relations*, Macmillan, London.

Collignon, S. (with Bofinger, P., Johnson, C. and de Maigret, B.) (1994) *Europe's Monetary Future: a study prepared at the request of the European Parliament*, Pinter, London.

Committee for the Study of Economic and Monetary Union (1989) *Report on Economic and Monetary Union in the European Union*, EC, Luxembourg.

Cooper, R. (1994) 'Yes to European Monetary Unification, but No to the Maastricht Treaty' in Steinherr, *op. cit.*

Cooper, R. and John, A. (1988) 'Coordinating Coordination: Failures in Keynesian Models', *Quarterly Journal of Economics*, 103, August; reprinted in Mankiw and Romer, *op. cit.*, vol 2.

Copeland, L. (1994) *Exchange Rates and International Finance*, 2nd edition, Addison-Wesley, Wokingham.

Corbett, J. (1987) 'International Perspectives on Financing: evidence from Japan', *Oxford Review of Economic Policy*, 3, 4.

Cuikerman, A. (1992) *Central Bank Strategy, Credibility and Independence: theory and evidence*, MIT Press, Cambridge, Mass.

Currie, D. (1995) 'UK and European Monetary Union: why we should not stand aside', *Economic Outlook*, 19, 3.

Currie, D. and Levine, P. (1993) *Rules, Reputation and Macroeconomic Policy Coordination*, CUP, Cambridge.

Deakin, S. and Wilkinson, F. (1996) *Labour Standards – Essential to Economic and Social Progress*, Institute of Employment Rights, London.

Debreu, G. (1959) *Theory of Value: an axiomatic analysis of economic equilibrium*, Wiley, New York.

De Grauwe, P. (1989) *International Money: post-war trends and theories*, Clarendon, Oxford.

De Grauwe, P. (1992) *The Economics of Monetary Integration*, OUP, Oxford (2nd edition 1994).

De Grauwe, P. (1995) 'Monetary Policies in the EMS' in Bordes, Girardin and Mélitz, *op. cit.*

De Grauwe, P. (1995a) 'Alternative Strategies Towards Monetary Union', *European Economic Review*, 39, 3/4, April.

De Grauwe, P. (1996) 'Monetary Union and Convergence Economics', *European Economic Review*, 40, 3–5, April.

De Grauwe, P. and Papademos, L. (eds) (1990) *The European Monetary System in the 1990's*, Longman, London.

De Grauwe, P. and van Santen, J. (1991) 'Speculative Dynamics and Chaos in the Foreign Exchange Market' in O'Brien, R. and Hewin, S. (eds) *Finance and the International Economy*, vol. 4, OUP, Oxford.

Delors, J. (1992) *Le Nouveau Concert Européen*, Odile Jacob, Paris.

Dobson, W. (1991) *Economic Policy Coordination: requiem or prologue?*, Institute for International Economics, Washington DC.

Dornbusch, R. (1976) 'Expectations and Exchange Rate Dynamics', *Journal of Political Economy*, 84.

References

Dow, J. and Saville, I. (1990) *A Critique of Monetary Policy*, 2nd edition, Clarendon, Oxford.

Downes, P. and Vaez-Zadeh, R. (eds) (1991) *The Evolving Role of Central Banks*, IMF, Washington.

Doyle, C. and Weale, M. (1994) 'Do We Really Want an Independent Central Bank?', *Oxford Review of Economic Policy*, 10, 3, Autumn.

Drèze, J. and Malinvaud, E. (1994) 'Growth and Employment: the scope of a European initiative', *European Economic Review*, 38, 3/4, April.

Driffill, J., Mizon, G. and Alph, A. (1990) 'Costs of Inflation' in Friedman and Hahn, *op. cit.*, vol. 2.

Dürkop, U. and Naser, R. (1995) 'Back to Basics – Reformen in Europäischen Währungssystem' in Thomasberger, *op. cit.*

Egebo, T. and Englander, A. (1992) 'Institutional Commitments and Policy Credibility: a critical survey and empirical evidence from the ERM', *OECD Economic Studies*, 18, Spring.

Eichengreen, B. (ed.) (1985) *The Gold Standard in Theory and History*, Methuen, New York.

Eichengreen, B. (1992) 'Should the Maastricht Treaty be Saved?', *Princeton Studies in International Finance*, 74, December.

Eichengreen, B. (1993) *Reconstructing Europe's Trade and Payments: the European Currency Union*, Manchester University Press, Manchester.

Eichengreen, B. (1994) *International Monetary Arrangements for the 21st Century*, Brookings, Washington DC.

Eichengreen, B. (1994a) 'Fiscal Policy and EMU' in Eichengreen and Frieden, *op. cit.*

Eichengreen, B. (1995) 'The European Payments Union: an efficient mechanism for rebuilding Europe's trade?' in Eichengreen, B. (ed.) *Europe's Post-War Recovery*, CUP, Cambridge.

Eichengreen, B. (ed.) (1995a) *Europe's Post-War Recovery*, CUP, Cambridge.

Eichengreen, B. and Bayoumi, T. (1994) 'The Political Economy of Fiscal Restriction: implications for Europe from the US', *European Economic Review*, 38, April.

Eichengreen, B. and Frieden, J. (1994) *The Political Economy of European Monetary Unification*, Westview, Oxford.

Eichengreen, B. and Portes, R. (1987) 'The Anatomy of Financial Crises' in Portes and Swoboda, *op. cit.*

Eichengreen, B. and Wyplosz, C. (1993) 'The Unstable EMS', *Brookings Papers in Economic Activity*, 1.

Emminger, O. (1986) *D-Mark, Dollar, Wärungskrisen*, Deutsche Verlags-Anstalt, Stuttgart.

European Commission (1990) 'One Market, One Money', *European Economy*, 44, October; published in book form as Emerson, M. *et al.* (1992) *One Market, One Money: an evaluation of the potential costs and benefits of forming an economic and monetary union*, OUP, Oxford.

European Commission (1993) 'The Economic and Financial Situation in Italy', *European Economy*, reports and studies, 1.

European Commission (1993a) *Employment in Europe*, Luxembourg.

European Commission (1994) *White Paper: Growth, Competitiveness, Employment: the challenges and ways forward into the 21st century*, EU, Luxembourg.

European Commission (1994a) 'Towards Greater Fiscal Discipline', *European Economy*, reports and studies, 3.

European Commission (1996) *Pact of Confidence for Employment*, Brussels.

Filc, W. (1994) 'Credibility of German Monetary Policy on the Road towards EMU' in Steinherr, *op. cit.*

Fitoussi, J.-P. (1996) 'L'économie européenne prise au piège', *Le Monde*, 29 August.

Fitoussi, J.-P. and Phelps, E. (1988) *The Slump in Europe*, Blackwell, Oxford.

Fitoussi, J.-P. *et al.* (1993) *Competitive Disinflation: the Mark and Budgetary Politics in Europe*, OUP, Oxford.

Frankel, J. (1993) 'Zen and the Art of Modern Macroeconomics: the search for perfect nothingness' in Frankel, J. (ed.) *On Exchange Rates*, MIT Press, Cambridge, Mass.

Fratianni, M. and von Hagen, J. (1990) 'Asymmetries and Realignments in the EMS' in De Grauwe and Papademos, *op. cit.*

Friedman, B. and Hahn, F. (eds) (1990) *Handbook of Monetary Economics*, 2 vols, North-Holland, Amsterdam.

Funabashi, Y. (1989) *Managing the Dollar: from the Plaza to the Louvre*, 2nd edition, Institute for International Economics, Washington DC.

Garber, P. and Taylor, M. (1995) 'Sand in the Wheels of Foreign Exchange Markets: a sceptical note', *Economic Journal*, 105, 428, January.

Gardiner, E. and Perraudin, W. (1993) 'Asymmetries in the ERM', *IMF Staff Papers*, 40, 2, June.

Gershenkron, A. (1962) *Economic Backwardness in Historical Perspective*, Harvard University Press, Cambridge, Mass.

Giavazzi, F. and Spaventa, L. (1989) 'Italy: the real effects of inflation and dis-inflation', *Economic Policy*, 8, April.

Giersch, H., Paqué, K.-H. and Schmieding, H. (1992) *The Fading Miracle: four decades of market economy in Germany*, CUP, Cambridge.

Gilbert, C. *et al.* (1996) 'The World Bank: its functions and future', *ESRC Global Institutions*, Working Paper 15.

Giovannini, A. (1989) 'National Tax Systems versus the European Capital Market', *Economic Policy*, 9, October.

Giovannini, A. and Mayer, C. (eds) (1991) *European Financial Integration*, CUP, Cambridge.

Goodhart, C. (1988) *The Evolution of Central Banks*, MIT Press, Cambridge, Mass.

Goodhart, C. (1994) 'Central Bank Independence', *Journal of International and Comparative Economics*, 3; reprinted in Goodhart (1995), *op. cit.*

Goodhart, C. (1995) *The Central Bank and the Financial System*, Macmillan, London.

Goodhart, C. (1995a) 'Money Supply Control: base or interest rates' in Goodhart (1995), *op. cit.*

Goodhart, C. (1996) 'European Monetary Integration', *European Economic Review*, 40, 3–5, April.

Goodhart, C. and Schoenmaker, D. (1995) 'Institutional Separation between Supervisory and Monetary Agencies' in Goodhart (1995), *op. cit.*

Goodhart, C. and Schoenmaker, D. (1995a) 'Price Stability and Financial Fragility' in Goodhart (1995), *op. cit.*

Grahl, J. (1988) 'Productivity Slowdown and Financial Tensions' in Arestis, P. (ed.) *Post-Keynesian Monetary Economics: new approaches to financial modelling*, Edward Elgar, Aldershot.

Grahl, J. (1990) 'Hard TERMS', *Marxism Today*, November.

Grahl, J. (1993) 'Labour and the Schuman Plan' in Fyrth, J. (ed.) *Labour's High Noon*, Lawrence and Wishart, London.

Grahl, J. (1995) 'Euroscepticism and the Major Government', *Annales de l'Université de Savoie*, 19.

Grahl, J. and Teague, P. (1989) 'Labour Flexibility in West Germany, Britain and France', *West European Politics*, April.

Grahl, J. and Teague, P. (1990) *The Big Market: 1992 and the future of the European Community*, Lawrence and Wishart, London.

Grahl, J. and Thompson, G. (1995) 'The Prospects for European Economic Integration: macroeconomics, development models and growth' in Arestis, P. and Chick, V. (eds) *Finance, Development and Structural Change*, Edward Elgar, Aldershot.

Greenaway, D. (ed.) (1992) 'Policy Forum: the determinants of economic growth', *Economic Journal*, 102, 412, May.

Greenaway, D. (ed.) (1995) 'Policy Forum: sand in the wheels of international finance', *Economic Journal*, 105, 428, January.

Grilli, V. (1989) 'Seigniorage in Europe' in de Cecco, M. and Giovannini, A. (eds) *A European Central Bank? perspectives on monetary unification after ten years of the EMS*, CEPR/CUP, Cambridge.

Gros, D. and Thygesen, N. (1992) *European Monetary Integration: from the European Monetary System to monetary union*, Longman, London.

Hahn, F. (1965) 'On Some Problems of Proving the Existence of an Equilibrium in a Monetary Economy' in Hahn and Brechling, *op. cit.*; reprinted in Clower (1969).

Hawtrey, R. (1932) *The Art of Central Banking*, Longmans, London (reprinted 1962 Cass, London).

Hayek, F. (1976) 'Choice in Currency: a way to stop inflation', *Occasional Paper*, 48, Institute for Economic Affairs, London.

Hellwig, M. (1991) 'Banking, Financial Intermediation and Corporate Finance' in Giovannini and Mayer, *op. cit.*

Henderson, R. (1993) *European Finance*, McGraw-Hill, Maidenhead.

Herr, H. (1991) 'External Constraints on Fiscal Policies' in Matzner, E. and Streeck, W. (eds) (1991) *Beyond Keynesianism: the socio-economics of production and full employment*, Edward Elgar, Aldershot.

Hicks, J. (1974) *The Crisis in Keynesian Economics*, Blackwell, Oxford.

Hirst, P. and Thompson, G. (1996) *Globalisation in Question*, Polity Press, Oxford.

Holtham, G. (1996) 'The Maastricht Conception of EMU is Obsolete', *Political Quarterly*, 67, 3, July–September.

Horwitz, S. (1992) *Monetary Evolution, Free Banking and Economic Order*, Westview Press, Boulder, Col.

Inman, R. and Rubinfeld, D. (1996) 'Designing Tax Policy in Federalist Economies: an overview', *Journal of Public Economics*, 60, 3.

Italianer, A. and Ohly, C. (1994) 'Towards Greater Fiscal Discipline: an overview', *European Economy*, reports and studies, 3.

Jeanneney, J.-M. (1994) 'De Bretton Woods à la Jamaique: contestations françaises', *Économie Internationale*, 59, 3me trimestre.

Johnson, C. (1996) *In with the Euro; Out with the Pound*, Penguin, Harmondsworth.

Jones, R. and Kenen, P. (1985) *Handbook of International Economics*, vol. 2, North-Holland, Amsterdam.

de Kam, C., Sterks, C. and de Haan, J. (1994) 'An Assessment of Margins for Consolidation in the Member States of the European Union', *European Economy*, reports and studies, 3.

Kaplan, J. and Schleiminger, G. (1989) *The European Payments Union: financial diplomacy in the 1950's*, Clarendon, Oxford.

Kenen, P. (1969) 'The Theory of Optimal Currency Areas: an eclectic view' in Mundell, R. and Swoboda, A. (eds) *Monetary Problems of the International Economy*, University of Chicago Press, Chicago.

Kenen, P. (1989) *Exchange Rates and Policy Coordination*, University of Michigan Press, Ann Arbor.

Kenen, P. (1995) *Economic and Monetary Union in Europe: moving beyond Maastricht*, CUP, Cambridge.

Kindleberger, C. (1978) *Manias, Panics, and Crashes*, Basic Books, New York.

Kindleberger, C. (1981) 'Quantity and Price, Especially in Financial Markets', in *International Money: a collection of essays*, George Allen and Unwin, London.

Kindleberger, C. (1987) *The World in Depression*, revised edition, Penguin, Harmondsworth.

Kiyotaki, N. and Wright, R. (1989) 'On Money as a Medium of Exchange', *Journal of Political Economy*, 97.

Knodell, J. (1994) 'Financial Institutions and Contemporary Economic Performance' in Bernstein, M. and Adler, D. (eds) *Understanding American Economic Decline*, CUP, Cambridge.

Kornai, J. (1982) *Growth, Shortage and Efficiency: a macrodynamic model of the socialist economy*, Blackwell, Oxford.

References

Kreisky, B. (ed.) (1989) *A Programme for Full Employment in the 1990's: report of the Commission on Employment Issues in Europe*, Pergamon, Oxford.

Kreps, D. (1990) *Game Theory and Economic Modelling*, Clarendon, Oxford.

Krugman, P. (1979) 'A Model of Balance of Payments Crises', *Journal of Money, Credit and Banking*, 11.

Krugman, P. (1989) *Exchange Rate Instability*, MIT Press, London.

Krugman, P. (1990) 'Policy Problems of a Monetary Union' in De Grauwe and Papademos, *op. cit.*

Krugman, P. (1992) *Currencies and Crises*, MIT Press, Cambridge, Mass.

Krugman, P. (1994) *The Age of Diminished Expectations*, MIT Press, Cambridge, Mass.

Krugman, P. and Miller, M. (1992) 'Why Have a Target Zone?', *Warwick Economic Research Papers*.

Krugman, P. and Miller, M. (1992a) *Exchange Rate Targets and Currency Bands*, CUP, Cambridge.

Kydland, F. and Prescott, E. (1977) 'Rules versus Discretion: the inconsistency of optimal plans', *Journal of Political Economy*, 85.

Lakatos, I. (1970) 'Falsification and the Methodology of Scientific Research Programmes' in Lakatos, I. and Musgrave, A. (eds) *Criticism and the Growth of Knowledge*, CUP, Cambridge.

Lakatos, I. and Musgrave, A. (eds) *Criticism and the Growth of Knowledge*, CUP, Cambridge.

Layard, R. *et al.* (1984) 'The Case for Unsustainable Growth', *European Commission Economic Papers*, 31.

Layard, R., Nickell, S. and Jackman, R. (1994) *The Unemployment Crisis*, OUP, Oxford.

Leijonhufvud, A. (1967) 'Keynes and the Keynesians: a suggested interpretation', *American Economic Review*, 57, 2; reprinted in Clower (1969).

Lewis, A. (1978) *Growth and Fluctuations 1870–1913*, Allen and Unwin, London.

Lipietz, A. (1985) *The Enchanted World: inflation, credit and the world crisis*, Verso, London.

Lipietz, A. (1987) *Mirages and Miracles*, Verso, London.

Lucas, R. (1977) 'Understanding Business Cycles' in Brunner, K. and Meltzer, A. (eds) *Stabilisation of the Domestic and International Economy*, vol. 5 of Carnegie-Rochester Series on Public Policy, North-Holland, Amsterdam; reprinted in Lucas, R. (1983) *Studies in Business-Cycle Theory*, MIT Press, Cambridge, Mass.

Lucas, R. (1983) *Studies in Business-Cycle Theory*, MIT Press, Cambridge, Mass.

Lucas, R. and Stokey, N. (1987) 'Money and Interest in a Cash-in-Advance Economy', *Econometrica*, 55.

McKinnon, R. (1993) 'International Money in Historical Perspective', *Journal of Economic Literature*, 1.

MacShane, D. (1996) 'Left out of Europe?', *Fabian Society Discussion Paper*, 26.

Makowski, L. (1989) 'Keynes's Liquidity Preference Theory: a suggested re-interpretation' in Hahn, F. (ed.) *The Economics of Missing Markets, Information and Games*, OUP, Oxford.

Mankiw, N. (ed.) (1994) *Monetary Policy*, NBER, Chicago.

Mankiw, N. and Romer, D. (eds) (1991) *New Keynesian Economics*, 2 vols, MIT Press, Cambridge, Mass. and London.

Marglin, S. and Schor, J. (eds) (1990) *The Golden Age of Capitalism: reinterpreting the postwar experience*, Clarendon, Oxford.

Marsh, D. (1992) *The Bundesbank: the bank that rules Europe*, Heinemann, London.

Mathes, H. (1994) '"Damocles Shadowing": an innovation in the second phase of EMU', *Intereconomics*, 29, 2, March/April.

Matzner, E. and Streeck, W. (eds) (1991) *Beyond Keynesianism: the socio-economics of production and full employment*, Edward Elgar, Aldershot.

Mayer, C. (1988) 'New Issues in Corporate Finance', *European Economic Review*, 32.

Meese, R. (1990) 'Currency Fluctuations in the Post-Bretton Woods Era', *Journal of Economic Perspectives*, 4, 1, Winter.

Meese, R. and Rogoff, K. (1983) 'Empirical Exchange Rate Models of the 1970's: do they fit out of sample?', *Journal of International Economics*, 14.

Mélitz, J. (1994) 'French Monetary Policy and Recent Speculative Attacks on the Franc', in Cobham (1994), *op. cit.*

Miller, M. and Modigliani, F. (1958) 'The Cost of Capital, Corporation Finance and the Theory of Investment', *American Economic Review*, 53.

Milward, A. (1992) *The European Rescue of the Nation State*, Routledge, London.

Minford, P. (ed.) (1992) *The Cost of Europe*, Manchester University Press, Manchester.

Minsky, H. (1982) *Inflation, Recession and Economic Policy*, Wheatsheaf, Brighton.

Minsky, H. (1986) *Stabilising an Unstable Economy*, Yale University Press, New Haven, Conn.

Mourmouras, I. (1997) *Greek Monetary Policy and EMU*, Springer, New York, forthcoming.

Muet, P.-A. and Fontenau, A. (1990) *Reflation and Austerity: economic policy under Mitterrand*, Berg, Oxford.

Mullineux, A. (ed.) (1992) *European Banking*, Blackwell, Oxford.

Mundell, R. (1961) 'A Theory of Optimum Currency Areas', *American Economic Review*, September.

Neumann, M. (1994) 'Reforming the European Monetary System', *Intereconomics*, 29, 2, March/April.

Oates, W. (1972) *Fiscal Federalism*, Harcourt, Brace, Jovanovitch, New York.

OECD (1993) 'Active Labour Market Policies: assessing macroeconomic and microeconomic effects', *Employment Outlook*, 11.

OECD (1995) *Economic Surveys: Germany*, OECD, Paris.

OECD (1995a) *Economic Surveys: Italy*, OECD, Paris.

OECD (1996) *Historical Statistics*, OECD, Paris.

Orléan, A. (1986) 'Mimetisme et anticipations rationnelles: une perspective keynesienne', *Recherches Economiques de Louvain*, 52, 1.

References

Ostroy, J. and Starr, R. (1990) 'The Transactions Demand for Money' in Friedman and Hahn, *op. cit.*

Palmer, J. (1996) 'Wanted: a compelling vision', *Political Quarterly*, 67, 3, July–September.

Panic, M. (1992) *European Monetary Union: lessons from the classical gold standard*, St Martin's Press, New York.

Patinkin, D. (1965) *Money, Interest and Prices*, 2nd edition, Harper and Row, New York.

Persson, T. and Tabellini, G. (1994) 'Does Centralisation Increase the Size of Government?', *European Economic Review*, 38, April.

Peston, M. (1959) 'A View of the Aggregation Problem', *Review of Economic Studies*, 27, 72.

van der Ploeg, R. (1991) 'Macroeconomic Coordination Issues during the Various Phases of Economic and Monetary Union in Europe', *European Economy*, special edition, 1.

Polster, W. and Voy, K. (1995) 'Öffnung der Märkte, Kooperation, Institutionalisierung: zur Gescichte der europäischen Wärungsintegration' in Thomasberger, *op. cit.*

Portes, R. and Swoboda, A. (eds) (1987) *Threats to International Financial Stability*, CUP, Cambridge.

Posen, A. (1993) 'Why Central Bank Independence Does not Cause Low Inflation' in O'Brien, R. (ed.) *Finance and the International Economy*, vol. 7, OUP, Oxford.

Radice, G. (1996) 'The Case for a Single Currency', *Political Quarterly*, 67, 3, July–September.

Riese, H. (1993) 'Scwäche des Pfundes und Versagen der Deutschen Mark: Anmerkungen zur gegenwärtigen Krise des Europäischen Währungssystems' in Bofinger, P., Collignon, S. and Lipp, E.-M. (eds) *Währungsunion oder Währungschaos*, Gabler, Wiesbaden.

Riese, H. (1994) 'Einkommensbildung als Entwicklungsproblem' in Hölscher, J. *et al.* (eds) *Bedingungen ökonomischer Entwicklung in Zentralosteuropa*, vol. 2, Metropolis Verlag, Marburg.

Rogoff, K. (1985) 'The Optimal Degree of Commitment to an Intermediary Monetary Target', *Quarterly Journal of Economics*, 100, November.

Rueff, J. (1967) *Balance of Payments: proposals for resolving the critical world economic problem of our time*, Macmillan, New York.

Sachs, J. and Sala-i-Martin, X. (1992) 'Fiscal Federalism and Optimal Currency Areas: evidence for Europe from the United States' in Canzoneri, M., Grilli, V. and Masson, P. (eds) *Establishing a Central Bank: issues in Europe and lessons from the United States*, CUP, Cambridge.

Selgin, G. (1994) 'Free Banking and Monetary Control', *Economic Journal*, 104, 427, November.

Sheffrin, S. (1983) *Rational Expectations*, CUP, Cambridge.

Shiller, R. (1989) *Market Volatility*, MIT Press, Cambridge, Mass.

Smits, R. (1994) 'A Single Currency for Europe and the Karlsruhe Court', *Legal Issues of European Integration*, 2.

Soskice, D. (1991) 'The Institutional Infrastructure for International Competitiveness: a comparative analysis of the UK and Germany' in Atkinson, A. and Brunetta, R. (eds) *Economics for the New Europe*, IEA/Macmillan, London.

Spahn, H.-P. (1995) 'Die Krise des EWS und die brüchigen Grundlagen der Leitwährungsordnung' in Thomasberger, *op. cit.*

Steinherr, A. (ed.) (1992) *The New European Financial Marketplace*, Longman, London.

Steinherr, A. (ed.) (1994) *30 Years of European Monetary Integration: from the Werner Plan to EMU*, Longman, London.

Steinherr, A. and Huveneers, C. (1992) 'Universal Banking in the Integrated European Marketplace' in Steinherr, *op. cit.*

Steinherr, A. and Weiserbs, D. (eds) (1991) *Evolution of the International and Regional Monetary Systems: essays in honour of Robert Triffin*, Macmillan, New York.

Stevenson, A., Muscatelli, V. and Gregory, M. (1988) *Macroeconomic Theory and Stabilisation Policy*, Philip Allan, London.

Stiglitz, J. and Weiss, A. (1981) 'Credit Rationing in Markets with Imperfect Information', *American Economic Review*, 71, June.

Streeck, W. (1996) 'German Capitalism: does it exist? can it survive?', Kellog Institute Working Paper, 218, University of notre Dame, Indiana.

Swann, D. (1983) *Competition and Industrial Policy in the European Community*, Methuen, London.

Temperton, P. (ed.) (1993) *The European Currency Crisis; what chance now for a single currency?*, Probus, Cambridge.

Thomasberger, C. (ed.) (1995) *Europäische Geldpolitik zwischen Marktzwängen und neuen institutionellen Regelungen*, Metropolis, Marburg.

Thomasberger, C. (1995a) 'Europäische Währungsintegration an der Wegscheide; Die Antinomeien des Leitwährunssystems und die Notwendikeit institutioneller Reformen' in Thomasberger (ed.), *op. cit.*

Tietmeyer, H. (1991) 'The Role of an Independent Central Bank in Europe' in Downes, P. and Vaez-Zadeh, R. (eds) *The Evolving Role of Central Banks*, IMF, Washington DC.

Tobin, J. (1978) 'A Proposal for International Monetary Reform', *Eastern Economic Journal*, 4.

Topol, R. (1991) 'Bubbles and the Volatility of Stock Prices', *Economic Journal*, 101, 407, July.

Triffin, R. (1961) *Gold and the Dollar Crisis: the future of convertibility*, Yale University Press, New Haven, Conn. and London.

Triffin, R. (1996) *The World Money Maze: national currencies in international payments*, Yale University Press, New Haven, Conn. and London.

References

Tugendhat, C. (1987) *Making Sense of Europe*, Penguin, Harmondsworth.

Vaciago, G. (1993) 'Exchange Rate Stability and Market Expectations: the crisis of the EMS', *Review of Economic Conditions in Italy*, 1.

Walters, A. (1992) 'Britain and the Exchange Rate Mechanism' in Minford, *op. cit.*

Weber, A. (1991) 'Reputation and Credibility in the European Monetary System', *Economic Policy*, 12, April.

Williamson, J. (1993) 'Exchange Rate Management', *Economic Journal*, 103, 416, January.

Williamson, J. (1994) 'The Rise and Fall of the Concept of International Liquidity' in Kenen, P., Papadia, F. and Saccomani, F. (eds) *The International Monetary System*, CUP, Cambridge.

Williamson, J. and Miller, M. (1987) *Targets and Indicators: a blueprint for the international coordination of economic policy*, Institute for International Economics, Washington DC.

Williamson, O. (1985) *The Economic Institutions of Capitalism: firms, markets, relational contracting*, Collier Macmillan, London.

Winkler, B. (1996) 'Towards a Strategic View on EMU: a critical survey', *Journal of Public Policy*, 16, 1, Jan–April.

Wolf, M. (1996) 'Why European Integration Cannot be Built on EMU', *Political Quarterly*, 67, 3, July–September.

Wray, R. (1984) 'The Political Economy of the Current US Financial Crisis', *International Papers in Political Economy*, 1, 3.

Wren-Lewis, S. *et al.* (1991) 'Evaluating the United Kingdom's Choice of Entry Rate into the ERM', *Manchester School*, 59, supplement.

Wyplosz, C. (1996) 'Un mark à 3.75 F pour sauver l'Union monétaire', *Le Monde*, 4 September.

van Ypersele, J. and Koeune, J.-C. (1984) *The European Monetary System: origins, operation and outlook*, EC, Luxembourg.

Index